Spinoza and the Politics of Renaturalization

Spinoza and the Politics of Renaturalization

HASANA SHARP

The University of Chicago Press
Chicago and London

The University of Chicago Press, Chicago 60637
The University of Chicago Press, Ltd., London
© 2011 by The University of Chicago
All rights reserved. No part of this book may be used or reproduced in any manner whatsoever without written permission, except in the case of brief quotations in critical articles and reviews. For more information, contact the University of Chicago Press, 1427 E. 60th St., Chicago, IL 60637.
Published 2011
Paperback edition 2021

30 29 28 27 26 25 24 23 22 21   1 2 3 4 5

ISBN-13: 978-0-226-75074-3 (cloth)
ISBN-13: 978-0-226-79248-4 (paper)
ISBN-13: 978-0-226-75075-0 (e-book)
DOI: https://doi.org/10.7208/chicago/9780226750750.001.0001

Library of Congress Cataloging-in-Publication Data

Sharp, Hasana.
  Spinoza and the politics of renaturalization / Hasana Sharp.
    p. cm.
  Includes bibliographical references and index.
  ISBN-13: 978-0-226-75074-4 (cloth : alk. paper)
  ISBN-10: 0-226-75074-4 (cloth : alk. paper) 1. Spinoza, Benedictus de, 1632–1677—Criticism and interpretation. 2. Hegel, Georg Wilhelm Friedrich, 1770–1831—Criticism and interpretation. I. Title.
  B3998.S56 2011
  199'.492—dc22
                                                                    2010054342

CONTENTS

Acknowledgments vii
List of Abbreviations xi

Introduction: The Politics of Renaturalization   1
A Practical Wisdom of Renaturalization   5
Impersonal Politics   10
Ingredients   15

PART I   RECONFIGURING THE HUMAN

1   Lines, Planes, and Bodies: Redefining Human Action   21
Action as Affect   25
The Transindividuality of Affect: Spinoza and Simondon   34
The Tongue   42

2   Renaturalizing Ideology: Spinoza's Ecosystem of Ideas   55
The Matrix   58
Ideology Critique Today?   61
The Fly in the Coach   64
"I am in Ideology," or The Attribute of Thought   68
What Is to Be Done?   75

3   Man's Utility to Man: Reason and Its Place in Nature   85
The Politics of Human Nature   87
Reason and the Human Essence   93
Man's Utility to Man   100
Nonhuman Utility   107

PART II BEYOND THE IMAGE OF MAN

4 Desire for Recognition? Butler, Hegel, and Spinoza — 117
Spinoza in Hegel *121*
Desire in Hegel *124*
Conatus and *Cupiditas* in Spinoza *132*
From Interpersonal Recognition to Impersonal Glory *139*
Judith Butler's Post-Hegelian Politics of Recognition *149*

5 The Impersonal Is Political: Spinoza and a Feminist Politics of Imperceptibility — 155
The Politics of Recognition *159*
Elizabeth Grosz's Critique of the Politics of Recognition *163*
Thinking beyond the (Hu)Man *169*
A Politics of Imperceptibility *175*

6 Nature, Norms, and Beasts — 185
The Beast Within *188*
Animal Affects (and) the First Man *201*
Ethics as Ethology? *210*

Works Cited 221
Index 235

ACKNOWLEDGMENTS

> Of all the things that are not under my control, what I value most is to enter into friendship with sincere lovers of truth. For I believe that such a loving relationship affords us a serenity surpassing any other boon in the whole wide world.
> —BENEDICT DE SPINOZA, Epistle 19

It is my good fortune to have little control over the circumstances and encounters that have nourished my thinking and writing, for I could not possibly have chosen a more exhilarating group of friends, teachers, and conversation partners.

For soul-inflaming friendship and encouragement over the years, I thank Will Roberts, Sara Brill, Lisa Guenther, Jason Read, Christina Tarnopolsky, and Chloë Taylor. I am also grateful to them for reading, discussing, hearing, and remarking on various parts of the manuscript. Their influence, love, and support are palpable on all of these pages. For perspicacious comments on various parts of my text, I am grateful to Jane Bennett, Charles Blattberg, Julie Cooper, Cristian Lo Iocano, Filippo del Lucchese, Erin Tarver, and Warren Montag. For reading a draft of the entire manuscript and providing meticulous, probing, and thought-provoking suggestions, I thank Will Roberts, Erik Stephenson, Lars Toender, and Caroline Williams. Even if my stubbornness did not always yield to their better judgment, the book owes a great deal to their reflections and challenges.

None of this would have been possible without the teachers who prompted and expanded my love of Spinoza. First and foremost, I was urged to understand why people fight for servitude as if it were their salvation by Warren Montag. I found further encouragement and instruction from Dan Conway, Emily Grosholz, Rick Lee, Pierre-François Moreau, and Shannon Sullivan. I would also like to acknowledge the early and formative intellectual stimulation and friendship provided by Alejandro de Acosta, Fouad Kalouche, Mufridah Nolan, Elizabeth Randol, Ben Swire, and Soenke Zehle. I surely would have found myself on a different path if it were not for them.

Earlier versions of parts of the manuscript were presented at the following institutions or associations: American Political Science Association, Canadian Society for Continental Philosophy, Canadian Society for Women in Philosophy, Concordia University, Historical Materialism, International Symposium for Phenomenology, Queen's University, Rethinking Marxism, Society for Phenomenology and Existential Philosophy, University of Guelph, and Vanderbilt University. I benefited immeasurably from the financial support, questions, encounters, and surprises these meetings provided. Ancestors of chapters 2 and 5 were published in *Political Theory* 35, no. 6 (December 2007) and *Hypatia* 24, no. 4 (October–December 2009), respectively. My writing, traveling, and research were supported generously by a grant for new researchers from the Fonds québecois de recherche sur la societé et la culture.

Bringing forth a first book, like a first child, is an exciting and frightening process. This book could not have had a better midwife than the expert and kind Elizabeth Branch Dyson at the University of Chicago Press. I am also grateful for the acuity of Susan Tarcov, without whom it would surely be less presentable.

I warmly acknowledge the supportive and exciting intellectual community of Montreal's four universities. I have benefited especially from the Groupe de recherche interuniversitaire en philosophie politique and the Montreal interuniversity history of philosophy workshop. I am fortunate to have too many interesting colleagues to be able to take full advantage of their gifts. The whole philosophy department at McGill deserves to be named, but, alas, they are too many. My colleagues in political theory, Arash Abizadeh, Jacob Levy, Catherine Lu, and Christina Tarnopolsky, are exemplary in every way, always ready with queries, conversation, and invitations to play. Montreal is a wonderful environment for the study of early modern rationalism, with interlocutors like Carlos Fraenkel, Alison Laywine, Christian Nadeau, and Justin Smith. In feminist philosophy, I rely on the solidarity and stimulation offered by Alia Al-Saji, Bettina Bergo, Marguerite Deslauriers, and Natalie Stoljar. Richer soil for a project on Spinoza, feminism, and political theory is scarcely imaginable.

For unwavering love and support, I am indebted to my parents, Joe and RoseMary Sharp, and, in ways they may not realize, to my sisters, Abigail and Michelle. For calling me out of myself and amplifying my power in so many ways, I owe my animal companions, my son, Emmett, and my partner. And, for innumerable joys, I thank Will Roberts, to whom this book (and so much more) is dedicated.

ABBREVIATIONS

Works by Spinoza

E	*Ethics (Ethica)*
Ep	*The Letters (Epistola)*
KV	*Short Treatise on God, Man, and His Well-Being (Korte Verhandeling)*
TIE	*Treatise on the Emendation of the Intellect (Tractatus de Intellectus Emendatione)*
TP	*Political Treatise (Tractatus Politicus)*
TTP	*Theological-Political Treatise (Tractatus Theologico-Politicus)*

Works by Descartes

Med	*Meditations on First Philosophy (Meditationes de Prima Philosophia)*
PS	*Passions of the Soul (Passions de l'âme)*

References to the *Ethics* employ the following system of abbreviations:

Roman numeral = part
ax = axiom
app = appendix
c = corollary
def = definition
def aff = definition of the affects

d = demonstration
ex = explanation
L = lemma
p = proposition
prol = prolegomenon
post = postulate
pref = preface
s = scholium

Notes

References to the *TP* and *TTP* denote the chapter and the paragraph (e.g., 2.6). References to the *TIE* cite section numbers from the Curley translation.

References to the *PS* cite the article number (e.g., a. 52).

Quotations are from the following translations, with occasional modifications: *Ethics* (*Collected Works*, trans. Curley), *TTP* (trans. Israel and Silverthorne); *TP* (trans. Shirley); *Ep* (trans. Shirley).

References to the *Med* cite page numbers from the Cottingham, Stoothoff, and Murdoch translation. Quotations from the *PS* are also from this translation.

All citations of French texts are translated by the author.

INTRODUCTION

The Politics of Renaturalization

Spinoza is a philosopher of many posthumous births. He was first viewed as an abominable atheist, then resurrected as the "God-intoxicated man," a romantic pantheist, the great thinker of the multitude, the advocate of the liberated individual, and most recently the most rigorous of the rationalists (to list only a few of his epitaphs). Even if there are many Spinozas, they all converge, at least on one point, his "naturalism." No one denies the twin pillars of Spinozism: the identity of God and Nature and the tenet that "man" is but a tiny "part of Nature."[1] Spinoza unequivocally rejects anthropomorphic portraits of God as a master artisan, legislator, commander, or king. Existence for Spinoza is horizontal. The infinite creative force of nature is not separable from the infinitely many beings that exist. Humanity receives no special metaphysical value and no privileged place in nature. Spinoza's naturalism denies human exceptionalism in any form. Like any other thing in nature, humans are corporeal and ideal, ineluctably immersed in a system of cause and effect, and each of us comprises a power that is infinitely surpassed by the totality of other beings. Famously, Spinoza avows that right is co-extensive

---

1. Throughout this study, I preserve Spinoza's sexist language when citing him and referring to his own claims in order to avoid giving a false and anachronistic impression of gender inclusiveness.

with power and thereby refuses a distinction between how things are in reality and how they ought to be by right. While readers share this general schema of Spinoza's portrait of reality, there is plenty of room for interpretive diversity when it comes to the question of what follows from his naturalism. Even if commentators agree that Spinoza's metaphysics is naturalist, we do not agree, for example, on whether he is an ethical or political naturalist.[2]

This book develops a politics of renaturalization from Spinoza's naturalism, especially its powerful redefinition of human existence and agency.[3] Spinoza's naturalism, I will argue, navigates between two dangers. On one side, Spinoza refutes any notion of humanity that implies supernatural qualities. As Michael Della Rocca put it recently, Spinoza's naturalism is grounded in the thesis that "everything in the world," human, animal, or mineral, "plays by the same rules."[4] During his own time, one scandalous implication of this thesis was that no volitional power, divine or human, can operate independent of the natural order of cause and effect. Importantly, for his time and ours, his attack on supernatural models of man refuses every dualism between mind and body, where mind and body are imagined to play by different rules. Spinoza's remains a potent challenge to the current consensus. Most philosophers today maintain a "compatibilist" idea of the person, a view of moral agency in which freedom of the will is seen to be compatible with natural determination. For compatibilists, one can view the natural world as entirely determined and predictable, according to the natural laws of cause and effect, and consistently maintain that rational beings are, as such, free and thereby morally responsible for their actions. Compatibilism is classically represented by Kant, for whom reason acts as a "special cause" of our actions, without which we cannot be considered moral actors.[5] This reconciliation of natural and moral causality is a clear violation of Spinoza's naturalism and, even if it has virtues in a court of law, is no solution to systemic ethical and political problems.

Descartes anticipates the compatibilist solution to the problem of free will with his understanding of corporeality as entirely mechanical and mentality as infinite (*Med* IV). For Spinoza, minds are equally submerged within a system of cause and effect, operating according to the same prin-

---

2. See Eisenberg, "Is Spinoza an Ethical Naturalist?"
3. Although Spinoza aims, above all, to alter human self-experience and life in common, the implications of his naturalism certainly extend beyond human existence.
4. Della Rocca, *Spinoza*, 5.
5. Kant, *Critique of Pure Reason*, A 448/B 476–A 452/B 480.

ciples as bodies (*E* II p9). Nevertheless, he denies that thought is reducible to extension, or mind to body. Mental power is distinctive and cannot be explained by bodily forces. Importantly for my purposes, Spinoza attributes thinking power (mind) to all beings in nature. Thus, there is no recourse to mind to explain human freedom, yet he does not eliminate the distinctive character of thought as a natural power animating all of existence.

Spinoza's "parallelism," whereby mind and body do not interact, sets the stage for a radical naturalism that redefines human existence and agency in several ways: (a) thought is irreducible to matter, and yet does not have a unique spiritual logic that distinguishes it from (other attributes of) nature; (b) mental life is not confined to human, rational, or spiritual beings; and (c) thought and extension, mind and body, are not involved in a struggle for control. Minds do not exercise their will over bodies, and bodies do not threaten the moral autonomy of minds. Since both thought and extension equally express substance (the universal power of nature), neither thought nor extension is subordinate to the other. Thought's role is therefore not to reflect the reality of extension, and the external world is not the stage upon which self-consciousness manifests its freedom. With this framework Spinoza paints a portrait of human existence that is entirely natural and yet preserves the unique character of thought. Because thinking power is universal in nature, Spinoza's redefinition of man at the very least unsettles most bases of human exceptionalism.

As if he realizes the implications of his erosion of human distinctiveness, Spinoza's naturalism militates against a second danger. If his first and most obvious concern is to reject any notion of man as supernatural, he is likewise wary, albeit to a lesser extent, of the elevation of pristine, wild Nature to the status of a norm. Just as we are undermined by measuring ourselves and one another against a standard of perfect rationality or disembodied freedom of the will, we likewise attenuate our own power by aspiring to resemble a noble lion or a self-sacrificing honey bee. His naturalism thus denies that humanity, civilization, or any other being might be found to be subnatural, lower than almighty Nature.

Although many commentators recognize Spinoza's opposition to supernaturalism, none have discussed his concern with what I am calling, if awkwardly, "subnaturalism." Indeed, ecological philosophers and democratic theorists treat nature in Spinoza's thought as a standard against which to judge certain political forms and ways of life as defective. According to the radical enlightenment portrait, for example, Spinoza's affirmation of the infinite diversity of existence is a basis for the most unequivocal form of tolerance the western canon has ever known.[6] Similarly, the ecological interpretation finds that Spinozism engenders a profound respect for each and every being's effort at self-actualization.[7] Although freedom's highest expression, for Spinoza, involves apprehending natural beings (above all, ourselves) as unique singularities and refusing to judge them against any external standard, Spinoza's metaphysics does not obviously entail a normative morality of respect for the flourishing of any and every being by virtue of its being a "part of nature." Although both the radical enlightenment traditions and deep ecology take inspiration from Spinozism and often deviate from the letter of Spinoza's text, it is important to guard against moralizing nature as a kind of authoritative design to which we ought to conform. Spinoza's naturalism forecloses appeals to either a spiritual or a natural order separate from the connection and order of finite things as they are. Neither God nor Nature commands us to fulfill a predetermined design.

Nevertheless, this book finds a tension within Spinoza's naturalism in that it points, concomitantly, toward and away from humanity. On the one hand, he redefines human agency as entirely natural, locating it within a system that reserves no special status whatsoever for humans. This denial of human exceptionalism serves, first and foremost, to attenuate a particularly destructive passion: hatred, directed at oneself or others. An account of how an understanding of reality such that all things play by the same rules mitigates hatred is one of the tasks of this study. The aspiration to attenuate hatred and misanthropy gives rise to a second strand of Spinoza's argument that can pull against his anti-anthropocentrism. Spinoza insists that humans need to come to love and regard themselves in their distinctiveness, *as* humans, both in order to increase their power as individuals and to relate to one another in increasingly enabling ways. The second half of the book underlines Spinoza's commitment to both (a) rejecting human exceptionalism and (b) heralding the necessity of what I call "philanthropy." The final chapter's examination of the human-animal relation examines (just) one place where we can gain a particularly illuminating perspective on Spinoza's own struggle to balance the aims of his ethics and politics, which point toward and away from human specificity.

In sum, I contend that Spinoza's naturalism provides the resources for a "philanthropic posthumanism," a collective project by which we can come

---

6. See the monumental studies by Israel, *Radical Enlightenment* and *Enlightenment Contested*.
7. For example, Mathews, *The Ecological Self*, which is indebted to a number of works by Arne Naess.

to love ourselves and one another as parts of nature. The position I glean is posthumanist, if by humanism we understand a philosophical tradition that aspires to a universal union of humanity on the basis of a shared characteristic that is not exhibited by nonhumans, like reason, moral sensibility, or a capacity for autonomy.[8] Even if humanism typically rejects a supernatural order in favor of human community on earth, from the perspective of Spinozism it relocates supernaturalism within the human mind. A view of human nature in opposition to the rest of nature inflames hatred, as we expect ourselves and one another to exhibit powers of infinite self-control, acting in radical contradiction to our circumstances. At the same time, Spinoza warns against a nonhuman stance, since a standard of nonhuman nature undermines our power in other ways.[9] The main interpretive thesis of this book is that Spinoza's naturalism aims to engender enabling self-love in humanity by eroding those models of man that animate hatred, albeit indirectly, by suggesting that we are, at one extreme, defective Gods or, at the other, corrupt animals who need to be restored to our natural condition.

A Practical Wisdom of Renaturalization

If neither Spirit nor Nature is a standard against which humanity or civilization might be judged, how do we understand Spinoza's political theory? I argue that Spinoza's view of "human actions and appetites just as if it were a question of lines, planes, and bodies" (*E* III pref) provides the basis for a practical wisdom of "renaturalization." It founds a new appreciation of ourselves as parts of nature, operating according to the same rules as anything else, invariably dependent upon infinitely many other beings, human and nonhuman. I call this "renaturalization" rather than naturalization, because Spinoza's is a strategic reversal of the scientific spiritualization that was gaining momentum in his time with Cartesianism. Cartesian dualism perseveres today in various forms and is manifestly a primary target of Spinoza's critique, even if he could not have written what he did outside of its wake. Spinoza's objection to dualism is not only metaphysical but also ethical and political. Renaturalization is a strategy to attenuate the antipathy that plagues our psyches and our life in common. A spiritual, antinaturalist logic in ethics and politics dominates our

---

8. See, e.g., Davies, *Humanism*.
9. Wolfe distinguishes usefully between being posthumanist and posthuman in *What Is Posthumanism?*

humanist tradition from Descartes to Kant to Hegel. Spinoza's approach reinserts human action into nature to undermine the sad passions, especially hatred, that attend attributions of exclusive moral responsibility. Renaturalization aims to cure social ills but involves broadening our frame of reference beyond social relations. The politics of renaturalization can thus promote alternative conceptions of political activity that connect us more palpably to nonhuman nature.

I borrow the term "renaturalization" from Elizabeth Grosz who advocates a conception of power *in* nature to transform debates about recognition and rights.[10] Whereas feminist and race theorists have long been concerned with *de*naturalizing our understanding of "man," Grosz insists on recuperating a view of ourselves as natural.[11] I agree and think Spinoza can help us. Yet he also warns us strongly against turning nature into a norm, such that we might aspire to better approximate some concept of nature. In navigating between supernaturalism and subnaturalism, I explore the promise *and* difficulty of theorizing politics when human distinctiveness has been comprehensively called into question.

Feminists, race theorists, Marxists, phenomenologists, and critical theorists, among others, have long been suspicious of any discourse of nature, or of what Judith Butler in her early work calls "naturalistic ideology."[12] Marx, Foucault, and many feminists pose a critical practice of "denaturalization" in opposition to ideological naturalization. These critical methodologies reveal how power structures depend upon their ability to mystify their historical and bloody origins. Occluding the contested processes by which capitalism, bourgeois sexuality, European superiority, or patriarchy is constituted, naturalistic ideologies represent such systems as unalterable expressions of human nature. Critical theories of denaturalization expose the normalizing impulse of so many appeals to nature. The introduction to a recent anthology on the co-articulation of race and nature aptly summarizes the suspicious stance toward "nature" among denaturalists.

> Imagined as an ontological foundation, nature has served as the generative terrain from which assertions of essence emerge. Nature appears to precede history, even as it wipes away the historical artifacts of its own fashioning. Race has provided mobile markers of identity and difference

---

10. Grosz, *Time Travels*.
11. Found Objects Collective, "An Interview with Elizabeth Grosz."
12. Butler, "Sexual Ideology and Phenomenological Description."

on this naturalizing ground, rationalizing orders of exclusion as laws of necessity. Race provides a critical medium through which ideas of nature operate, even as racialized forces rework the ground of nature itself. *Working together*, race and nature legitimate particular forms of political representation, reproduce social hierarchies, and authorize violent exclusions—often transforming contingent relations into eternal necessities.[13]

This tradition of critical theory, a form of social constructivism, persuasively demonstrates how discourses of nature often function in oppressive ways, ascribing a necessity and teleology to (human) nature in order to justify domination. It is thus my conviction that we cannot advocate the naturalization of humanity without taking the history of naturalistic ideology seriously. I opt for the less elegant term "renaturalization" to distance my approach from naturalistic ideology. I cannot simply bring "nature," "the body," or "matter" back without reworking them in response to the concerns of feminists, race theorists, or the Marxist traditions of critical theory. Although one can never be confident of having exorcised all vestiges of ideology, I hope to contribute to a less oppressive imaginative horizon in which to challenge the human-nature divide.

Although appeals to nature are never without risks, the critical impulse of denaturalization has generated a set of polemical binaries that, even if necessary in certain contexts, merit challenge and reconceptualization. For these critics, "nature" signifies changelessness, teleology, simplicity, and normative holism, to which they oppose historical contingency, open-ended development, complexity, and asystematicity. From this point of view, Spinoza's naturalism is in the enemy camp, since his metaphysics is necessitarian and exhibits totalizing tendencies, even if he is a staunch critic of teleology and natural simplicity. Moreover, Spinoza views human relations in terms of cause and effect, a "scientific methodology" to which a number of critical theorists object. Butler, for example, praises Foucault for exposing "sex" as a discursive effect of religious and secular sciences of the soul, rather than treating it as a natural cause of desire and sexuality.[14]

There are practical and theoretical reasons, however, that argue for the critical alternative of renaturalization. As mentioned, Spinoza contends that regarding ourselves as special beings inflames odium. Understanding humanity as vulnerable to the same determinations as beasts, rocks,

---

13. Moore, Kosek, and Pandian, *Race, Nature, and the Politics of Difference*.
14. Butler, *Gender Trouble*, 31.

and vegetables facilitates social harmony and political emancipation. Only when we consider ourselves to be constituted by our constellations of relationships and community of affects can we hope to transform the forces that shape our actions and characters. When we regard ourselves as beings within nature, we affirm the passionate basis of activity and respond more effectively and knowledgeably to harms, sorrows, and threats, as well as to pleasures, joys, and promises.

Avowing humanity as part of nature entails understanding individuals as beings with complex histories, exposed to many diverse bodies and minds, and ever open to forming new compositions with ambient forces. Nature, on Spinoza's model, is not opposed to history. A Spinozist can agree with the notion that man is a historical being, while insisting that history is not the product of overcoming nature. History is not a progressive spiritualization of nature, where humans, through working together, come to master, bring under control, and "interiorize" biological need, instinct, and other "external" elements of our existence. Nature, for Spinoza, names the necessity of ongoing mutation and the inescapability of dependence among finite beings. Rather than serving to prescribe the entelecheic unfolding of a thing's essence, Spinoza's nature affirms the variability intrinsic to relational existence. To be a relational being is to undergo a history of constitutive affections and transformations in response to encounters with other beings, human and nonhuman.

The mutable aspect of Spinoza's notion of nature underscores that renaturalization is not necessarily incompatible with denaturalization. Spinoza's analysis of scripture as a natural rather than a supernatural artifact suggests significant overlap with a denaturalist approach, insofar as it involves revealing the sociopolitical genealogies of what appears to be given. Among other things, Spinoza recommends studying the original language in which it was written, the precise meanings of the idioms at the time they were recorded, who the particular audience was, and the political circumstances the stories aim to address (do they pertain, for example, to just or oppressive conditions?) (*TTP* 7.5). Renaturalizing scripture does not produce a naturalistic ideology whereby its decrees appear eternal, necessary, and immune to challenge. On the contrary, Spinoza's approach calls much of its authority into radical question. Given that most of ancient Hebrew is lost, interpretation of scripture is necessarily partial and ought to be responsive to new knowledge about ancient peoples and languages. Being natural means being situated within a particular time, place, and causal nexus. The encounter between reader and text, a complex meeting of composite individuals, engenders still further effects to be explored and understood, if always incompletely.

Spinoza's naturalism, likewise, shares with Marxism and feminism an emphasis upon the relational character of existence, while offering some practical guidance for negotiating life within a causal community. Marxism and feminism focus on the institutional and ideological character of social relations, but Spinoza presents a broader perspective that includes our relations with all of nature. The virtues of an extrasocial perspective, as I see it, are as follows: renaturalization combats voluntarism more effectively than a denaturalizing approach, which, as a variant of social constructivism, implies that social artifacts are products of human actions and institutions. The core thesis of renaturalization is the radical redefinition of human agency as part of nature. Spinoza refuses to distinguish between natural and social forces, or mental and physical determination.[15] Renaturalization differs from many approaches to social construction in that it does not aim to revolutionize consciousness alone or to relabel objects that once appeared natural as social (i.e., effects of human agency). Rather, it is a practical theory that seeks the nonhuman forces operating within everything we think is ours, or our own doing.

That is, renaturalization maintains that there is an irreducible power of external causes, within and without each of our bodies. The constitutive aspect of nonhuman powers points to the second major advantage of a renaturalist approach: anti-anthropocentrism. Denaturalization and social constructivism meet criticism from an ecological perspective for promoting an anthropocentric worldview in which everything appears to be a human artifact. Nevertheless, many environmental thinkers confirm, with this very criticism, an opposition between humanity and nature. Although Spinoza has been an inspiration for ecological thought, "nature" must not be understood to imply whatever is nonhuman.[16] It should already be clear that Spinoza challenges all of our usual distinctions between mind and body, "man" and nature, culture and wilderness, artifice and adaptation. As long as we keep in mind that cyborgs, landfills, and leviathans are just as natural as tides, forests, and flocks of birds, I hope to contribute to the ecopolitical ambition to rethink nature. In an epoch that threatens environmental catastrophe and mass extinction, we must marshal theoretical

---

15. On this model, social construction as the complex *interaction* of ideas and objects over time does not make sense. Cf. Haslanger, "Social Construction," 315.

16. See Houle, "Spinoza and Ecology Revisited."

resources for thinking and speaking about nonhuman nature, in political as much as in ethical theory. Not only do we have obligations to nonhuman nature, we have reasons to amplify the power of nonhuman nature. Our collective power, our politics, depends upon becoming a part of nature differently. For the politics of renaturalization, our agency, perseverance, and pleasure depend upon affirming and nourishing the nonhuman in and outside of ourselves. The relations that matter to our intellectual and our corporeal well-being are far from exclusively human.

Rather than merely defending Spinoza's concept of nature against the denaturalist accusation that invocations of "nature" are oppressive—something that can perhaps too easily be done—this book explores the emancipatory promise of the politics of renaturalization. In the end, admittedly, any concept of nature is a blunt tool that is only as valuable as its effects, its ability to generate other concepts and tools that fortify our ability to think and act (*TIE* §§30–31). In an age that continues to view human existence as an "empire within an empire" (*E* III pref), however, critical political thought urgently needs a sense of freedom compatible with our character as corporeal, affective, and sensuous beings, invariably embedded in relations with other beings, human and nonhuman.

Impersonal Politics

From a contemporary perspective, however, much of what I have said may not sound especially political. Contemporary political theory is overwhelmingly concerned with questions of justice and legitimation rather than with ontological accounts of what kinds of beings we are. Normative political theory, for good reasons, is also wary of deriving political principles from nature or metaphysics. Contemporary debates occur largely within the categories of normative political and moral thought, which pertain to conventional human practices and the criteria for just procedures within institutions that engender and regulate what Hegel calls "ethical life." As a result of this powerful philosophical tradition, we lack a sophisticated political language to address either our own naturalness or our relationship to nonhuman nature. The discourse of animal rights, for example, succeeds, to the limited extent that it does, by arguing for the extension of the definition of humanity to include a tiny elite of nonhuman animals in the sphere of moral concern and juridical standing. There are, simply put, no words flowing in mainstream currents to express a politics of intimacy, power, and connection with nonhuman forces, even with those nonhuman companions to which we have profound attachments and bonds.[17]

It has been argued that Spinoza's philosophy is free of normative elements.[18] Although it is true that there is no room in Spinoza's politics for a conception of rights separable from their exercise, presenting his thought as a radically antinormative program or a thoroughgoing critique of juridical power is not my project.[19] Moreover, despite his notorious critique of the separation of right and power, Spinoza's practical philosophy involves an affirmation of the necessity of both (provisional) morality and juridical politics, but the precise approach to political institutions of legitimation in his political treatises is highly complex and somewhat elusive. While I often refer to the political treatises for support, my study emphasizes the political implications of the naturalist ontology in the *Ethics*. My considered conviction is that the normative and juridical lens in contemporary political theory needs to be supplemented and challenged by what I call an "impersonal" perspective. Although I do not mean to claim that it represents the totality of Spinoza's political philosophy, throughout the book I develop an impersonal perspective on ethics and politics. His philosophy provides resources for unsettling the presumptions of "personal politics" and thereby altering current debates in feminist and critical theory.

Hegel claims that the "commandment of right" is to "be a person and respect others as persons."[20] "Person" for Hegel is a technical term that refers to the "capacity for rights" through which human individuals and societies represent themselves as free and equal. Rather than representing a simple recognition of a given, essential human freedom, personhood for Hegel is a historical achievement, possible only in "postconventional" societies. Persons are equal precisely because modern institutions and ways of life liberate them from natural determination, allowing them to grasp the universal aspects of their selfhood. Recognition of oneself and others as persons involves knowledge of those so recognized as finite and infinite at once, as natural beings who can nevertheless sustain the radical infinity of self-consciousness. When we achieve consciousness of ourselves as

---

17. Haraway and other posthumanists have gone considerable distance in rethinking human-animal relations, but their efforts have gone unrecognized in mainstream ethical and political thought. While this Spinozan critique I offer here is unlikely to revolutionize the mainstream, I aspire to add water to these alternative currents.

18. Den Uyl, *Power, State, and Freedom*.

19. Compelling interpretations of Spinoza in this vein include Montag, *Bodies, Masses, Power*, and Negri, *The Savage Anomaly*.

20. *The Philosophy of Right*, §36.

moral agents through juridical representation, we grasp ourselves as persons rather than as things.

Personhood is a normative rather than a purely descriptive category. It designates how we ought to see ourselves and others in order to recognize one another as free beings. With the notion of personhood we represent ourselves as freed of natural determination and thereby morally responsible for our actions. Not only, then, are we persons rather than things, we are rational and not merely human. Whereas *human* names a biological organism, person, strictly speaking, designates only rational beings. Children and the cognitively impaired who cannot will their actions in accordance with universal rules are not persons, but extraterrestrials (and possibly higher animals) and corporate entities ("artificial persons") may be.[21] A virtue of Hegelianism is to insist that personal politics approximates universality only when the multifarious social institutions and dimensions of collective life allow for inclusive and expansive representation of the diverse constituents of the social body. A collection of particularities needs to become universal. The normative function of "personhood" has force for Hegel only insofar as it also reflects powers that are actualized by some meaningful (in his time, male and propertied) portion of a community. The affirmation of personhood in oneself and others is far from the totality of ethical life for Hegel, but contemporary political philosophy nevertheless has come to preoccupy itself above all with this "moment" of politics.

Personal politics, like denaturalization, is important and indispensable. Throughout this book, I often contrast Spinoza to Hegel because they are very close in some respects and mutually illuminating opponents in others. Moreover, I take neo-Hegelianism to be the best expression of normative political thought today, especially from a feminist perspective. As I remark in chapter 5, the emphasis in neo-Hegelian politics of recognition upon the arduous and delicate intersubjective processes of establishing relationships of respect, equality, and sympathy among people with distinct languages, cultures, histories, and perspectives is invaluable. Likewise, the neo-Hegelian politics of recognition appreciates the psychic damage caused by oppressive sociosymbolic regimes, which cannot be captured by a theory that focuses on the just distribution of goods or the rights owed to individuals. Because, as I discuss in chapter 4, Hegel's political ontology is thoroughly relational, like Spinoza's, Hegelianism regards freedom as a

---

21. For a genealogy and critical discussion of the term, see Poole, "On Being a Person."

complex process that cannot be understood independently of historical conditions or relations with others.

Yet personal politics is essentially antinatural. To be a person is to be free from nature, to have transubstantiated one's animality into humanity. Even if personhood does not embody the totality of ethical life, neo-Hegelian political theory emphasizes the representation of humanity and personhood. Thus, Butler's post-Hegelian politics of recognition, as she notes, returns again and again to "the question of the human."[22] Personal politics cannot avoid restricting the domain of the political to an interrogation of the normative criteria that guarantee and foreclose personhood, the representation of distinctively human freedom. Without arguing for a displacement of normative political theory—something that is as unrealistic as it is foolhardy—I claim that an impersonal perspective opens up a new continent of political theory and practice. Indeed, to transform a phrase, I contend that the *impersonal* is political.

Impersonal politics does not necessarily oppose but is different from a politics of rights and representation. Impersonal politics will not be televised. Impersonal forces include those affects that circulate in the social body, enabling and constraining the powers of bodies and minds, often without anyone's awareness or knowledge. Impersonal politics happens, whether we are aware of it or not, but we can cultivate a practical wisdom of renaturalization by which we seek out new sources of agency, connection, and energy. Rather than a politics of rights and representation, impersonal politics is a project of composition and synergy.

Let me offer an example. A group of five hundred thousand people assemble on the National Mall to protest a bill being considered by Congress. They gather, sing, chant, present their signs, and socialize. They receive disappointing media coverage and the opposed bill passes easily. From the perspective of strictly personal politics, the rally failed. The demands of the protestors were not represented to a larger public, nor did they come to be reflected in the law; the contours of the legal person and mass understandings of freedom were not altered. From an impersonal political perspective, however, the primary sites of concern are different. Rather than a concern with whether representations were contested or confirmed, an impersonal lens is trained upon the affects that concretely determine individual and collective power. Insofar as individuals were exhilarated and forged connections pregnant with unknown futures, this event contributed to the agency of those involved, engendered the basis of new forms

---

22. Butler, *Undoing Gender*.

of shared power, and thereby "succeeded." Such connections may not have taken the form of email addresses exchanged or future meet-ups established but may be nothing other than a coagulation of joyful affect that enabled ambient bodies and minds to think and act more effectively or, in Foucault's words, to engage in an "art of not being governed quite so much" in their everyday lives.[23]

On the other hand, the event may have amplified sad passions, entrenched divisions between social groups with different demands and self-conceptions, and foreclosed certain alliances that had seemed replete with possibility beforehand. Nevertheless, the affective therapy that emerges from a politics of renaturalization offers the following counsel:

> It should be noted that in ordering our thoughts and images, we must always attend to those things that are good in each thing so that we are always determined to acting from an affect of joy. For example, if someone sees that he pursues esteem too much, he should think of its correct use, the end for which it ought to be pursued, and the means by which it might be acquired, not of its misuse and emptiness, and men's inconstancy, or other things of this kind. (*E* V p10s)

The practical wisdom of renaturalization depends upon an affective orientation toward joy, which indicates an augmentation in one's power or agency. Impersonal politics takes its point of departure from the desire to enhance one's pleasure and power through encounters with other bodies and minds. It is an affective politics that privileges enabling relationships, wherever they may be found, rather than particular identities or institutions. Such an orientation cannot simply be willed but must occur by virtue of myriad impersonal factors in one's environment over which one cannot exercise sovereign control. The impersonal perspective encourages one to be attuned to those sources of strength and vitality that generally fly below the radar of theoretical or even conscious scrutiny. I have already noted that one of the virtues of the neo-Hegelian tradition of political theory is that it does not dismiss unconscious and affective elements of agency and ethical life as irrelevant. Yet Spinoza advocates a shift from understanding affective and psychic life in terms of representation to thinking in terms of natural forces combining or combusting. Spinoza encourages an attentiveness to affect as an indication of whether and how ambient forces enhance one's power of existing. Spinoza hopes

---

23. Foucault, "What Is Critique?" 193.

that each affect, whether painful or pleasurable, if considered in terms of both its natural multiplicity (E V p9) and its "correct use," can animate and support a "love of freedom" (V p10s). This book endeavors not only to describe but to be such an exercise in the love of freedom.

Ingredients

The first part of the book interprets three central concepts in Spinoza's ontology—affect, idea, and reason—to establish the theoretical lexicon on which the second, more argumentative half of the text relies. I begin with an examination of how the "spiritual" principles in Spinoza's thought can be understood within his naturalistic framework. Each chapter in part 1 relates the concepts to discussions in current philosophy and political theory—the politics of emotion, ideology critique, and moral theory, respectively—but the primary aim is to illustrate Spinoza's redefinition of humanity through his peculiar understanding of familiar terms. While a number of thinkers find ample resources in Spinoza for addressing current political concerns, their analyses often take the continuity of his concepts with our own for granted, neglecting the peculiarity of their meaning within his system. Yet Spinoza's concepts of affect, idea, and reason should not be assimilated to current post-Cartesian, post-Kantian, and post-Hegelian categories. Spinoza's thought weaves familiar terms into a surprisingly novel web of conceptual relationships, which can challenge and supplement if not displace current debates within liberal and democratic theory that founder on traditional oppositions and inferences. In contrast to recent books that celebrate Spinoza's protoliberalism or radical enlightenment principles, the second half argues that his alternative vision of affect and reason grounds, not a better politics of representation and rights, but a posthumanist politics of composition and synergy.

In chapter 1, I contend that Spinoza's portrait of affect redefines human action and freedom. Spinoza declares his understanding of affect to be entirely novel. His new conception, first and foremost, undermines any notion of "men's way of living" as unnatural, supernatural, or antinatural, expressive of an absolute freedom of mind and will. As long as our understanding of humanity is opposed to nature, we are in opposition to ourselves and the conditions of our freedom. His notion of affect within a field of powers and counterpowers that enable and constrain us aims to mitigate antipathy with an alternative conception of human freedom that is inextricable from ambient powers, human and nonhuman. I contend, with Etienne Balibar, that human freedom is best understood in "transindividual" terms. I examine the consequences of his ontology of affect through a discussion of his claim that we have nothing less in our power than our tongues. As a paradigmatic sign of human distinctiveness, Spinoza refigures speech as something that follows from a network of affections far beyond our sovereign control. I conclude that it is precisely because speech is so far beyond our control that he insists so frequently on the importance of collective conversation in the political writings. Because affect reveals us to be beyond ourselves, we can construct meaningful forms of freedom only together.

Chapter 2 presents Spinoza's theory of ideas in terms of natural power. Ideology critique typically "denaturalizes" ideas that are taken to be obvious, true, and natural by revealing them to be historically specific expressions of economic and cultural power. I argue that Spinoza offers a complementary "renaturalization" of ideology whereby social critics and political activists can grasp how ideas grow, survive, and thrive, or shrink and die, like any other natural being. The consideration of ideas in terms of force and vitality figures ideology critique as a struggle to give life support to some ideas within the power of thought while starving others. Because ideas, considered absolutely on Spinoza's terms, are indifferent to human flourishing, they survive, thrive, or atrophy on the basis of their relationship to ambient ideas. Thus, the effort to think and live well requires attention to the collective dimensions of thinking life, where "collective" refers to a transpersonal accumulation of ideal power that includes human as well as nonhuman beings. Because it is primarily a matter of force and power rather than truth and falsity, the project of thinking otherwise entails an effort to displace and to reorganize ideas that is best undertaken by coordinating and galvanizing many thinking powers. To illustrate this I consider how social movements, in addition to explaining how pernicious ideas come into being, might endeavor to reorganize relations among ideal powers to be more enabling.

Chapter 3 further develops the notion of renaturalization through an examination of the character of reason in Spinoza's ethics. I examine the argument that despite Spinoza's ontological egalitarianism, by which everything is equally part of nature, his morality appears to be irredeemably anthropocentric. If, as I claim in chapter 1, "man" has come to mean something different for Spinoza, the character of anthropocentrism takes on a new meaning as well. And if, as I contend in chapter 2, we ought to reimagine thought itself, what it means to be rational must likewise be reconsidered. This chapter resituates Spinoza's appeals to "human nature," his unequivocal and profound valorization of human association and friendship, and his understanding of reason as the foundation of ethical practice. I argue that Spinoza's understanding of reason is far more local and contextual than has been recognized. I claim that reason is constituted rather than discovered, which opens the way for a critical appraisal of questions of human utility and the norms implicit in Spinoza's own invocation of "man."

Chapter 4 examines Judith Butler's claim that Spinoza's *conatus* (striving) and *cupiditas* (desire) prefigure Hegel's understanding of desire and thus support her own reconstruction of a politics of recognition. Through an analysis of Spinoza's and Hegel's conceptions of desire, this chapter ascertains the basis of the heretical alliance that Butler forges between Hegel and Spinoza in the service of her own political theory. I argue that what is at stake in posing Spinoza and Hegel as alternative foundations for social and political theory is less a matter of joy versus despair or positivity versus negativity (as many Spinozists have claimed) than a question of two competing models of relationality. Spinoza and Hegel inscribe their conceptions of desire within relational ontologies, but their different understandings of the character of relationships among finite beings entail distinct conceptions of power, agency, and thus of politics. Butler is correct to identify each thinker as an alternative to mainstream liberalism. However, she underestimates Spinoza's challenge to any politics grounded in representation, including her own.

In chapter 5, I further the argument that Spinoza challenges rather than supports a politics of recognition. I begin with a consideration of Elizabeth Grosz's provocative claim that feminist and antiracist theorists should reject a politics of recognition in favor of "a politics of imperceptibility." Her alternative proposal of imperceptibility, although suggestive, remains inchoate and difficult to grasp. I turn to Spinoza to develop and explore its possibilities. Spinoza's political writings, far from according priority to individual or group recognition, provide structural means for reorienting the multifarious desires for recognition so that they may be transformed and fulfilled in alternative ways. Even if the desire to be esteemed remains very powerful, it cannot become a force of freedom as long as it depends upon the desirer's being seen as an absolutely special genre of being, elevated out of nature by virtue of rationality, consciousness, free will, or anything else. My contention is that the self-love—and the production of collective power and pleasure—at which the desire for recognition aims requires a nonhumanist theory of agency and desire. I explore what this means through the consideration of an example from feminist politics.

This study of Spinoza is inspired throughout by the various attempts to reimagine and reorganize our lived relations and connections to human and nonhuman beings in light of posthumanist critiques of human exceptionalism. Spinoza's ontology of relations troubles species boundaries and opens the way to consider linkages of power with nonhuman beings. Nevertheless, in investigating Spinoza's words on beasts in chapter 6, I encounter some cautionary notes for ethical and political turns to the nonhuman. Spinoza's words on beasts demand that we investigate the affective orientation that draws us to nonhuman figures like the animal. Spinoza diagnoses the desires and affects engendering the figure of the animal as a model for human agents. The image of the animal is not an animal in its own right but a wild, uncultivated anti-man, and therefore always an image *of* man (in both senses of the genitive). Spinoza's remarks on animals concern the misanthropic despair that can erupt as a reaction to the impossible ideals implicit in humanist politics. I conclude chapter 6 and the monograph with a critical exploration of the limits and promises of an ethics and politics that are not governed by the image of man.

PART I

Reconfiguring the Human

1

Lines, Planes, and Bodies:
Redefining Human Action

In the preface to his study of affect in the *Ethics*, Spinoza famously remarks that he will "consider human actions and appetites just as if it were a question of lines, planes, and bodies." With its redefinition of *humanas actiones*, the perspective of lines, planes, and bodies is the fundamental basis for the politics of renaturalization. According to Spinoza,

> Most of those who have written about the affects and men's ways of living, seem to treat, not of natural things, which follow the common laws of Nature, but of things which are outside Nature. Indeed, they seem to conceive man in Nature as a dominion within a dominion [*imperium in imperio*]. For they believe that man disturbs, rather than follows, the order of Nature, that he has absolute power over his actions, and that he is determined only by himself. (*E* III pref)

It is only in this preface that Spinoza draws attention to the peculiarity of his geometrical method.[1] He remarks that those who "prefer to curse or laugh at the affects and actions of men" will find his approach both strange and futile, for what is irrational is not susceptible to rational demonstra-

---

1. As noted by Cooper, "Freedom of Speech and Philosophical Citizenship in Spinoza's *Theological-Political Treatise*," 101.

tion. Yet he insists that everything operates according to the same rules, and "hate, envy, anger, and the like . . . follow with the same necessity and force of Nature as other singular things." Notably, the justification for the geometrical method is not that it engenders a scientific perspective on external reality. Geometry is invoked not to measure the earth (*ge*), external nature, or physical as opposed to spiritual reality but to make possible a new measure of ourselves, a new measure of "man." The lens of geometry exposes humanity as continuous with nature, operating according to the same norms and regularities.

Viewing humanity in terms of lines, planes, and bodies aims to correct the psychology that leads each to invent "from his own temperament different ways of worshipping God, so that God might love him above all the rest, and direct the whole of Nature according to the needs of [his] blind desire and insatiable greed" (*E* I app). Spinoza declares that a narcissistic understanding of reality might have imprisoned us forever if mathematics "had not shown men another standard [*norma*] of truth" (I app). Yet mathematics is not the sole measure of reality, the key that unlocks the mysteries of the universe. Math provides a distinctive standard of truth, an alternate angle that enables us to see ourselves and our place in nature in a different light. Unlike the imaginative perspective that sees everything as being "for or against us," the geometrical perspective examines things in terms of their definitions, or self-relations. Among the most difficult things to aspire to know in terms of their self-relation rather than their relation-to-me are human action and passion. But Spinoza hopes the geometrical method will allow us to understand rather than "bewail" affects. Thus, beyond teaching us the properties of triangles, geometry paves the way for the politics of renaturalization, a new perspective on "hatred, anger, envy, and the like."[2] Spinoza mobilizes mathematics to reinsert human action into nature, so that "man" is no longer understood to be an empire within an empire, operating according to uniquely human laws and norms.

Those who imagine man to be "determined only by himself" (*E* I app) misunderstand humanity as something opposed to nature. As a consequence, human viciousness is frequently blamed on affects and passions, understood to be the animal eruptions that stain spiritual and rational man, marking his this-worldly existence and lamentable distance from God. Freedom of the will, in other words, belongs to an anthropology in

---

2. I elaborate on "the ethical function of mathematics" in "'*Nemo non videt*.'"

which humanity is both exceptionally free and defective. This is a recognizably Christian view of postlapsarian man, free to earn or to lose the grace of God. On this model, Spinoza contends that the task of moral and political thought is reduced to denunciation or approbation instead of understanding and action. This view of human nature persists in "scientific" attempts to grasp human passions and actions.[3] Thus, perhaps even more effectively than his predecessors, "the celebrated Descartes" and his new natural science sever the spiritual from the natural, maintaining that even if our bodies are knowable machines, "the mind has absolute power over its own actions." Spinoza's study of the affects comprises a novel effort to reinsert human action and existence into nature. "So the way of understanding the nature of anything, of whatever kind, must . . . be the same, namely, through the universal laws and rules of Nature." A view of action as affect opposes the emerging scientific spiritualism by rejecting any implication that "men's way of living" is unnatural, supernatural, or antinatural, exempt from the order of cause and effect.

Spinoza's treatment of affect in the final three parts of the *Ethics* engages directly with Descartes's *Passions of the Soul*, opposing its conclusions point by point. It remains relevant in our time as a challenge to mainstream approaches to both political theory and social constructivism, which persist in the view, however complicated, that the world in which we live is an artifact of human agency. Even if denaturalization upsets some understandings of autonomy through analyzing social institutions, it retrenches oppositions between humanity and animality, culture and nature. Spinoza's analysis of action as a kind of affect grounds his effort to renaturalize humanity.[4] I say that he "renaturalizes" rather than "naturalizes" humanity, since he is engaged in a strategic reversal of the particular form of spiritualization gaining momentum in his own time. Spiritualization is most evident in the postulate of a mind equipped with a radically free will, which operates in an entirely different way than its body. Although the notion of free will long precedes Descartes in the Christian tradition, the secular version of Cartesian dualism persists today, for example, such that most philosophers identify themselves as

---

3. Heidi Ravven argues that putatively secular ethical and political theory remains Christian insofar as it preserves the notion of an absolutely free will. "What Spinoza Can Teach Us about Embodying and Naturalizing Ethics."

4. For other approaches to Spinoza's theory of affect, see Damasio, *Descartes' Error* and *Looking for Spinoza*; Negri, "Value and Affect"; Massumi, *Parables of the Virtual*; and Clough, *The Affective Turn*.

"compatibilists."[5] Most believe, like Descartes and Kant, that total determination in the realm of nature is compatible with radical human freedom in the realm of the mind. Although the term suggests a "compatibility" between mind and matter, spirit and nature, moral responsibility and causal determinism, it disguises an opposition between rational and natural life. This book aims to show why such an opposition, for Spinoza, yields self-hatred, misanthropy, and civil unrest, and to begin to think our way beyond it.

I proceed in this chapter to outline Spinoza's understanding of action as affect and its place in his system. I thereby introduce the working vocabulary upon which the remainder of the book depends. The second section outlines how the perspective of affect displaces methodological individualism. To think in terms of affect is necessarily to think in terms of "transindividuality," such that forms of individuality are necessarily incomplete and variable in response to other beings. The third section examines one major consequence of Spinoza's revision of human action. I ascertain what becomes of verbal expression and mental decision in Spinoza's thought when action becomes affect. For Aristotle and many following him, including Hobbes, what makes us human is a power to deliberate and use language. Spinoza, however, treats both decision and speech as radically natural phenomena, which do not make humans exceptional. This example highlights the political implications of the perspective of lines, planes, and bodies. Renaturalization prompts Spinoza to counsel governments to safeguard the freedom of expression, while insisting on the universal inability to control our tongues. While other Spinoza commentators emphasize the futility of the sovereign repression of free expression, the politics of renaturalization underscores the lack of control from the other side. The limitations that Spinoza recommends upon sovereign power emerge from the lack of sovereignty in each and every one of us. Understanding human expression in terms of natural forces and affective determination urges us to conceive of speech as something that emerges by virtue of a complex play of contact and contiguity with other beings, human and nonhuman. In what may seem to be a paradoxical gesture, I suggest that, precisely because we have so little power over our tongues, Spinoza advocates institutions that promote collective conversa-

---

5. In a recent survey of 3,226 professional philosophers and graduate students, 59 percent "accept or lean toward" compatibilism, while the next most popular answer, "other," was selected by fewer than 15 percent of respondents. See http://philpapers.org/surveys/ (accessed December 17, 2009).

tion. This chapter thus provides the basic schema for a politics of renaturalization, which begins to disrupt the voluntarist and anthropocentric bases of current ethical and political thought.

Action as Affect

When redefining human action, Spinoza's target is most obviously Descartes. Many today also identify Descartes as their antagonist. André Gombay notes that there is something shocking and even abhorrent to most people about the Cartesian dictum "I think therefore I am."[6] Aren't we also embodied, feeling beings who relish the experience of awe before natural beauty and artistic expression? The restriction of what is essentially and distinctively "me" to thought and thought alone continues to disturb readers of Descartes.[7] Yet this has not prevented the vast majority of political and moral theorists from drawing lines around the human community with precisely such an understanding. Even animal rights theorists argue for including animals on the basis of their "relevant similarities" to human beings, all of which pertain to consciousness and thought.[8] Thus, even as the narrow vision of humans as essentially and exclusively thinking beings raises so many objections, political and ethical theory often remains confined to this vision.

With Spinoza's theory of affect, we have a comprehensive redefinition of human agency. More than an affirmation of our corporeality, Spinoza's theory of affect gives rise to a notion of agency that is in no way exclusively human. The conception of the human that emerges is a being around whom lines cannot be definitively drawn and whose powers cannot be preemptively defined. As he insists on the inability of the mind to master its body, he declares that "no one has yet determined what the body can do" (*E* III p2s). Mind-body identity entails that, likewise, no one knows what the mind can do. These limitless possibilities ascribed to mind and body include not only those we call human but also the ideal and corporeal powers of beasts, computers, and collectivities. "Affect" names those changes in power that belong to finite existence by virtue of being connected necessarily to other beings, immersed in a field of powers and counterpowers that cannot be entirely inventoried, anticipated,

---

6. Gombay, *Descartes*, ix.
7. Recent Descartes scholarship, however, has been dedicated to revising this portrait of Descartes, especially through interpretations of *Passions of the Soul* and the correspondence with Princess Elisabeth. See, e.g., Deborah J. Brown, *Descartes and the Passionate Mind*.
8. See the now classic texts of Regan, *The Case for Animal Rights*, and Singer, *Animal Liberation*.

or circumscribed by "human nature," a term we will explore in depth in chapter 3. Let us carefully examine the term "affect" and its place in Spinoza's system.

It would be difficult to overestimate the importance of affect in Spinoza's philosophy as a whole. The final three of the five parts of the *Ethics* focus on "affect." *Affectus* is the first word of the *Political Treatise* and remains a protagonist throughout the text.[9] The *Theological-Political Treatise* begins with a vivid portrait of the misery provoked by hope and fear, the affects that nourish the superstition and despotism that are the treatise's objects of critique. Since my first concern in this chapter is how affect redefines human action, I will restrict myself here to describing its centrality to his ontology.

Recent scholarship on Spinoza often understands affect to be interchangeable with emotion.[10] Even if he catalogues many affects that we identify as emotions,[11] affect is not *reducible* to our emotional lives. The term was translated into English by both Samuel Shirley and R. H. M. Elwes as "emotion," but the term "emotion" misleadingly applies only to human beings and perhaps "higher" animals. Emotion likewise suggests irrationality and bondage, but Spinoza links affect to action, reason, and freedom as well. Most basically, affect refers to a universal power to affect and be affected, to the fact that finite beings enhance and diminish one another's power necessarily, by virtue of their inescapable interdependency. An affect is an encounter between bodies that involves a change in one's power, for better or for worse, together with an idea of that change (*E* III def3). Spinoza's ontology views affects as pertaining to all bodies in nature, sentient or not. To make his unorthodox portrait of affect clearer, I will draw a brief sketch of his ontology.

Existence, according to Spinoza, consists of the infinitely complex, unbounded totality he names "Nature," "substance," or "God," which is most basically all there is and all there could ever be. Nature is "expressed" in infinitely many "attributes," or ways of being, of which we know two, thought and extension. Each way of being is articulated into infinitely many "modes." Most of what we recognize as "things" at the level

---

9. As I mentioned, however, the English translations obscure the importance of affect, properly speaking, in the political writings. *Affectus* is rendered variably as "passion" or "emotion" but almost never as "affect," making it impossible for the casual reader to identify it as a term of art.

10. For example, Damasio, *Looking for Spinoza*; Nussbaum, *Upheavals of Thought*.

11. At the same time, it is an exaggeration to claim that Spinoza's theory of affect has *nothing to do with* emotions, as some imply, following Deleuze and Guattari's remarks and Massumi's translator's note in *A Thousand Plateaus*.

of phenomenal experience are finite "modes" (also called "affections" or "modifications"). Importantly, since there is nothing outside of the infinite system of relations (nature), all modes are bound to one another in relationships of cause and effect. Each and every finite thing is bound to every other finite thing (E I p28), as well as to the infinite force of nature (I p15). Substance, God, or nature does not exist apart from but exists in and as this inexhaustible system of horizontal, mutual causality among infinitely many beings (I p18).[12] Yet the doctrine of the attributes, to be discussed further below and explored in the following chapter, maintains a distinction between the causal community of bodies (modes of extension) and that of ideas (modes of thought). This has the very important result for the politics of renaturalization that each idea is situated within a network of ideas in which it exists and acts. An idea's action and existence are restricted to its attribute (thought), such that it neither moves nor is moved by bodies. Likewise, each body exists and acts within a force field of bodies, affected by and affecting other bodies, but its actions and passions cannot be explained by virtue of the impact of ideas (I def2; II p7; III p2).

Each mode exists and acts because it has, concomitantly, the power to affect (E I p36) and to be affected by others (I p28). This is as true of rocks and surfboards as it is of squirrels and humans. The only difference is that "in proportion as a body is more capable than others of doing many things at once, or being acted on in many ways at once, so its mind is capable of perceiving many things at once" (II p13s). Insofar as human bodies can undergo more affections and are able to affect more bodies in nature, they exhibit greater powers of mind. Such powers reflect only a relative complexity of body and mind rather than a difference in kind from other natural beings. Nothing prevents some animals from exhibiting greater mental power than some humans, and perhaps even less prevents some collective bodies, like civil institutions or electronic networks, from exhibiting mental power superior to that of a particular human. All beings are "animate," or minded, in precisely the same measure as their bodies "can be disposed in a great many ways" (II p14).

We must be cautious, however, in our understanding of this coveted spiritual power that we call "mind." As mentioned above, in the order of being, "a body is not limited by a thought nor a thought by a body"

---

12. This story, which is often referred to as Spinoza's "doctrine of immanence," is necessarily simplified but will be developed throughout this study. For helpful treatments of Spinoza's ontology that have an immediate bearing on political theory, see Montag, "Spinoza: Politics in a World without Transcendence," and Negri, *The Savage Anomaly*.

(*E* I def2). Thus, the relationship between mind and body is not one of "psycho-physical interactionism." In what has become known as his doctrine of "parallelism," Spinoza contends that "[t]he order and connection of ideas is the same as the order and connection of things" (II p7). He reiterates this several times, sometimes altering his formulation to read that any thing in nature expresses "the same order and connection of *causes*" (II p7s; II p9d; my emphasis). The notion of parallelism, attributed to Spinoza by Leibniz, misleadingly suggests that for each material "thing" in the world, there is a representation, or idea, in the universal intellect, or mind of God. For the human being, parallelism implies that there are ideas in the human mind reflecting each body part. The imagery of parallelism, as others have pointed out,[13] is thereby easily misconstrued, since it suggests that ideas exist in order to represent bodies and are valid insofar as they do so accurately. Since the attributes are metaphysically independent of one another, ideas and bodies do not express or explain *one another* but rather express one and the same order and connection of *causes*.[14] Parallelism risks reducing one dimension of natural reality to a state of functional dependency on the other. Yet, by virtue of their infinity, the attributes of thought and extension are not ontologically dependent upon one another. Each attribute exhaustively expresses nature in its own terms and is thereby irreducible to any other form of natural power. Neither ideas nor bodies have a functional purpose outside of their respective attributes. Ideas strive to exist as powerfully as they can within the causal order of ideas, and bodies strive to do the same within the causal order of bodies.

This autonomy of the attributes prompts Spinoza to assert frequently that the mind aims at understanding and nothing else. This has the attractive consequence that the mind's powers are valuable not only insofar as they allow us to subordinate nature to our purposes. Nevertheless, it appears to be a typical philosopher's reduction of human aspiration to philosophy. Yet the mind's drive to understand is simply a restriction imposed by the doctrine of the attributes. The restriction's primary function is not to denigrate bodily power or activity but to deny the power of the will to impose itself upon the body. If minds can act only on other ideas, they cannot govern bodies. Full self-understanding involves a notion of the body as self-organizing and capable of coordinating its powers among other bodies. Indeed, "the body itself, simply from the laws of its nature,

---

13. For example, Harris, *Spinoza's Philosophy*, and Macherey, *Introduction à l'Ethique de Spinoza, La seconde partie*.

14. I owe this point to Macherey, *Introduction à l'Ethique de Spinoza, La seconde partie*, 72.

can do many things which its mind wonders at" (*E* III p2s). Bodies, no less than minds, strive to act and to amplify their existence within the realm of bodies. Bodies and ideas each serve themselves.

While Spinoza's presentation sometimes goes awkwardly back and forth between mental and corporeal explanations of various phenomena,[15] his treatment of affect provides us a way to think about "the order and connection of causes" insofar as it involves variations in the intensity of power belonging to mind and body at once. Descartes wrote about the passions in order to explain how mind and body communicate and form a unit despite their duality.[16] When Spinoza turns to affect, however, he describes the necessary identity of body and mind, their perfectly symmetrical activity and passivity. "By affect [*affectum*] I understand affections [*affectiones*] of the body by which the body's power of acting is increased or diminished, aided or restrained, and at the same time, the ideas of these affections" (*E* III def3). Note that an "affection" or modification of the body entails an affect only when it includes a change in power. There can be bodily transformations (affections) that do not include affects, because the body's power does not become greater or less (III post1). An affect always names an alteration, for better or worse, of one's agency. In contrast to contemporary philosophical understandings of emotion, an affect is not a *response* to an event "triggering bodily changes."[17] An affect *is* that event; it is a qualitative change, equally corporeal and mental, in the intensity of a being's power to persevere. Because the mind and the body are the same thing, a bodily event does not provoke a mental state or "passion of the soul." Whereas, for Descartes, when the body acts, the mind usually receives, and vice versa,[18] Spinoza's view is that mind and body are powerful or weak, free or servile, in precisely the same measure.

Although this definition of affect applies equally to any and all bodies, Spinoza's primary concern is to redefine human action. His account dis-

---

15. One of the most awkward and problematic examples is the kind of thought experiment in part V of the *Ethics* where Spinoza proceeds to talk about the mind's duration independent of the body (*E* V p20s) and then to "feign" *as if* mental eternity begins with a certain achieved consciousness of God (V pp31–33).

16. See his fascinating correspondence with Princess Elisabeth of Bohemia.

17. I am referring to de Souza's definition of "emotion" in the *Stanford Encyclopedia of Philosophy*.

18. Descartes remarks that "a passion in the soul is usually [*communément*] an action in the body" (*PS* a. 2). Although the use of "communément" does not appear to suggest that it is ontologically necessary for one part of the self to act and the other to receive, I am not aware of any examples that he offers where the mind and the body are simultaneously active. He does provide several examples, however, of the soul acting on itself through volition, which, because the soul is metaphysically indivisible, names an action.

places a notion of unconstrained volition that might impose itself upon the extended universe. Spinoza presents the power of the mind so that it is opposed neither to the power of the body nor to the determinate power of nature. The mind's power, far from being a spiritual force that acts despite corporeal nature, is entirely natural and fully coincident with the actions of its body. In part IV, dedicated to human servitude, Spinoza notes that "[a]n affect, insofar as it is related to the mind, is an idea by which the mind affirms of its body a greater or lesser force of existing than before" (*E* IV p7d). Insofar as one is conscious of them, affects alert us to our "force of existing," our current ability to survive and thrive. Affects, properly understood, have immediate and vital importance. As we learn more about our affects, we are better able to gauge our particular "force of existing" and whether certain kinds of affections, certain encounters and relationships with others, amplify or diminish our vitality. To what precisely ought we to be alert?

Spinoza's account of the affects is, in a way, reductive. He names only three "primary affects," fewer than anyone before him: joy, sadness, and desire. Desire names the striving to persevere in one's being; joy is "that passion by which the mind [and body] passes to a greater perfection"; and sadness is "that passion by which it passes to a lesser perfection" (*E* III p11s). All affects, according to Spinoza, "arise from these three." The economy of his treatment of the affects, I suggest, reflects the primary function of his analysis. Spinoza's discussion of affects does not, for example, provide a moral catalogue of good and bad, praiseworthy and blameworthy emotions. His aim is, as he notes, not to "curse or laugh at the affects and actions of men" but to understand them (III pref). His particular understanding of affects centers the problem of power, or agency, within the framework of a radically relational ontology. Joy and sadness name the two fundamental ways that power varies by virtue of the constant modifications provoked by our being with others. There are infinitely many ways in which a complex being's activity can be enabled or constrained, but the economy of analysis reflects the supreme importance of tracking the depletion and animation of power ("force of existing") proper to each of us. This focus guides an examination of action in a deterministic universe, where "every singular thing, or any thing which is finite and has a determinate existence, can neither exist nor be determined to produce an effect unless it has been determined to exist and produce an effect by another cause" (I p28).

While I will examine desire in greater detail in chapter 4, for now I will note that all beings are provisionally individuated by their striving to persevere in being, and this endeavor to exist is their essence (*E* III p6). A human essence, or appetite to live, is called "desire" insofar as we are conscious of it (III p9s). It might strike some as peculiar that desire is an essence. The identification of essence with desire highlights that "natures" (synonymous with essences) are neither stable nor self-same. The essence of a complex being like man is not best understood as the "eternal truth" of human nature, since an essence includes whatever contributes, however temporarily, to the appetite by which beings strive to promote their preservation.[19] Understanding the singular essence of a complex, conscious existent entails undertaking what Balibar calls a "natural history of desire," an examination of the actions and passions that shape desire and its vicissitudes.[20] A natural history would be a developmental account of the transformations of a body from that of a profoundly dependent infant to that of a differently dependent adult, capable of undergoing and engendering an increasingly diverse range of affects (V p39).

Leaving aside further consideration of desire, let us turn for a moment to the other two basic affects: joy and sadness. The experience of joy (*laetitia*) signals that an encounter with another or a change within one's body has enhanced one's power in some way. The experience of sadness (*tristitia*), or some species of it, reveals the opposite. Love, hate, jealousy, envy, humility, abjection, glory, and self-satisfaction are contextualized permutations of joy and/or sadness, fused always with desire, and hence fall into one of two classes, joyful or sad, depending upon whether they amplify or diminish one's power on balance. Complex bodies are affected by joyful and sad passions simultaneously, but one class may dominate and prompt us to refer to our condition as depressed, elated, angry, grateful, and so on.

Alerting us to things that might aid or threaten our vitality is likewise the primary function of the passions for Descartes. However, on his account, the passions have special regard for bodily welfare (*PS* aa. 52, 137). As a result, Descartes's theory of passions introduces a difficulty alien to Spinoza's approach: sometimes what is primary and valuable for the body is actually harmful to the soul. For the body, "[s]adness is in some way primary and more necessary than joy, and hatred more necessary than love" (*PS* a. 137), even though hatred and sadness are anathema to the virtue of the soul (*PS* aa. 140–41). When there is a conflict between the good of the

---

19. Note that the proposition elaborating on the human essence includes adequate and inadequate ideas (*E* III p9).

20. Balibar, *Spinoza: From Individuality to Transindividuality*.

mind and that of the body, we must strive to order life, as far as possible, in accordance with the needs of the "better part of ourselves." Yet, as long as we are bound to this mortal coil, sadness and hatred often outweigh the impulse of rational love. Hatred prompts us to separate from what might harm us, to consider ourselves isolated and "alone" (PS a. 80). In a dangerous world, Descartes fears that our finitude demands the primacy of these isolating passions, but if we were only minds, "we could not abandon ourselves too much to Love and Joy, or shun Hatred and Sadness too much" (PS a. 141). This conflict prompts an arduous project of total mastery over one's passions (PS a. 212), sacrificing the immersion in love and joy that the soul desires to the demands of bodily health (PS a. 141).[21] The Cartesian project of liberation entails the subordination of one part of the self by the other, the government of body by mind and of passion by volition. On such a dualistic model, the two parts of oneself are not only distinct but, at least sometimes, opposed.[22] Freedom depends upon the extent to which the rational soul can order nature according to its distinctive requirements.

Whereas for Descartes it is the volitional soul that ought to become as active and Godlike as possible, for Spinoza the mind and the body are necessarily in it together, and the active thriving of one is always simultaneously the active thriving of the other. For Descartes, the opposition between mind and body leads sadness and hatred to retain primacy as long as we remain embodied. In contrast, for Spinoza, since minds and bodies are the same thing with identical requirements, "[h]ate can never be good" (E IV p45). Hate is a problem not because Spinoza advocates apathy, as some commentators suggest, but simply because "we strive to destroy the man we hate" (IV p45d). Spinoza's theory of affect correlates mental and bodily well-being and demands an alternative to self-prophylaxis, an impossibility for natural beings, for overcoming hatred. We cannot overcome hatred by reordering the world to protect the life of the mind, the solitary world of the sage. Rather, we must begin by forging a new perspective on human action and affect. The politics of renaturalization is thus anti-antipathetic in two senses: first, in the obvious sense of striving to displace antipathy with more powerful affects (IV p7); and, second, by

---

21. It was not so arduous, however, that Descartes did not boast of having achieved it by controlling even the disturbing images of his own dreams. Letter to Princess Elisabeth, 1 September 1645.

22. On dualism versus dichotomy, see Plumwood, *Feminism and the Mastery of Nature*, chap. 2.

opposing the extirpation of passions, becoming anti-anti-pathos, which can only mean the transcendence of nature (IV p4c).

Action as affect, then, does not entail *apatheia* for two reasons: (a) passions and the ability to be affected are the condition of possibility for action, and (b) passions themselves are not entirely passive. Immediately following the definition of affect, Spinoza notes that "if we can be the adequate cause of any of these affections, I understand by the affect an action; otherwise, a passion" (*E* III def3). We remain "partial causes" of our passions, for they express our power to be affected, a power that we must expand and diversify rather than overcome in order to become more powerful thinkers and actors (II p14). Indeed, joyful passions largely support our efforts to amplify our strength and self-understanding. Even sad passions are, in many circumstances, indirectly enabling.[23] Spinoza does not designate a class of harmful passions, even as he singles out hate as uniquely problematic. Rather, on a case-by-case basis, we can identify affects as noxious only when they entirely foreclose our power of thought (V p10), which would also mean a massive diminution of our corporeal power. Hate poses particular dangers to our powers of discernment and our ability to act in ways that improve our conditions, but if it can move us to understand and transform the conditions that make us feel hateful, it too might have a "correct use."

Action as affect views either mental or corporeal action as "adequate" rather than absolute. Only the totality of nature is absolute, unconstrained by external forces, since there is nothing external to the whole of reality. Finite modes like ourselves cannot hope to be absolute. We can only be adequate causes, comprising more of the force that contributes to an effect than do "external" causes, which never cease to contribute something (*E* III def1). Affect allows us to sense, gauge, and speak about activity and passivity, while affirming the irreducibility of passion for finite beings. There is no action without passion, and no passion without action. Activity and passivity do not simply map onto agency and patience, since enabling passions are often the eventual source of action. If an adequate cause is primarily but not exclusively responsible for an effect (i.e., if we never act alone), how do we determine when we act? This is a difficult question in Spinoza's philosophy. Spinoza claims that "if a number of indi-

---

23. It is impossible to make an absolute statement about the virtues of particular affects without reference to an individual and its unique circumstances. Thus, humility might be good in a culture that overemphasizes pride and narcissism, even if, as a sad passion, it cannot be said to be good in itself. One requires a contextual analysis to assess the work being done by any given affect in a particular situation.

viduals so concur in one action that together they are all the cause of one effect, I consider them all, to that extent, as one singular thing" (II def7). Does this suggest that what I am changes with every concurrence in bringing about some effect? Am "I" nothing more than these various concurrences, these abilities to compose, decompose, and recompose "singular things" by virtue of the power of affect?

The complexities of Spinoza's theory of affect deserve a book of their own, but we can observe at least its polemical function and thus the politics of renaturalization that it inspires. Spinoza's treatment of action as affect begins with an intervention: "the body cannot determine the mind to thinking, and the mind cannot determine the body to motion, to rest, or to anything else" (*E* III p2). Spinoza's positive argument for a fully affective notion of action is less visible than his critical stance. An understanding of free human action emerges more fully in the difficult "remedy for the affects" described in the final part of the *Ethics* and the political writings. According to my interpretation, one important outcome of his account of action as affect is that one cannot enjoy freedom alone. Human action is not an individual exercise but the consequence of an enabling affective milieu, comprising infinitely many human and nonhuman forces. As we have glimpsed, however, this affective account of freedom raises tricky questions about identity and individuation. In the following section, I will proceed to examine how these questions might be addressed by Spinoza's renaturalization of action, according to which human freedom must be reimagined as freedom-within-relation.[24]

The Transindividuality of Affect: Spinoza and Simondon

The ontological status of individuals in Spinoza's philosophy prompts a great deal of debate among scholars, with clear implications for notions of human freedom. Is something an action only if a discrete individual completes it without the assistance or impediment of others? The stakes, for some, are clear. If Spinoza believes that individuals are parts that belong essentially to a whole and act only by virtue of that larger power, then his philosophy belongs to an organicist tradition that culminates in Hegel and leads to Marxism. If, on the other hand, he treats individuality as original and psychologically irreducible, Spinoza grounds a liberal or libertarian

---

24. I thus agree with Aurelia Armstrong that Spinoza's notion of freedom has affinities with a feminist ethics of care that emphasizes connection, relationality, and dependency. See her "Autonomy and the Relational Individual."

politics for which independence is paramount.[25] What if neither of these alternatives adequately describes Spinoza's ontology? What if, as Etienne Balibar suggests, Spinoza's philosophy is better understood to anticipate the strange theory of ontogenesis outlined by French phenomenologist and philosopher of science Gilbert Simondon?[26] In particular, what if the main individuals in question (i.e., humans) are understood, neither as parts of wholes nor as irreducible atoms, but as "transindividuals"? This section will explore how Simondon's idiom of "transindividuality" illuminates Spinoza's view of human action in terms of affect. The removal of the traditional binaries part-whole and individual-aggregate reorients debates about whether Spinoza's philosophy belongs essentially to a "collectivist" or an "individualist" tradition of ethical and political thought. Disrupting the polarized debate provides the conceptual resources for the politics of renaturalization. The "third way" made possible by reading Spinoza through Simondon opens up a consideration of relationality beyond a dialectic of dependence and independence. Moreover, Spinoza's understanding of power relations implicit in his account of affect points toward the political implications of the concept of transindividuality, implications Simondon himself never considers expressly.

Simondon's basic innovation is to insist on a third approach to understanding individuality. According to his scheme, the history of philosophy tends either to presume a substantialist notion of uncreated unitary being or a hylomorphism in which individuals emerge from the coming together of form and matter. In either case, thinkers presume the reality of the given individual and seek to determine its conditions of existence. The individual, whether it is essentially a part of a whole or the spiritual formation of matter, is the point of interest for the metaphysician.[27] The viewpoint of Simondon's metaphysician, we might add, is likewise the perspective of the political theorist: How can the given freedom of the constituted individual be fostered or preserved? How can the individual subject to the determinations of life in common with others acquire moral autonomy with respect to her choices? Whether one takes a liberal approach, in

---

25. See, again, Armstrong, "Autonomy and the Relational Individual," as well as Matheron, *Individu et communauté chez Spinoza*, for the organicist interpretation, and Barbone, "What Counts as an Individual for Spinoza?"; Mara, "Liberal Politics and Moral Excellence in Spinoza's Political Philosophy"; Rice, *Tanquam Naturae Humanae Exemplar*"; Smith, *Spinoza, Liberalism, and the Question of Jewish Identity*; and West, "Spinoza on Positive Freedom," for the (far more common) liberal and libertarian interpretations.

26. Balibar, *Spinoza: From Individuality to Transindividuality*.

27. See the introduction to Simondon, *L'individuation à la lumière des notions de forme et d'information*.

which the integrity of the self is taken for granted as a normative description, or a "relational" approach, where dependencies are treated as central to the selfhood of individuals, it is still the individual that matters. The individual is the point of departure insofar as it is her freedom and ability to act autonomously that are sought.

Simondon suggests that an "ontogenetic" approach in which we seek "to know the individual through individuation, rather than the individuation through the individual," engenders an alternative lens.[28] When we seek out the *process* of individuation, we will find an always incomplete operation of differentiation and relation. Most of those beings we call "individuals"—human or nonhuman, organic or machinic, natural or political—are better described as "transindividuals." "The individual would then be grasped as a relative reality, a certain phase of being that presupposes a preindividual reality, and that, even after individuation, *does not exist on its own*, because individuation does not exhaust at one stroke all of preindividual reality."[29] The transindividual can be grasped only along with its preindividual conditions of existence and the incipient differentiations to come. Such an understanding is not merely an affirmation of ineluctable dependency or of the inexhaustible potentiality of becoming. It is an insistence that the individual is not available to knowledge *simpliciter*. The concept of the individual cannot be thought independently of what it is not. At the level of existence as well, a being always retains a preindividual "charge," an index of the fact that energetic relations are never resolved prior to death.[30] The transindividual is a paradoxical concept that defers perpetually the affirmation of individual reality per se. For Simondon, we can acknowledge distinctive agencies but never as anything other than relational phenomena. There simply are no atoms, originary or produced.

But neither are there wholes. Whole is another word for individual, that which is not divided. "In order to think individuation, being must be considered . . . as a system that is charged and supersaturated, above the level of unity."[31] Being is a system of relations that is excessive, always incomplete and uncompleted, and perpetually differentiating. It is not a unity because it is "supersaturated," replete with energetic force that is composing and recomposing in new forms, in response to new tensions, at all times. In Simondon's terms, living is "problematic," un-

---

28. Simondon, "The Position of the Problem of Ontogenesis," 5.
29. Ibid., 5.
30. Simondon, *L'individuation à la lumière des notions de forme et d'information*, 252.
31. Simondon, "The Position of the Problem of Ontogenesis," 6.

derdetermined, and unresolved. A fully coordinated unity or a completed individual never crystallizes. To live is to relate. Transindividuality names a collective agency, an always provisional and never isolable operation of action and differentiation. Transindividuality points up the "problematic" character of life as "a permanent activity of individuation"[32] and the systematic character of existence, which is likewise never finalized.

What might these strange ideas have to do with Spinoza, *the* thinker of substance, unity, and systematicity? After all, Spinoza is the point of departure for Hegel precisely because of the totalizing character of the One substance that admits of no negation, no true difference. Spinoza's substance is said to be that darkest of nights in which all cows are black.[33] Spinoza uses the language of individuality, refers to nature as a kind of totality, and treats particular beings as "parts." Many have recognized, however, the strategic character of Spinoza's discourse. *Deus sive Natura* is only the most famous of Spinoza's many translations of transcendent, supernatural categories into the language of immanence and nature. From his letters, we have a clue that his language of individuality may also involve a sleight of hand, a surreptitious translation of the transcendent notion of spiritual independence into the immanent terms of relation and composition. In fact, it is precisely when differentiating himself from Hobbes that Spinoza insists that "God can only improperly be called one or single" (*Ep* 50). Both the claim and its context lend support to interpretations such as Antonio Negri's whereby Spinoza subtly exposes the unity and simplicity of representations, including especially those of sovereigns and states, as imaginative constructions concealing the irreducible difference and antagonism constitutive of any body.[34]

But let us look more closely at Spinoza's text. In *Ethics* II, he identifies three levels of individuality: (a) simple bodies (*corpora simplicissima*) are the most basic individuals (*individua*); (b) complex, composite bodies made up of many simple bodies are themselves individuals; finally, (c) "the whole of nature is one individual, whose parts, that is, all bodies, vary in infinite ways, without any change of the whole individual" (*E* II p13s). Most everything we encounter in daily life, including one another, is of the middle sort. Spinoza insists that there are not limits to nature and that there is no void (I p15). His appeal to something like atoms with the notion of *corpora simplicissima*, as well as his image of nature as a "whole"

---

32. Ibid., 7.
33. See Hegel, *Phenomenology of Spirit*, preface, and *Lectures on the History of Philosophy*.
34. Negri, *The Savage Anomaly*.

or "totality," is thus perplexing. If nature is an infinite plenum with no empty space, it is hard to understand how simple bodies could exist on the model of atoms. Likewise, a grasp of nature's inexhaustible infinity and lack of borders makes it "one" or a "whole" in only a peculiar sense. Unbounded infinity is not part of a series, and thus the idea of either oneness or wholeness seems to be something like an auxiliary of imagination: useful but not precisely correct. Even if I can only gesture at the vexing metaphysical questions concerning the status of atoms and totality here,[35] we are justified in focusing on what matters to the politics of renaturalization: the middle sort of composite individual.

"The human body," Spinoza tells us, "is composed of a great number of individuals of different natures, each of which is highly composite" (*E* II p13sL7). Many different "individuals" compose what we think of as a human being. Among the composite individuals composing a human body we might include, along with our cells and organs, the various microorganisms that live on our skin and within our intestines, and without which our bodies could not persevere as the bodies that they are. Importantly, those microorganisms do not strive to be in order that *we* may live—their being is not a function of ours—but we form a composition with them, and thus our bodies and theirs persevere. The compositions that we pick out as discrete individuals and the dependencies that we regard as essential vary according to habit and cultural milieu. What this notion of composition foregrounds is that while the beings that constitute an "individual" could not exist without one another, this does not entail that any member of a composition has an instrumental purpose in relationship to another or to the total composition that is nature. Thus, it is justified to say that Spinoza's thought is not holistic; parts are not servants of the whole. Finite modes do not exist for the sake of the totality of nature, and neither does nature exist so that finite beings can. Neither serves the other. The relationship is more complicated than Spinoza's own language of parts and wholes suggests.

Simondon refers to transindividuals as "collectives," and we can fruitfully consider the human body in his terms. Simondon's insistence that transindividual collectives are "problematic" figures rather than sovereign wholes helps us to guard against the tendency either to discover atomic individuals as the basic units of nature (as liberal and libertarian interpreters do) or to view humans as subordinated to the seamless and irresistible

---

35. Cf. Josef Moreau, "Spinoza: est-il moniste?"

laws of the whole (as the neo-Stoic portrait maintains). Avoiding either extreme facilitates a better understanding of Spinoza's controversial doctrine of *conatus*. Spinoza maintains that the infinitely many finite modes of nature are singular "things" with unique strivings, but that modes cannot be understood in isolation from one another or from the infinite force of existence (God/Nature) (*E* III pp6–9). Since desire is a human's essence, affect is central to Spinoza's account of individuation. Recall that affect signals changes in the intensity of corporeal and mental power produced by encounters among bodies internal or external to a transindividual (III defs2–3). Composite bodies must undergo constant change in order to remain themselves, and the more complex they are, the more changes they must undergo. In order for the body of an infant to become the body of an adult, it must become capable of relating affectively to an increasingly diverse cast of beings. The more a being is able to be acted upon, the more it is activated. The more affects it can undergo, the more it can perceive, and the more it can affect others (III p 13s). The more complex a being is, in other words, the more it depends upon transformative involvements with other beings to preserve its characteristic arrangement of motion and rest. If humans are distinguishable from other beings by virtue of our relative complexity rather than an atomic spiritual principle, we are also distinguished by being constituted by a *greater* need of others. As feminist theorists have long argued, it is to the intensity of our dependency and involvement with one another that we owe our agency. We act only because we are perpetually "joining forces" with myriad beings in complex ways (IV p37s). Precisely because we cannot exist or act alone, human bodies and minds tend to be "capable of a great many things" (V p39s).

It is Spinoza's doctrine of *conatus*, his affective account of essences, that prompts Balibar to link Spinoza's ontology to Simondon's. What Balibar doesn't develop is the fact that Simondon's insistence on the reality of relation pertains as much to psychic as to physical phenomena. Simondon understands thoughts, perceptions, and affects in terms of processes of individuation, becoming more or less distinctive by virtue of a play of various potentialities within a preindividual field. Perceptions, thoughts, and feelings come to stand out through a preconscious resolution of "tension" within a force field of primordial relations. He thereby recasts knowledge as a relation between relations, rather than a relation between a subject and object. One identifies a feeling or perceives an object not by virtue of a coming into contact with an external reality (*Gegenstand*). Knowledge, Simondon suggests, may better be understood as "sympathy," or co-feeling, among living beings.³⁶ Consciousness is not a different kind of existence but a particular expression of ontogenetic relationality.

The term "transindividual" preserves some of the strangeness of Spinoza's system. In particular, it treats individuality as something that emerges from a "preindividual reservoir" from which it cannot finally be distinguished. The highest form of knowing in Spinoza's taxonomy, intuitive science, similarly involves the grasp of singular essences as determinate expressions of the essence of God/Nature. Intuitive science thereby refigures the notion of our dependency on God, such that it is equally valid to affirm that nature requires singular individuals in order to be what it is, in order to be infinitely diverse. The distinction between nature as the cause of each essence and singular essences as causes of nature's infinite variability ultimately becomes a heuristic rather than an ontological one. Ontological difference—the distinction between Being and beings—is thereby called into question. We regard ourselves as transindividuals, beings who come to exist and act more determinately by virtue of the increasing concurrence of other beings. Precisely insofar as a being can affirm and coordinate a multiplicity of agencies is it individuated. Affect receives a special place in Simondon's ontological schema, because the "charge" of emotional energy that we experience alerts us to how we are fueled and nourished, or burdened and diminished, by relations with others. To consider the problem of the affects, Muriel Combes notes, is to attend to "the experience in which a being appreciates that it is not only individual."³⁷ "Affective life, as a 'relation to oneself,' is a relation to what, *in oneself*, is not of the order of the individual."³⁸

Affect has a privileged place for both Spinoza and Simondon because affect discloses something essential about the kinds of beings we are. Affect points to the ultimate indiscernibility of activity and passivity that belongs to relational beings. Only by affirming that we cannot exist and act except by virtue of others may we gain greater power of individuation, while, concomitantly, acknowledging that complete separation can only mean death. What Spinoza alerts us to more than Simondon, however, is that affects express variations in agency. Simondon introduces a comprehensive paradigm of relational being, and Spinoza underscores the fact that relations are never neutral. Precisely because individuation is never complete, relations are power relations.

---

36. Simondon, *L'individuation à la lumière des notions de forme et d'information*, 249.
37. Combes, *Simondon: Individu et collectivité*, 55.
38. Ibid., 56.

From Spinoza's protovitalistic perspective, being as a constellation of power relations does not imply that nature is intrinsically violent, a perpetual war of all against all. Power (*potentia*) should be understood as the capacity, vitality, or "force of existing" that belongs to ideas as much as to bodies. At the same time, from the perspective of finitude, we cannot escape a fundamental *agon* of forces. While there is no teleology of conflictual relations necessary for either nature's or humanity's self-development, finite beings cannot but struggle against other finite beings that oppose their perseverance in being (E III p6). Each singular thing is vastly outnumbered by others that will not necessarily concur with its endeavors (IV ax1); thus Spinoza insists throughout his work that each of us remains necessarily exposed to passions and "man" can never bring it about that "he should be able to undergo no changes except those that can be understood through his nature alone" (IV p4). Passivity and vulnerability are irreducible aspects of finitude. While we can never free ourselves of subjection to antagonistic forces, under the best circumstances we can become increasingly attuned to those kinds of encounters that generate joyful, enabling passions and those that entrench and amplify sad, diminishing, and violent passions.

The vulnerability to others that the concept of transindividuality highlights is the very condition of possibility for life, strength, and wisdom. Spinoza's ethical subject still strives to become increasingly active and individuate itself. When one acts, or produces an effect that "can be understood through his nature alone," however, Spinoza still identifies adequate or virtuous action as an "affect." Action remains affect (a modification of the body by which its power is increased), because any and all action within an ontology of relation is, concomitantly, a coordination of activity with other beings. As Balibar puts it, "to be active or to be an adequate cause is *also* to establish a relationship with others, albeit not one of dependency (not even 'mutual' dependency) but of *convenientia* or synergy."[39] Thus, the task of becoming active and engendering freedom is not one of self-fortification against the influence of affects. Activity is a form of affection that becomes possible by virtue of combining energies effectively with ambient beings, human and nonhuman.

A relational ontology of transindividuals entails a complicated understanding of freedom for which we barely have the vocabulary. In an age in which rational choice and methodological individualism reign over the scientific study of human life, we strain to conceive of a nonvolitional free-

---

39. Balibar, *Spinoza: From Individuality to Transindividuality*, 24.

dom in which one negotiates, consciously and unconsciously, one's constituent relations with others, rather than transcending the natural realm of cause and effect. Simondon's language of transindividuality elaborates a distinctive understanding of relational individuation that points toward a politics of affect. These insights support a politics of renaturalization, which redefines agency to emphasize concrete problems of synergy and composition, rather than questions of rights and representation with respect to individuals and states. Rather than the traditional standoff between atomism and holism, we have a project of feeling and living otherwise, together. The following section will consider the renaturalization of what is so often considered a uniquely human act: speech.

The Tongue

Speech is one of those activities that are very difficult to renaturalize. Few prejudices are more pervasive than the view that we are masters of our tongues, and yet, for Spinoza, there is nothing over which we have less power. Our clichés indicate that there are all too many loose-lipped people whose imprudent utterances sink ships. Yet it remains difficult to persuade ourselves that we are not exceptions to this rule. The conviction that speech is by its nature free and that we, by virtue of being speaking animals, are free is but a stubborn case of the prejudice according to which men are "firmly persuaded that the body now moves, now is at rest, solely from the mind's command, and that it does a great many things which depend only on the mind's will and its art of thinking" (E III p2s). Spinoza's redefinition of freedom involves, first and foremost, an attack on the belief that our bodies are our instruments, the executors of our wills. Yet even if experience frequently belies our convictions, even if we, albeit ashamedly, acknowledge involuntary bodily acts, speech remains a special locus of our sense of liberty.[40] For Spinoza, this feeling of lack of constraint—like other experiences of what is called "negative freedom"—betrays an ignorance of the causes that move us to speak and act. The feeling that speech is free, however, is so tenacious and dear to us that Spinoza warns that any effort to curb it will be seen as tyrannical and met with ferocious resistance (*TTP* 20.4). We will accept that a governing body has a right to constrain much of our action, but we will fiercely resist the imperial management of our tongues. Strict censorship is a death sentence for any commonwealth. Even if it is a chimera, people will fight to

---

40. Pierre-François Moreau, *L'expérience et l'éternité chez Spinoza*, 375.

the death for the freedom "to think what they wish and to say what they think" (*TTP* 20.17).

Not only do we experience speech to be devoid of external constraint, we like to express ourselves. We enjoy making ourselves visible to others, revealing our inner lives. Yet despite being called a philosopher of expression, Spinoza rejects any model of free expression implying that a cause is whole and intact prior to its effect. With his claim that the body's actions do not spring from the mind's direction, Spinoza rejects a "technical" view of freedom, according to which intentions order and govern the practices of the body. The practical wisdom of renaturalization critiques the tendency to imagine either God or man on the model of the craftsman, as beings that inform the material world in accordance with their preexisting ideas. The craftsman model governs our views of speaking as much as our notions of making (transforming matter in accordance with the demands of spirit). We believe that we deliberate internally and proceed to externalize our mental process in the form of speech. Speech is treated as an expression, a publication of our interiority. On this artisanal model, ideas precede and govern actions, thoughts precede utterances, and minds command tongues. This is one of the several reasons speech is viewed as an essentially human action, the privileged mode by which we make manifest our rich internal lives.

An expressive understanding of speech has been called into question on many fronts in the past century. To take but one well-known example from feminist theory, Judith Butler treats language, gestures, and corporeal self-stylization as "performative" rather than "expressive."[41] Speech is not something personal and individual but a "citation" of social practices, constrained by the norms and linguistic structures that it also produces. One can observe generally that Butler insists upon the social character of language, that speech acts are "scripted" in advance by conventions and power relations, and that language itself contains myriad rules to which speaking subjects invariably submit. This model calls our agency into question and views speech as a site of subjection (which may be more or less liberatory). Speech is not merely epiphenomenal with respect to given power relations, since subjects can cite norms subversively and disrupt social scripts, especially once they have become critically aware of them. Nonetheless, subversion is reiterative of the structures it subverts, and there is no room in such a poststructuralist account for something like radically "free expression" absent of all constraint.

---

41. Butler, "Performative Acts and Gender Constitution."

The perspective of renaturalization supplements this tradition by calling attention to the natural forces enabling and constraining speech rather than the socially constructed character of language and speech acts. Spinoza's analysis of affect underscores the irrepressibility of the tongue rather than the intractable government of The Symbolic. Renaturalization emphasizes the local transmission of affect that belongs to embodied and finite existence, rather than the larger structures of humanly constituted authority. It thereby directs us to alternative sites of intervention. Rather than focusing our energies upon transforming representations of humanity or oedipal structures, as many feminists in the denaturalizing tradition advocate,[42] renaturalization suggests that we experiment with the affective aspect of collective conversations. Yet if Spinoza affirms that "men have nothing less in their power than their tongues" (*E* III p2s) and that "it is a universal failing in people that they communicate their thoughts to others, however much they should keep quiet" (*TTP* 20.4), why does he emphasize public and collective speech for the production of a powerful commonwealth above any other practice? If the tongue is most elusive of our control, why is its animation the key to collective self-determination? In this section, I propose the counterintuitive thesis that it is precisely our lack of sovereignty with respect to our tongues that lends them power to construct collective sovereignty. Although the tongue escapes our conscious control, it has the potential to reveal those affects and forces that contour our imaginations. Such disclosure, however, is possible only when we come to affirm that the tongue, speech, and language are not our own. We need the renaturalist perspective that reveals us, when considered as individuals, to be dispossessed of control over our bodies. Only then can speech, face to face and body to body, generate the affective conditions of a qualified and precarious collective self-possession. What this implies is thinking outside a politics of rights and representation and moving toward an experimental art of composition and synergy. Before making suggestions about new ways of animating our tongues, however, I will rehearse briefly the basis of Spinoza's critique of free will that prompts his remarks on speech.

Humans cannot control their tongues, according to Spinoza, as long as by "control" we mean predict and direct, in accordance with preformed reason or transparent intention. As I contend above, our bodies simply are not the instruments of our minds. Spinoza's treatment of the mind in part II of the *Ethics* concludes with a well-known criticism of Descartes's

---

42. For example, Cornell, *The Imaginary Domain*, and Oliver, *Family Values*.

view that judgments are exercised by human volition. Descartes maintains that the mind has two basic kinds of thoughts: perceptions and volitions (actions). Perceptions depend upon the body and are therefore passive. Volitions, in contrast, originate in the mind and are fully active (*PS* a. 18). They include desires, aversions, affirmations, denials, and doubts. The will is the only human power that is infinite, and Descartes therefore likens it to divine power. A judgment is an enactment of the will, by which a subject affirms or denies a perception, assesses it to be true or false, or decides to suspend his or her belief.

Spinoza denies that the mind has two fundamentally distinct kinds of thoughts, one that might be entertained independently of affect and another that involves desire. Rather, Spinoza claims that "will and intellect are one and the same" (*E* II p49c) and that all ideas, by their nature, involve affirmation and some measure of affective force. When one doubts, it is not by virtue of some power of self-restraint with respect to a representation that the body prompts in the mind. A doubt reflects conflicting affects that move the individual such that she affirms X and not-X at the same time. Far from being the expression of the one human power worthy of divinity, doubt signifies the co-presence of conflicting ideas and the subject's impotence to determine their causal history. In the *Theological-Political Treatise*, doubt appears not as a power of resistance with respect to suspect representations but as a highly vulnerable state in which "the slightest impulse can steer [the mind] in any direction" (1.1). Doubt is an affective condition that inclines one to yield to the strongest passion rather than to act from one's own resources and knowledge.

All ideas affirm the existence of something. Whereas Descartes notes that we can perceive our bodies and yet call their existence into radical question, Spinoza claims that our perceptions include the notion of existence, whether what we perceive is a triangle or our leg (e.g., *E* II p11). Spinoza offers the example of "a mode of thinking by which the mind affirms that the three angles of a triangle are equal to two right angles" (II p49d). In conceiving the idea of a triangle, one cannot deny that the measure of its three angles equals two right angles, since that idea belongs to the definition of a triangle. One is not free to entertain the possibility that a triangle might be configured differently, since one cannot separate the concept triangle from its essential properties. Insofar as one actually has the idea of a triangle, one must assent to all that is included in the idea. While an idea of a triangle is not an especially affectively charged one for most people, his point is that no idea, no matter how basic, is simply a "mute picture on a panel" that may be accepted or rejected by an independent act of the mind. One affirms or negates an idea based on the force it exerts within one's mind and not based on a neutral observation of its veracity. Whether one judges an idea to be true or false is not affected by the impact of "animal spirits" or some other corporeal determination, but rather reflects the power of the idea itself within the causal order of thought. The force of an idea is experienced affectively, by the whole individual, such that Spinoza ultimately assimilates judgment to affect. Affect is, therefore, not opposed to reason. Instead, reason names an active affect, an action (*E* V p3).

The politics of renaturalization challenges the portrait of humans as authors of unconstrained decisions. Spinoza hopes that the denial of free will, together with the affirmation that judgments are affectively necessitated, "contributes to social life, insofar as it teaches us to hate no one, to disesteem no one, to mock no one, to be angry at no one, and to envy no one" (*E* II p49s). This claim is key to the politics of renaturalization as I understand it. Viewing ourselves through the les of "lines, planes, and bodies" attenuates antipathy. It is an anti-antipathy strategy, as I mentioned, in two senses: by denying free will, the politics of renaturalization (a) mitigates hatred and (b) denies an ability to transcend *pathos*, our subjection to passions. It urges us to build a culture that affirms the necessity rather than the arbitrariness of the will in order to counter the hatred and sadness that arise from viewing ourselves and one another as uniquely responsible for our actions. If we can acknowledge the ineradicability of passions and the external determinations of fortune for all, our judgments, especially of our own misfortune, will lose some of their power to deplete us. Spinoza's geometric method promises to deliver an affirmation of necessity in all beings—God, triangles, humans, and praying mantises, alike. Only when we can see minds as much as bodies in terms of the constellations of powers and counterpowers in which they are embedded can we cease to hold the mind uniquely responsible for the acts of its errant instrument, its body.

Spinoza anticipates vehement objection to his claim that the body does not follow the mind's command. He expects the most pressing objections to be based on examples from the crafts. Isn't it the case that artists and architects devise ideas in accordance with which they guide their bodies' actions? Warren Montag notes, however, that one requires a notion of corporeal discipline, the determination of bodies by bodies, in order to account for something like the building of temples.[43] A body never simply

---

43. *Bodies, Masses, Power*, chap. 2.

carries out the desires of a mind. Bodies need certain habits and capacities that can be produced only by being disposed over time in ways that engender the forces necessary for building a complex artifact. The design envisioned by the mind cannot explain how bodies act on bodies, human and nonhuman, in order to erect a building. The temple's design emerges from and contributes to a history of bodily encounters and is better explained as a causally produced and productive desire than an originary intention (*E* IV pref).

Spinoza treats speech as, above all, corporeal. He declares that

> human affairs, of course, would be conducted far more happily if it were equally in man's power to be silent and to speak. But experience teaches all too plainly that men have *nothing less* in their power than their tongues, and can do nothing less than moderate their appetites. (*E* III p2s; my emphasis)

We like to imagine that our words express thoughts that precede and govern them. Perhaps not always, but we think that we sometimes succeed at speaking our minds. Spinoza claims that much of the time we are more like the drunk, madman, and gossip, who "believe they speak from free decision of mind [*ex libero mentis decreto*], when really they cannot contain their impulse to speak." Like those of drunks, lunatics, and chatterboxes, our words are, more often than not, spoken passions, responses to ambient forces.

Our bodies move in response to other bodies, not in response to our minds. Proximate bodies affect us in myriad ways, many of which we remain unaware of. It is not impossible for our tongues to move by virtue of bodily motions that are primarily internal to us rather than external to us, such that we might be the adequate cause of lingual motion. Yet, usually, we imagine ourselves to cause our words, when we have little if any understanding—let alone mastery—of the vast multiplicity of causes that incite our speech. If we consider Spinoza's rather sexist example of the gossip for a moment, he may be invoking cultural notions that women lack self-control and get "carried away" in the presence of others. Rather than expressions of his profound philosophical wisdom, Spinoza's own examples might be seen as "citations" of cultural norms *and* as consequences of having been affected by proximate bodies in his own environment. Perhaps he was conditioned to use such a stock example by teachers, parents, books, or by virtue of a complex reaction to being in the presence of vocal women he considered incontinent. (This is not to excuse his choice of example, of course, but only to consider the character of an explanation in his own terms.) Perhaps this example would not have occurred to him had he spent more time with philosophical women, as Descartes did. This is mere speculation, of course. My point is only that the speech of Spinoza, no less than that of the gossip or the schizophrenic, issues from a complex constellation of affects, rather than self-transparent intentions.

Feminists, by contrast, have analyzed gossip as a valuable form of social knowledge rather than a mindless occupation of bored housewives.[44] From a feminist perspective Spinoza's chatterbox may be seen in terms of her desire to be a bearer of valuable information. Such a desire will be more or less inflamed by proximate bodies. Someone she wants to bring nearer to herself may prompt increased speech, or she may speak of others as a way to deflect attention from herself when anxious. We cannot make general claims about which affects animate gossip, but we might consider the various affective and bodily forces moving our tongues and those of others when gossip happens. Gossip, like any other mode of speech, issues from a complicated constellation of passions to be listened to, shape social relations, and enjoy contact with another. Feminist analyses suggest that in contexts that encourage rather than foreclose women's speech, these same social passions might contribute to rational public deliberation, a mutually enlarging conversation with a loved one, or a galvanizing activist speech. What Spinoza underscores is that the affects exciting tongues are as powerful as an alcoholic's urge for whiskey or an infant's yearning for milk. They can hardly be resisted.

Speech, therefore, is no different from anything else we do, which we typically imagine to be free only by virtue of our ignorance of antecedent causes. Because we experience an impulse to say or to do something, we imagine that our desire arises from within us, a "within" that we construe as mental. Yet Spinoza claims that "decisions of the mind are nothing but the appetites themselves, which therefore vary as the disposition of the body varies." "Decisions of the mind," our own personal mental decrees, remain among our preferred examples of free will. We see that here, Spinoza like Hobbes reduces deliberation to appetite (*E* III p9s).[45] Yet in contrast to Hobbes, for whom bodies are all that there is, Spinoza does not maintain that the mental medium of decision is irrelevant.

---

44. See, for example, Code, *Rhetorical Spaces*, chap. 7.
45. Hobbes famously refers to the will as "the last Appetite, or Aversion, immediately adhering to the action, or the omission thereof." *Leviathan*, 127.

Both the decision of the mind and the determination of the body by nature exist together—or rather *are one and the same thing*, which we call decision when it is considered under, and explained through, the attribute of thought, and which we call a determination when it is considered under the attribute of extension and deduced from the laws of motion and rest. (III p2s; my emphasis)

In his own time, I suspect, Spinoza was eager to undermine, above all, the prejudice of free will. Thus, rather than treating speech as an expression of a human nature belonging to *logos*, Spinoza examines speech as it follows from the tongue. While the irreducibility of thought to extension entails that a decision of the mind has a distinctive reality of its own, perhaps Spinoza chooses the corporeal register of analysis because there is less danger of an overemphasis on bodily determination.

Some current theorists of affect, inspired by Spinoza, examine the corporeal to the utter exclusion of the mental, and the passive to the exclusion of the active.[46] There is a danger that, in our time, the notion of natural determination may overwhelm the imagination, such that an invocation of the body eclipses any consideration of the mind. To say that what is called "decision" in the realm of thought is called "determination" in the realm of extension is not, however, to reduce mind to body. Affect names the source of change in a way that points to mind and body at once, even if it doesn't solve the problem of their coexistence or relation.[47] Spinoza aims not to eliminate the reality of decision (*decreto*), or mental determination, but to redefine it. Decisions and "speech acts" become forces embedded within a constellation of cause and effect; they disclose our variable power to affect and be affected. Even if words and decisions issue from a heteronymous body and mind rather than a sovereign will, one alcohol enthusiast, for example, will not be affected in the same ways as another. Each of us is involved as a causal agent in the constitution of her unique disposition. Our words and deeds are necessarily constrained by our histories, but we are not hollow effects of a causal chain. Each finite mode is also a cause (*E* I p36) and was involved in the past that has contoured its disposition. What follows, then, for procedures of decision-making? If Spinoza emphasizes the affective aspect of decisions and utterances, how ought we to comport ourselves toward these phenomena in our individual and

---

46. See Clough's introduction to *The Affective Turn*.
47. Hardt, "Foreword: What Affects Are Good For," x.

collective lives? How do we address what might be considered unequal dispossessions? Are not some groups systematically deprived of autonomous self-expression, even on this revised model of freedom? Are not some, by virtue of their place in the social structure, more likely to be alcoholics or madmen or perceived as annoying chatterboxes?[48]

Even if it does not obviously tell us what to do, the lens of renaturalization retrains our focus. It calls our attention to the disposition of the body, fluctuations in its capacity, its particular history of experiences, and the milieu in which it is affected and able to affect others. It rejects the idea of a mind that intervenes in the causal order of bodies and decides to act upon it. "For each one governs [*moderatur*] everything from his affect; those who are torn by contrary affects do not know what they want, and *those who are not moved by any affect are very easily driven here and there*" (*E* III p2s; emphasis added). With this, Spinoza does not dismiss every notion of self-government, or self-moderation, but rather denies that we control our affects with nonaffects (IV p7). We do not impose order upon our affects with a different kind of power (e.g., reason). Our power, as well as our lack of power, is to be understood in terms of affect. Self-cultivation is not antipathetic. It does not entail extinguishing one's affects and discovering an alternative mode of self-determination.[49] The minimization of affect, as he states clearly, renders one the mere plaything of fortune. Lack of determination by either desire or joyful passions makes one more, rather than less, vulnerable to the influence of external causes, especially those sad passions like hatred, fear, anxiety, and melancholy. This should not be surprising given that, for Spinoza, self-determination emerges from our receptive powers to be affected and to coordinate multiple diverse agencies. Nevertheless, we tend to imagine falsely that less determination, less affect, or weak desire constitutes greater freedom to decide. Yet indifference is not freedom.[50] On the contrary, freedom is accompanied by

---

48. I thank Erin Tarver for asking me to consider this issue explicitly, even as I do not answer these questions in a satisfying way.

49. Spinoza's ontology makes the extirpation of affect impossible, which renders his own claim that "those who are not moved by any affect are very easily driven here and there" strange. It would seem that being driven here and there entails being moved by passions, or external causes. He notes that we can undergo many changes that are not affects, since they do not involve a transition in power (*E* III postI). Perhaps it is possible to be "easily driven here and there" without an increase or decrease in one's ability to think and act, but it seems unlikely. My suspicion is that "those who are not moved by any affect" refers to those who do not represent themselves as being moved by any desire or aversion.

50. Cf. Descartes, *Med* IV.

strong inclination, articulate desire, and discerning differentiation. Reason names mental actions accompanied by strong affect, determined such that one cannot even contemplate doing otherwise.[51] Necessary, determinate, desirous action is freest. "Freedom does not remove the necessity of action, but imposes it" (*TP* 2.7).

Whether absinthe or sober conversation with our most sympathetic and thoughtful interlocutors animates our tongues, our mental decrees are, at the same time, bodily appetites. It is from their affect that each—philosopher, statesman, or madman—"governs everything." The Latin term for "governs" (*moderor*) suggests the establishment of boundaries, regulations, and restraints. It recalls the Greek term *nomos*, naming the physical boundary, often a hedge or stone marker, that delineated property, and from which we get our word "autonomy." It is from one's affect that individuation—the boundaries of things and selves—emerges. One is rendered distinct not by a simple soul but by how one's affective composition yields to or enjoins others, distinguishes good from bad, beneficial from harmful, and de-cides (Latin: *cædere*), cuts things off from each other, however provisionally. Affect marks differences between things, evaluates encounters as pleasant or painful, energizing or depleting, determines the "mind to think this rather than that" (*E* III app), and arouses the tongue to utter this rather than that.

Spinoza has long been celebrated as an advocate of free speech and a forerunner of liberal tolerance.[52] The *Theological-Political Treatise* is interpreted to support "almost complete freedom of expression" since the state can never extinguish our natural right to "exercise our judgment."[53] Yet judgments, as we have seen, do not necessarily signal human freedom. Spinoza's support of a right to judge should not be viewed as the protection of either a naturally given individuality or a uniquely human capacity worthy of respect. Judgments are affirmations or negations intrinsic to our ideas; they are properties of mental life that no positive law could alter or eradicate any more than it could stop the sun from setting. Spinoza's argument against government attempts to control speech acts, therefore, does not rest upon a distinctively moral commitment to tolerance, understood as a principled respect for the diversity of human beliefs and

---

51. See *E* IV p66. We will examine this in greater detail in chapter 3.

52. Recent examples include Smith, *Spinoza, Liberalism, and the Question of Jewish Identity*; Israel, *Radical Enlightenment*.

53. Pitts is here interpreting remarks in chapter 20 of the *TTP*. "Spinoza on Freedom of Expression," 26.

practices.[54] Although Spinoza avows the inevitability of radical natural diversity, he advocates "free speech" precisely because human speech is *not free*, at least not as freedom is commonly understood. Since what we say does not flow from mental decrees over which we have independent control—again, "men have *nothing less* in their power than their tongues"—it is futile and self-undermining for a government to legislate the appropriateness of speech acts, or spoken passions. But, more than that, were it possible, it would be undesirable for either sovereigns or citizens to attempt to legislate over their speech acts. Our words, like the images that populate our minds, even if they don't point to nature as it is in itself, reveal ourselves to ourselves, disclose our passionate character and that of our milieu (*E* I app).

It is no accident that with his attack on the freedom of the will, Spinoza goes after *logos* itself. Speech is often seen to be the index of our humanity, because it is an intimate experience of freedom we all know. The most human thing we do, speak articulately, and that most remarkable edifice of human construction, language, however, are at the same time *most* elusive of our power. For as long as we persist in an understanding of agency on the model of the anthropomorphic individual, we can never reappropriate our power within the medium of speech. As long as we imagine speech to flow from an independent and isolable mind, we are drunk on self-delusion, unable to control our declarations. Nevertheless, my contention is that our unfreedom with respect to our tongues is precisely why speech is central to the displacement of imaginary by real freedom. Given that speech is caused by the forces operating in our environment, even if we do not reveal a discrete interiority upon speaking, we might view the scene of debate as a theater illuminating these very forces, the affects, and images moving us. Speech, beyond our sovereign control, reveals the powers that enable and constrain us. The theater of affect surely unveils as many causes of antipathy and dissatisfaction as sources of joy, strength, and rejuvenation. It might even reveal all too many chatterboxes, drunks, and madmen in our ranks, but, properly understood, it could indicate the conditions that incline us toward incontinence. The perspective of affect, moreover, demonstrates that none of us is ever inoculated against debilitating forces. Speech, viewed as disclosive passion, might reveal what disables us as well as what fortifies us.

Speech is liberating, from the perspective of the politics of renatu-

---

54. This has been regarded as a weakness of his defense of tolerance. Rosenthal, "Spinoza on Why the Sovereign Can Command Men's Tongues but Not Their Minds."

ralization, only when we cease to see it as free. When we see words as bodily motions caused by our mutual involvement with one another, we can discover ourselves, not as individuals, but as situated within a complex constellation of causes. We can then, together, endeavor to transform that environment and build the conditions of genuine freedom, which will necessarily be a freedom of degree rather than an absolute power to determine ourselves. Deliberation and communication might be interesting, from the perspective of renaturalization, not primarily for the content of the words uttered, but for the affects they uncover and the energetic resources they foreclose or offer to a community.

Despite the fact that Spinoza thinks our tongues to be one of the most wild and uncontrolled features of the human body, his primary recommendation for good government in his political treatises is the constitution of large deliberative assemblies. Whether he is discussing monarchy, aristocracy, or democracy, he recommends putting as many people as possible in a room together to speak. He prefers democracy on the basis that it potentially brings the whole commonwealth together to speak, side by side, in proximity to one another. These experiments in collective speech yield, importantly, "what no one had previously thought of" (*TP* 9.14). In speaking together, then, we are not discovering a rationality always already present, but constituting new ideas aroused by many minds and bodies encountering one another, speaking, debating, and listening. Inequalities in power and struggles to speak and to be heard are surely ineradicable for Spinoza, but the only mechanism he installs for preventing an unhealthy pooling of power within the political body is structured public decision-making by a large and diverse (in terms of trade or "clan") group of constituents. The ultimate virtue of deliberation is the production of a sharper and more discerning common agency through collective, open-ended speech. Especially through deploying that power over which we as individuals have so little control, we produce a mutually enlarging power together. Speaking is the primary way to expose entrenched antipathies, the main obstacles to joining forces, which, because such passion exceeds individual agents, can be countered only *en masse*.

Spinoza's redefinition of human action offers a vision of power for finite beings like us as power sharing. The renaturalization of humanity entails that humans are not different in kind from other finite beings: we all act by virtue of one another, by virtue of a power to be affected and to affect others. If we were different in kind, we could neither undergo passions provoked by others, nor could we define and constitute part of nature.

The continuity of all that exists serves as the basis for a new vision of power and of activity as power-in-connection, acting as plugging-in.

One is said to act, according to Spinoza, when an effect can be understood "through one's nature." Balibar rightly emphasizes that Spinoza never characterizes acting "through one's nature" as acting "alone."[55] Indeed, many individuals can act together and thereby be understood as one singular thing (*E* II def 7). Likewise, two individuals can have sufficiently similar natures so as to combine and "compose an individual twice as powerful as each one" (IV p18s). Spinoza explains that "the power [*potentia*] of each thing, *or* the striving [*conatus*] by which it (*either alone or with others*) does anything, or strives to do anything . . . is nothing but the . . . actual essence of the thing" (III p7d; emphasis added). Beings, in their essence, act and strive "either alone or with others." Acting "alone," moreover, never entails exiting the realm of causality. The most potent action is always one that links to others. In the *Ethics* as much as in the political writings, freedom is a project of coordinating a system of relationships among ambient beings, of acting in concert.

The most important natural forces, Spinoza avers, are fellow human beings, by which he meant especially fellow men. To forge the most enabling relationships with our fellows, however, his philosophy endeavors to renaturalize man and to arrive at a new understanding of human power. A vision of human agency that is not opposed to nature is more urgent today than ever. Even as Spinoza is an invaluable resource for reconfiguring our ideas of humanity, we certainly need to go further than Spinoza himself did by overturning the masculine assumptions undergirding his treatment of man. Spinoza's ontology is broad enough to support many new figures of the human, some of which will certainly be counter to his own vision. But, to alter a phrase, Spinozism falls behind history, and even behind itself, if it ever thinks it has arrived.

---

55. Balibar, *Spinoza: From Individuality to Transindividuality*, 24. Chapter 3 discusses the idea of a "nature" further.

2

Renaturalizing Ideology:
Spinoza's Ecosystem of Ideas

What becomes of ideology critique when minds are considered to be parts of nature and social forces are not different in kind from natural ones? Ideology critique typically involves a practice of "denaturalization" in which certain ideas that are taken to be obvious, true, and natural are shown to be historically specific expressions of economic and cultural power. Feminist ideology critics reveal that the ostensible obviousness of the need for women to remain in the domestic sphere, to take a well-known example, is a culturally variable product of hetero-patriarchal structures of power that contributes to women's subordination. Thus, for most feminists, the idea that women are *naturally* relational, nurturing, and cooperative conceals the institutional mechanisms that produce feminine subjects who are useful to the dominant class insofar as they cultivate such characteristics.[1] In this chapter, I argue that in Spinoza we find an alternative "renaturalization" of ideology whereby social critics and political activists can grasp how ideas grow, survive, and thrive, or shrink and die, like any other natural being. Rather than uncovering the synthetic basis of ostensibly natural facts, the politics of renaturalization

---

1. For example, MacKinnon, *Toward a Feminist Theory of the State*. Of course, feminist theorists of care, among others, valorize women's nurturing and relational capacities, but they do not claim that such skills are naturally prevalent in women.

seeks to identify the "ecological" factors that contribute to the vitality of oppressive ideas.

"Renaturalization" is not a direct antonym to the critical tradition of denaturalization. It does, however, resist the notion, implicit in social constructivism, that beneath any idea of nature, we will find only human agency. The imperative to expose the man behind the curtain often yields "intellectualist" and voluntarist strategies for challenging domineering constellations of ideas. It is important to denude truth claims as "truth-effects," but we ought not to think that we are the sole authors of such effects. Humans are dangerous animals who play games with truth, don infinitely many masks rendering us unrecognizable to ourselves, and transmute history into farce. Nevertheless, ideology critique offers too few resources for disarming tenacious, oppressive ideas. As Foucault observes, critique has trouble moving beyond the project of exposing lies, challenging distortions of reality, speaking truth to power, even as it calls for overturning the (institutional, material, structural) conditions of destructive ideologies.[2] Yet even Foucault's insights about the "politics of truth" overlook the force of ideas themselves, the power ideas have *qua* ideas.

In this chapter, I contend that understanding ideas as striving natural forces refigures ideology critique as a project of resistant reconstruction within an "ecosystem of ideas." Considering ideas in terms of force relations challenges received interpretations of Spinoza's ethical program as quietist and intellectualist, concerned only with the private enjoyment of truth and beatitude.[3] Although Spinoza obviously values true ideas, truth does not, alone, set anyone free (*E* IV p1). True or adequate ideas often fail to determine individuals and collectivities, such that we "see the better, but do the worse."[4] In order to be effective, true ideas require a favorable affective environment. The virtue, or power (IV def8), of true ideas is to be found in their affective more than their representational character. A project of ideology critique, therefore, becomes less a question of truth and falsity and more a matter of which constellations of ideas are enabling and which disabling. Moreover, when ideas are grasped in terms of energy and force, the self-emancipating practices of a solitary sage make

---

2. See Foucault, "Two Lectures," in *Power/Knowledge*.

3. For example, Yovel, *Spinoza and Other Heretics*, 1:154. This view is shared by many commentators, including, Smith, *Spinoza, Liberalism, and the Question of Jewish Identity*, and Wetlesen, *The Sage and the Way*.

4. Spinoza cites this phrase from Ovid's *Metamorphoses* several times in the *Ethics*.

little sense without a broader account of the relations (ideal and material, at once) that fortify her or his thinking power.

Marxist philosopher Louis Althusser, several of whose students became important Spinoza interpreters,[5] claims to have found in the appendix to part I of Spinoza's *Ethics* "the matrix of every possible theory of ideology."[6] Taking his cue to read Spinoza in these terms, I develop an interpretation of Spinoza's theory of ideas pertinent to ideology critique. Althusser highlights Spinoza's treatment of imagination and how the world "spontaneously" appears to human subjects, but I contextualize imagination within Spinoza's portrait of mental life more generally. Examining Spinoza's framework as a whole, we discover "Ideology"[7] to be a feature of natural rather than exclusively social (human) existence, and the project of critique becomes an engagement with the "life force" of ideas. The renaturalization of ideology critique is still a struggle for freedom, but it entails a reconception of freedom. Critical practice of renaturalization cannot hope to transcend determination, but neither is it a Stoic submission to the status quo, with only the solace of enlarged understanding. Freedom must be produced through an immanent displacement and reorganization of our constituent relations with others, including other ideas. Mitigation of the servile aspects of imagination entails, rather than an extirpation of any and all partiality or distortion (Ideology), "a new form . . . of appropriation" of one's imaginary life, a new grasp of the peculiar force of ideas, the way that we live and have our being in "the attribute" of thought.

My argument hinges upon an interpretation of Spinoza's difficult concept of the attributes, in particular the attribute of thought, and the portrait that emerges of what it is to be a finite thinking power in the infinite totality of nature's thought. Spinoza asks us to consider ideas in terms of their force, vitality, and power rather than *primarily* in terms of their truth and falsity. Such an emphasis leads me to conclude that the effort to think and live well requires attention to the collective dimensions of thinking life, where "collective" refers to a transpersonal accumulation

---

5. Most notably, Balibar and Macherey.
6. Althusser, "The Only Materialist Tradition," 7.
7. I use ideology in the broadest possible sense, which I defend below. It is closest to Althusser's use of "Ideology" in his essay "Ideology and Ideological State Apparatuses," even as I refer to something excessive of human representation. Althusser distinguishes between "Ideology" in the capitalized singular and "ideologies." Ideology is the invariant fact that human representations are mediated by the peculiar character of the social structure in which subjects live. Ideologies, on the other hand, refer to particular discourses that are motivated by a set of interests. Following Althusser, I consider ideology in the singular to refer to the more neutral sense of the "social" determination of ideas.

of ideal power that includes human as well as nonhuman beings. Ideology critique becomes a project of ascertaining particular disabling assemblages of thought, which must be countered through the mobilization of alternative constellations of thinking force. I come to this conclusion by way of an interpretation primarily of Spinoza's metaphysics rather than the more obvious route of his political writings, but it serves to make his frequent counsel for large deliberative assemblies in the latter far from surprising.

Spinoza offers a kind of "materialism" of ideas that underscores the exigency of joining forces to counter harmful ideas and the ways of life that correspond to them. Much attention has been given to Spinoza's materialism of bodies, but one can articulate an analogous field of determination among ideas. The enhancement of freedom requires attention to the distinctive characteristics of either mental or corporeal life, even as transformation necessarily occurs in each realm of life concomitantly. This chapter considers how to act in light of being given over to a power of thought that far exceeds our minds.

The Matrix

Let us briefly rehearse Althusser's argument for deeming Spinoza the inventor of "the matrix of every possible theory of ideology." Althusser derives "the matrix" primarily from the appendix to part I of Spinoza's *Ethics*. In these few pages, Spinoza traces the superstitious belief in a capricious and anthropomorphic God back to a spontaneous misrecognition of an individual's freedom and place in nature. Spinoza critiques the notion of humans as the center of a universe in which God rewards and punishes our deeds in accordance with his absolute pleasure. He treats the image of God as an all-powerful parent as entirely natural, however, a product of the embodied apprehension of our desire. In Spinoza's words, "men think themselves free, because they are conscious of their volitions and appetite, and do not think, even in their dreams, of what moves them to wanting and willing." We humans take our desire to be in front of us, representing something to which we are freely attracted, rather than behind us, as it were. Such a perspective "turns Nature completely upside down. For what is really a cause, it considers as an effect, and conversely." Spinoza calls this spontaneous perception "imagination," which discloses a great deal about the dispositions, desires, and passions of imaginers, without revealing much about the things imagined. We require the remedial intervention of other forms of knowing in order to modify the imaginative constitution of the world as something God, inspired by love for his subjects, laid out for human use.

The matrix of ideology follows from the conviction that the human individual is "the center and origin of every perception, of every action, of every object, and of every meaning."[8] An anthropocentric and individualist perspective derives from this "spontaneous" reversal of the order of cause and effect in which a subject's desire appears as the exclusive cause of her initiatives, ideas, and actions. This phenomenon may be familiar from Warren Montag's account in his work on Spinoza and Althusser.[9] Thus, I review it only briefly.

Althusser finds in Spinoza's portrait of the imagination the basic structure of ideology. Spinozan imagination, Althusser emphasizes, is not the first step on a ladder that comprises a "theory of knowledge," understood as a guarantee of truth.[10] Imagination, rather, names the "apparatus" that induces subjects to suffer a nearly endemic "slavelike subjectivity" precisely insofar as we regard ourselves to be undetermined. Without attention to what moves us to think and act, to our constraint and lack of freedom, we cannot modify our situation and hope to become freer. The apparatus of imagination performs two basic functions: first, it locates the human subject as the center of its thoughts, actions, desires, and meanings; second, it reverses the order of nature such that effects appear to be causes and reality seems to be organized teleologically in the service of human ends.[11] Readers of Althusser will recognize this as the apparatus of subjection described in the well-known "Ideology and Ideological State Apparatuses" essay. The description in the "ISAs" essay resonates with assertions Marx frequently makes, especially in the first volume of *Capital*. The reality of subjection is visible in the ambiguity of the term: one is a free subjectivity, an agent of thought and action, who is nevertheless subject to systematic and inescapable constraints on thinking and acting. As the story goes in *Capital*, the subject-worker is "interpellated" as free and responsible, as a peer in a legal exchange, precisely in order to contract away her freedom. Juridical freedom conceals that workers are free *from* the means of production and thereby constrained to consent to their own servitude.[12]

8. Althusser, "The Only Materialist Tradition," 6.

9. See especially chapter 2 of *Bodies, Masses, Power*. For other examinations of the relationship between Spinoza and Althusser, see Thomas, "Philosophical Strategies"; Norris, *Spinoza and the Origins of Modern Critical Theory*; Caroline Williams, *Contemporary French Philosophy*; Cotten, "Althusser et Spinoza"; and Althusser himself, "On Spinoza."

10. Althusser, "The Only Materialist Tradition," 5.

11. Ibid., 6, and E I app.

12. Marx, *Capital*, 1:280.

Juridical freedom brilliantly refigures the servile class as authors of their own subjection and marks a transformation in the historical struggle between master and slave. Legal, theological, and metaphysical discourses of inalienable, God-given freedom reshape the network of forces that determine the horizon of imagination, desire, and action.

The "illusion of subjectivity" to which Althusser refers is not, as many have feared, the illusion of agency. We act both because and in spite of ideology. Capitalism would not function without the activity of a multitude of workers, but our activity remains overtly and covertly forced in important ways. The illusion of subjectivity is the fantasy that each of us is the exclusive origin of her mode of imagining, that ideas and desires emanate outward from isolable minds and wills. Montag points out that, with Althusser, ideology ceases to be a question of beliefs and false consciousness.[13] I will go as far as to claim that on a broader reading of Spinoza, ideology ceases to be a question of minds at all. Althusser shows persuasively that ideology must be explained by relations of force, the practical discipline and arrangement of bodies, and the unconscious, affective structure that mediates the appearance of our lived world.[14] Thus, Montag emphasizes that ideology, for Althusser, is not a matter of subjective illusion but a matter of practice, ritual, and gesture.

Nevertheless, the fact that Althusser locates Spinoza's "matrix" in the appendix to part I of the *Ethics* suggests a faithfulness to Marx's (and Feuerbach's) emphasis upon the anthropo-theological fantasy as the necessary structure of any and all ideology, indeed "every possible theory of ideology." A more promising route for considering how we are subject to the force of ideas, in my view, lies in Spinoza's larger ontological picture. Rather than take aim exclusively at the religious form of our illusory autonomy (even as that was also Spinoza's explicit target), I examine the more neutral account of what it means to be a tiny particle of an infinite power of thought. In so doing, I offer an interpretation of ideology even further beyond the problematic of false consciousness. Spinoza's unique contribution to ideology critique lies not merely in his exposure of consciousness itself as spontaneously theological, as an originary and irrepressible belief in a transcendent and goal-directed human nature and its divine correlate. Rather, Spinoza's offers an examination of the life force of ideas, the way that ideas *qua* ideas behave and interact, and the way that humans live among and as ideal powers. Before discussing the fine

---

13. Montag, *Louis Althusser*, 78.
14. Ibid., 63.

details of Spinoza's portrait of the life of ideas, I will distinguish the notion of ideology critique I am sketching here from other major conceptions of it.

Ideology Critique Today?

Ideology critique has been all but abandoned in political theory,[15] even as it is practiced under other names. Although some eloquent and persuasive defenders remain,[16] it has been declared a victim of its own "imperialistic success,"[17] since a clever critic can determine anything whatsoever to be ideological. If there is no statement or image, for example, that cannot be said to be ideological, the category loses its analytic power. In its so-called vulgar Marxist formulation, ideology critique is denounced for expressing a naïve hope for a transparent social order, devoid of either distortion or domination. Paradoxically, while ideology critique takes its specific form as *critique* in Marx and Engels's *The German Ideology*, Marxism itself is often seen to be the supreme representative of ideological theorizing. In its vision of a social order that delivers a community of free producers at home in the world, Marxism exemplifies for many the problems intrinsic to aspirations of perfect impartiality and universality that such critique so effectively exposes.[18] Prompted by Foucault, many have shifted the rubric of their analyses away from ideologies toward regimes of discourse. Foucault associates ideology critique with the assumption that truth is opposed to domination and thereby emancipatory. In contrast, for Foucault, the production of truth, especially about the character of the human, is a major tool of domination. In fighting oppression, then, we should not see ourselves as missionaries of power-innocent truth. Rather, to live otherwise is to engender countertruths, nonneutral apparatuses of power-knowledge.[19]

Although I argue below that Spinoza also similarly objects to an under-

---

15. E.g., Sharpe, "The Aesthetics of Ideology."
16. Most notably, Eagleton, Laclau, and Žižek. See *Ideology*, "The Death and Resurrection of the Theory of Ideology," and the introductory essay in *Mapping Ideology*, respectively.
17. Laclau, "The Death and Resurrection of the Theory of Ideology," 202.
18. Although Marx's texts themselves are more complicated than many of the traditions to which they gave rise, his writings can be understood, at least partly, to be objectively responsible for the effects they produced. From a Spinozan perspective, texts are bodies that affect and are affected by other bodies, some of which accord with the striving unique to them (their particular "nature") but most of which are unanticipated products of energetic interactions between myriad forces.
19. See Foucault, "Truth and Power," in *Power/Knowledge*.

standing of truth independent of force relations, I do not join the many critics who, following Foucault's astute criticisms, abandon the term "ideology" altogether. I retain the term for two reasons: First, the notion of ideology, in contrast to discourse, preserves the centrality of an examination of ideas *qua* ideas. Spinoza's metaphysics maintains an analytic separation between ideas and bodies. There is a tendency in the studies of Spinoza to which I am most indebted to emphasize determination at the level of bodies. Yet Spinoza insists that since there is no *causal* relationship between the order of thought and the order of extension, the life of ideas cannot be explained *through* the life of bodies, and vice versa.[20] Ascertaining only corporeal determination risks suggesting that the order of bodies is the order of reality, while ideas compose the order of fiction. Although the theorists explicitly turn to Spinoza to avoid a simplistic model of the superstructure as epiphenomenal with respect to the base,[21] privileging corporeal determination without an analysis of ideal power implies that a consideration of ideas can be ideological only in the pejorative sense. Yet in no sense are ideas either secondary or derivative for Spinoza. Rather, thought names a way of being that is enacted by every existent thing. The omission of an analysis of (power) relationships among ideas risks leaving the philosophy of mind to the philosophers, as the interpreters of Spinoza's political thought restrict themselves to the plays of force in the putatively real world of bodies and affects.[22]

Moreover, in contrast to the Lacanian tradition of ideology critique, in Spinoza there is no unbridgeable distance between representation and "the Real," symbolization and that which it symbolizes. The order of extension, or matter, is not the ghostly specter of being that can take the form of thought only at the cost of its fictionalization. The fact that Spinoza's metaphysics forbids any kind of exit from thought to matter, insisting upon the irreducibility of one to the other (except perhaps in "the last instance" in substance), suggests an affinity to the Lacanian tradition, which finds expression in Althusser's creative fusion of Lacan and Spinoza.[23] Yet it is important not implicitly to give extension the status of "the Real," since ideas are equally real, determinate, and definitive of

20. Evidence for this claim can be found throughout the *Ethics*, but especially *E* I def2, II p7, III p2.

21. See, e.g., Montag, *Bodies, Masses, Power*.

22. This is a bit of an overstatement, since Balibar, Gatens, Montag, and Negri all examine the play of imagination and reason in political life, but the sensual, affective, and corporeal remain privileged sites of explanation.

23. In addition to the "ISAs" essay, see his contribution to Althusser and Balibar, *Reading Capital*.

existence. Thought is its own peculiar reality rather than a reflection of something other than itself. The task, then, is to understand the reality of ideas, which cannot be explained by a science of bodies. This chapter is precisely an effort to consider what it's like to be an idea on Spinoza's account. My hypothesis is that a truly materialist critique of ideology does not consist in confining analysis to the realm of bodies, matter, or even "material conditions" understood as nonideal determinants. On the contrary, Spinoza's strange materialism is one that reveals the force of ideas, their proper power, activity and passivity, in nature. The renaturalization of ideology provides a way to think about how to be part of an ecosystem of thinking forces.

The second reason I preserve the term "ideology" may strike readers as counterintuitive. Ideology renaturalized is less anthropocentric than discourse analysis, which examines statements and sign systems. Admittedly, Foucault's examination of discursive regimes is far from being subject-centered, phenomenological, or psychological (as in the Lacanian and Frankfurt School traditions). Foucault examines how discourses traffic through various institutions with conflicting aims and techniques, yielding effects that may have little to do with the self-evident intentions of the dominant class, the state, or a particular association of scientists but that nevertheless produce normalizing power relations. Neither Foucault nor Marx constrains himself to an examination of the aims or self-representation of subjects, and each attributes determinate power to impersonal, unconscious institutions and structures. Yet the bailiwick of discursive analysis, as much as Marxist ideology critique, is confined to human relationships.[24]

Ideas and minds, for Spinoza, belong to any and all existent beings, be they rocks, cars, birds, or chewing gum. The critique of ideology, therefore, entails more than an examination of human imagination and regimes of signification. Certainly, Spinoza privileges human relations, and the *Ethics* comprises a manifesto for human freedom, even as he redefines both humanity and liberation. Yet a premise of the politics of renaturalization is that we cannot understand either our power or lack of power before affirming that each of us is but a tiny part of nature (*E* IV p4), a nature that is indifferent to human aspiration (I app). Importantly, our ideas are no less natural than our bodies. Being parts of nature, our ideas encounter resistance and assistance to their thriving from nonhuman as well as human sources. Although such a perspective on ideology critique risks becoming

---

24. Cf. Bennett, *Vibrant Matter*, xiv.

even further stretched to meaninglessness than the discarded version that encompasses all human statements, I wager that it is worth entertaining this peculiar picture in order to challenge our anthropocentric psychology. I have been steeped in Spinoza long enough to no longer find strange the notion that ideas generated by nonhuman and inorganic life affect and are affected by my power of thinking, but I acknowledge that such a metaphysical assertion seems ridiculous to many.[25] Nevertheless, I entreat my readers to consider this strange view of existence precisely because it is strange and may thereby shed new light on more familiar assumptions. The renaturalization of ideology underscores the exigency of caring for our enabling ideas, nurturing them, and joining them to others for the sake of their survival. This vision of reality yields promising effects even if one may not readily accept that shoes have minds. Thus, into Spinoza's strange world we go.

The Fly in the Coach

Reflecting on Spinoza in his essay "The Underground Current of the Materialism of the Encounter," Althusser cryptically remarks that "consciousness is only the Fly in the Coach."[26] He alludes to the fable by Jean de La Fontaine in which a stagecoach struggles to mount a steep hill drawn by several strong horses. The fly believes that by stinging everyone in the coach and buzzing around she will impel the coach toward its destination and expects to be rewarded for her efforts when the horses finally succeed. Because the fly desires the forward motion of the coach, she imagines her endeavors to be its motor. If the coach had fallen irretrievably into a ditch, however, the fly would have searched for an external cause to hold responsible for thwarting her aim. The realization of her goal, in contrast, appears as her accomplishment alone.

Consciousness resembles a fly in a coach in that it finds itself in a situation already in motion and is immediately aware only of its own desires and ideas. A relatively small animate power of thinking, which describes any human in the "immense forests" of nature and history, cannot possibly be aware of the innumerable powerful forces generating and determining its motion and existence. Antonio Gramsci, alluding to the same fable, likens the proletariat to the horses and accuses the bourgeoisie of resem-

---

25. For example, Wilson, "Objects, Ideas, and 'Minds.'"
26. Althusser, "Underground Current of the Materialism of the Encounter," 183.

bling the fly.[27] The bourgeoisie congratulates itself for moving history, as it ignores the workhorses heaving it forward in a well-appointed coach. Althusser's remark, in contrast, is directed at Marx himself, thereby implicating all consciousnesses, even that of the most powerful founder of scientific materialism, in both the fly's ignorance and the exaggeration of her self-generated power. The insistence that we are all flies in coaches—not only the privileged and foolish are ignorant of what determines them to act—reflects Althusser's Spinozan conviction that to be a human mind is to be a tiny and often confused agency amidst immeasurably many other forces.

In a famous letter, Spinoza likens the notion of human freedom to the consciousness a stone might have as it flies through the air. The soaring stone is determined by an external cause, along with the laws of motion and rest that pertain to its body and the medium through which it glides, to continue in motion in a "fixed and determinate way." Spinoza urges his interlocutor:

> Furthermore, conceive if you please, that while continuing in motion the stone thinks, and knows that it is endeavoring, as far as in it lies, to continue in its motion. Now this stone, since it is conscious only of its endeavor [*conatus*] and is not at all indifferent, will surely think that it is completely free, and that it continues in motion for no other reason than it so wishes. This, then, is that human freedom which all men boast of possessing, and which consists solely in this, that men are conscious of their desire and unaware of the causes by which they are determined. (*Ep* 58)[28]

This analogy is not as hyperbolic as it seems at first glance. For Spinoza, all beings, including stones, are to some degree "animate." All beings include a power of thinking that corresponds exactly to the power of their bodies to be disposed in different ways, to act and be acted upon

---

27. Gramsci, "Fable of the Beaver," in *Selections from the Prison Notebooks*.

28. Although I do not address this here, I should note that Spinoza and Althusser have somewhat different targets in their critiques of conscious freedom. Althusser is likely critical of a phenomenological or existentialist model of "consciousness" as radically free interiority, which originates in Descartes. Althusser rather polemically equates Ideology in the omnihistorical sense to consciousness itself, suggesting that the celebrated consciousness of his peer intellectuals is invariably an expression of its social relations structured by domination. Spinoza, however, is concerned with a superstitious portrait of human and divine freedom as unconstrained caprice rather than natural necessity.

(*E* II p13s). Likewise every being, to the extent that it preserves its integrity amidst infinitely many other beings, as a stone surely does, is endowed with a *conatus*, or an endeavor to persevere in being, to remain what it is, to preserve and enhance its life to the extent that its nature allows (III p7). A human *mens*—usually translated as "mind," but which Althusser claims can be understood only as a "power of thinking"[29]—is different only in degree, not in kind, from the power of thinking that belongs to a stone. The body of the stone is far less capable of acting and being acted upon than a human body, but it is only its relative lack of complexity that accounts for its unconsciousness of the effort it exerts against disintegrating into earth or dissolving into air.

This analogy might seem to suggest that humans are entirely devoid of freedom and dumb as rocks when it comes to the appreciation of their own agency in the world. Yet the power by which rocks persevere in being is their proper freedom, even if the ability to fly through air involves a minimal amount of their peculiar power. Rocks require a certain degree of power and freedom to be rocks, even if they cannot fly without a great deal of external assistance. Similarly, all human activity involves a determinate and irreducible measure of power, but it is often *not* the power we attribute to ourselves and "boast of possessing." Yet this is not a moral failure. Just like the rock flying through the air, we are determined to imagine that we are "completely free." We cannot think otherwise without developing the powers that allow us to experience ourselves differently. We are not simply the arrogant bourgeoisie or the silly insects that neglect to look outside the window of the stagecoach. Our power of thinking is constrained to apprehend our desire as self-generated, just as we are determined to consider the actualization of our desires to be unaided by a multiplicity of ambient powers that can never be fully acknowledged. Although we do not immediately recognize this fact, everything we do is, at the same time, both a product of some degree of freedom and in large measure a gift that can never be repaid. (Of course, these gifts, being from amoral nature rather than divine grace, include the capacity to destroy, maim, and exploit.) Yet, at the level of uncorrected imagination, we remain like flies in stagecoaches and rocks hurdling through space: we imagine ourselves to be the origin of our power, thought, and action.

Peppered throughout Althusser's corpus are comparisons between Ideology, as he reconceptualizes it, and Spinoza's imagination, or "first kind of knowledge." As with Ideology, imagination conveys the world as we

---

29. Althusser, "The Only Materialist Tradition," 12.

find it, and ideas present themselves as "conclusions without premises" (*E* II p28d).[30] In the "Underground Current," Althusser sketches Spinoza's version of "man's" thinking life.

> That he starts to think by thinking confused thoughts, and by hearsay, until these elements 'take' form, so that he can think in "common notions" . . . is important, for man could well remain at the level of hearsay, and the thoughts of the first kind might not "take hold" with those of the second. Such is the lot of most people, who remain at the level of the first kind and the imaginary—that is, at the level of the illusion that they are thinking.[31]

The illusory aspect is multiple. First, as will be familiar by now, "they" misapprehend the subject of thought. The illusion is that *they* are thinking. Individuals imagine themselves to be the origin of their ideas, when, in actuality, they do not think independently of myriad other beings, especially those of their immediate surroundings, social milieu, and political environment. Second, their ideas do not originate fully formed and coherent but are the "crystallizations" of a primitive accumulation of impressions, experiences, affects, and similar ideas. An accretion is observed and undergone as a discrete idea, but imagination alone does not apprehend the process of accumulation, the fact that any given idea is the result of a complex set of encounters and relationships among ambient ideas. Just like all accumulations in human history, an idea is the outcome of a decentralized play of human and nonhuman forces, direct and indirect violence, as well as pleasure and strength. Third, we experience the illusion that we have discrete minds, understood as autonomous agencies, forms of self-awareness that transparently disclose our mental contents.

Althusser reminds us, however, that for Spinoza, there is no *cogito*, nothing to guarantee that a thinker will generate true and adequate ideas.[32] As I emphasize in chapter 1, the modal nature of human existence entails that we cannot exist in isolation from one another, or from any mode within our vicinity, such that it is never a matter of *ego cogito* but always and necessarily a matter of *homo cogitat* (*E* II ax2): I think if and only if we think. Moreover, the politics of renaturalization insists that

---

30. "Conclusions without premises" is a notion from Spinoza that recalls Althusser's notion of "symptomatic reading" as the investigation of answers to questions unconsciously or not yet posed. Cf. Althusser and Balibar, *Reading Capital*.

31. "Underground Current," 178.

32. Ibid., 178.

homo cogitat only because *natura cogitat*. Nature, human and nonhuman, organic and inorganic, has its being in and as thought (I p15). While the human individual is affected most powerfully by those modes most similar to her,[33] her power to think is very much determined, amplified, and constrained by those around her, whatever those proximate beings may be. The transindividual character of knowledge is neither accidental nor optional. It is an ontological fact, belonging to the nature of minds, along with the bodies of which they are ideas. To better understand the ontology of minds, we must turn to the dreaded conception of the "attributes."

"I am in Ideology," or The Attribute of Thought

There are few concepts in Spinoza's ontology as difficult as the "attributes." To review briefly from chapter 1, reality is the infinitely complex, unbounded totality called "Nature," "substance," or "God," which contains all there is and all that could ever be. Nature is expressed in infinitely many attributes, or "ways of being," of which we know two, thought and extension. Each way of being is differentiated into infinitely many modes. Thus, there are infinitely many bodies within the attribute of extension and infinitely many ideas within the attribute of thought. Spinoza defines an attribute as "what the intellect perceives of a substance, as constituting its essence" (*E* I def4). While attributes are perceived by the intellect, they constitute the "essence" of substance. The essence of substance, unlike that of modes, necessarily includes "existence" (I p20). This entails that attributes are real, actual constituents of nature.[34]

Because thought and extension are "essences of substance," Gilles Deleuze explains that they are not accidents or qualities *attributed to* substance but rather *attributive* powers that give their way of being to something else, their affections or modes. Thought is an active power of being, not a property that a mind predicates of substance. Thought is something that nature does, a "dynamic form" of reality.[35] While it is tempting to conclude that attributes are products of our minds or subjective "perspectives" on substance, the attributes name distinctive ways of *being* the same thing and not merely diverse ways of *knowing* the same

---

33. That is, usually other humans, but Spinoza would hardly be surprised by wolf and bear children, since corporeal similarity is something that emerges as much through repeated contact as from given biology. There is no such thing as an essential human, bear, or wolf nature, but only infinitely many individual natures or essences.

34. Macherey, *Hegel ou Spinoza*, chap. 4.

35. Deleuze, *Expressionism in Philosophy*, 45.

thing. "Man," according to Spinoza, "consists of a mind and a body," which are the same thing (*E* II p13c). We can study nature differently, however, if we attend to the reality of thought, which is irreducible to extension, and vice versa. Thought and extension cannot account for one another because attributes and their modes do not interact; bodies do not move minds and minds have no power over bodies (I def2).

Below, I ascertain the power of thought independent of the realm of extension, but it should be borne in mind that, for any given mode, they can be separated only for analytic purposes. The body is powerful in precisely the same measure as the mind, just as the mind is passive in the same measure as the body. The problem of mental liberation, therefore, is the same as the problem of corporeal liberation, but described, apprehended, and analyzed in different terms.[36] Although other readers of Spinoza's politics emphasize corporeal determination, my task is to renaturalize precisely the spiritual dimension, the medium of thought. In so doing, we will see that the concepts that typically justify human privilege and distinctiveness are for Spinoza entirely natural and predicable of every other finite mode. Nevertheless, his naturalism does not reduce ideality to corporeality. To keep it real, for Spinoza, one need not exit thought. This is not to say that analysis should be restricted to thought or that questions of liberation ought to accord priority to mental life. Rather, I insist only that the "conditions" of freedom and servitude are as ideal as they are corporeal. The politics of renaturalization strives to avoid opposing thought to nature, or freedom to determination.

Thought is the specific kind of being of which ideas are modifications (affections, or modes). For Spinoza, every intellect, or mind, whether finite or infinite, is an affection of thought: "By intellect (as is known through itself) we understand not absolute thought, but only a certain mode of thinking" (*E* I p31d). Even the infinite intellect, the mind of God, is a modal determination of thought, which Spinoza identifies as *natura naturata*, an effect of nature, rather than *natura naturans*, a primordial causal expression of nature. Consequently, in the metaphysical order, thought precedes and exceeds minds. Thought is an absolute activity of being, unlimited by any of its particular determinations. Deleuze claims that Spinoza subordinates consciousness to thought. He remarks that Spinoza takes the "body as a model," which has its parallel in thought. "It is a matter of showing that the body surpasses the knowledge we have of it, *and that thought likewise surpasses the consciousness that we have of it.*" Just as we

---

36. Cf. Montag, *Bodies, Masses, Power,* xxi.

remain unconscious of the activities of our organs, bloodstream, immune system, and so on, we also remain unconscious of the various ideas that impact and circulate within our minds.[37] Deleuze asserts that Spinoza, against much of the tradition of philosophy, radically devalues consciousness in favor of thought—indeed, Spinoza does not use the substantive term "consciousness" but only the adjective "conscious"—and thus furnishes "a discovery of the unconscious, of an *unconscious of thought* just as profound as *the unknown of the body*."[38] Minds always belong to a power of thinking that infinitely surpasses their own.

The unconscious that constitutes the unknown of the mind belongs to thought itself rather than to individual minds. Each mode is in a relationship of reciprocal dependence most profoundly with its immediate "neighbors," to speak somewhat loosely, and ultimately with every other affection (mode) within its attribute. "Thought" describes the being in common that unites all of its modes, all ideas, in a particular causal community of interdependence. Since minds are modes, they, by definition, exist conditionally rather than autonomously. "Singular things," Alexandre Matheron notes, "cannot exist but *in community*." This community of "universal interaction" is such that each being acts upon every other and is in turn acted upon by every other.[39] Minds are naturally and necessarily subject to other minds, along with infinitely many other ideas within the productive and infinite power of thought. The parallel I offer above of our ignorance of the various activities within our individual bodies is somewhat misleading. Not only are we ignorant of what might be said to be within our minds or bodies, we are also ignorant of the myriad relationships and forces that make our minds and bodies what they are.

Perhaps the notion of a power of being in which minds dwell, exist, and act is what prompts Althusser to note in the "ISAs" essay that only a Marxist or a Spinozist affirms that "I am in Ideology."[40] To think at all is for one's existence to be given over to thought, to be composed of rather than endowed with ideas, to live in a medium that is an a-centric force field of powers far exceeding one's particular being. The only way to gain a critical

---

37. To preserve the irreducibility of the attributes to one another, however, one must bear in mind that the "body as a model" is an analogy with the figure of the idea. Taking the body as a model entails understanding something by way of something else. The story of the body in Spinoza may even more properly be called "allegorical." Allegories are indicative and useful ways of understanding things, but the difference (allegory from *allos*, other or different) that holds apart the phenomena must be kept in mind.

38. Deleuze, *Spinoza: Practical Philosophy*, 18–19.

39. Matheron, *Individu et communauté chez Spinoza*, 19.

40. Althusser, "Ideology and Ideological State Apparatuses," 175.

purchase on Ideology is to affirm that one cannot be but *in* thought, in this determinate and infinite form of nature's power. One becomes "rational," or "scientific," only on the condition that one grasps the *mens* (power of thinking) for what it is. As Spinoza avers, "it is necessary to come to know both our nature's power and its lack of power, so that we can determine what reason can do in moderating the affects, and what it cannot do" (*E* IV p17s). One of the first conditions of ideology critique, therefore, is a certain measure of self-knowledge. We must recognize the finitude of our thinking power by virtue of our locus in causal networks, our exposure to passions, and our irreducible dependence upon neighboring ideas. In the terms of chapter 1, the renaturalization of ideology begins by recognizing the transindividual character of our minds.

According to Althusser, "mind" and "soul" are poor translations for the concept of *mens*, since they imply images of human thought entirely alien to Spinoza's system. Spinoza redefines thinking in a way that is even more foreign today than it was in his own time, when mental dependence upon God, a larger cosmic force, was a popular view. Spinoza's particular version of radical belonging to God was heretical in his own time, but it is even more so in ours. Are we not individuals, however interdependent with respect to our bodily requirements? Are we not ultimately free to think and choose as we please? Even as many continental and feminist philosophers have long rejected the model of the self-sufficient individual, such a self-understanding remains tenacious. In North America we typically retool our minds with individualistic cognitive behavior therapy and pharmaceuticals rather than by mobilizing many thinking powers (except perhaps on Facebook). Such a mechanical and individualistic perspective on mental life makes the renaturalization of ideology particularly difficult.

For Spinoza, a *mens* is a radically dependent singular thing, an idea composed of many ideas, that desires to persevere in being. It preserves and enhances its being only by coordinating its activity and undergoing enabling encounters with other ambient ideas. It never acts alone. The ideas of any given individual are the result both of some bare measure of its proper activity, its singular "essence," and of the accumulation of haphazard and deliberate encounters with other ideas. The ideas that gain force and power in the mind are, to a large degree, indifferent to the particular mind or its strivings. Ideas, like bodies, are augmented by amenable encounters with similar ideas and weakened by destructive, contrary encounters. The ideas that most occupy the mind are not necessarily the truest ideas but the ideas with the most life support, as it were, from fellow ideas.

The true ideas of finite modes should not be understood on a correspondence model of truth. Spinoza refers to our true ideas as "adequate." In his words: "By adequate idea I understand an idea which, insofar as it is considered in itself, without relation to an object, has all the properties, *or* intrinsic denominations of a true idea" (*E* II def4). This is not an especially helpful definition, except to indicate that the truth of an adequate idea does not depend upon its correspondence to an object. An idea is adequate when a mind, a particular finite mode of thought, can be said to be its adequate cause. "I call that cause adequate whose effect can be clearly and distinctly perceived through it" (III def1). Adequation as a criterion for truth maintains the distinction between the attributes. True ideas are not measured by something outside the attribute of thought. Adequation might even be understood to lower the bar for truth. My mind serves as the adequate cause when it acts, that is, when the idea it produces follows more from its power and the ideas included in it than from external sources. This notion of truth production coheres with the ontology of affect described in the previous chapter, in which action is a matter not of absolute activity but of proportionally greater activity. Thus, if my mind contains more than 50 percent of the premises, it may be the adequate cause of a conclusion. Containing the totality of premises would amount to being aware of all existing ideas and their interrelation, and thus I would be the absolute cause of an idea. An adequate, true idea follows *more* from my "nature" (essence) than from external causes. Thus, an adequate idea expresses the virtue, which Spinoza defines (perhaps with Machiavelli) as the power, of a particular mind (IV def8).

Yet even if an adequate idea implies virtue and power, Spinoza asserts that "[n]othing positive which a false idea has is removed by the presence of the true insofar as it is true" (*E* IV p1).[41] Truth or true ideas have no superadded power by virtue of their veracity. There is no force proper to truth *qua* truth. To use Althusser's interpretive vocabulary, truth is not a "gel." True ideas do not "take hold of" or exert themselves upon subjectivities any more forcefully than do absurdities. How can this be? How can a rationalist philosopher claim that truth is impotent? My suggestion is that ideas, no matter how clear and distinct, cannot take root in the mind without a fertile environment. True ideas, in order to avoid being overwhelmed by contrary ideas, need other compatible ideas to sustain them.

---

41. In citing this same proposition, Gatens emphasizes that imaginary ideas constitute a different perspective on things encountered, but are not opposed to true ideas. "The Politics of the Imagination," 199–200.

Let me suggest an example. In the Danish film *The Celebration* (*Festen*), a family gathers to celebrate the sixtieth birthday of its patriarch (plot spoiler ahead). It is tradition for the eldest son to give a toast that honors the father. Prompted by the recent suicide of his sister, the son's speech begins to echo the ritual and praise his father but includes the shocking revelation that the great man being celebrated raped him and his sister as children. The many guests and family all laugh and treat it as a provocative joke, which prompts another to join in and tell an audacious story. The son must try again and again to communicate his true idea, an idea that correctly explains a series of causes. The family and the constellation of ideas that compose it, however, form a resilient composition that absorbs these assertions and retains its structure initially. In the face of threats, the family continuously recomposes itself, remembers itself, by resisting and reconstituting the corrosive force that threatens its coherence. The true idea cannot take hold within the minds of the guests and fellow family members before a great deal more counterforce is gathered to oppose the family's self-conception, upheld by tradition, ritual, habit, and a complicated set of psychic attachments. The son must reorganize the local environment, a wide range of ideas and affects, before being able to render his idea thinkable let alone adequate in others. To be adequate in the minds of others, the idea has to become compatible with their dispositions; it needs to be upheld by other ideas present in their minds. Because adequate ideas are ones that include their causes, the guests at the celebration need the premises in order to be able to grasp the conclusions. Importantly, for my purposes, the premises are more than facts. The premises are the affective conditions, the ability to perceive and be transformed by an alien set of ideas and the bodies to which they correspond. The film dramatizes the struggle of reordering the affects and minds of a powerful set of ideas animating this (dys)functional family.

To further illustrate, picture the attribute of thought as various ecosystems of ideas, where the mind of God represents the total ecosystem of all ideas together. The image of the ecosystem highlights the fact that ideas, like all natural things, desire to persevere in being and survive only in a favorable environment. They endeavor to continue to exist and, like any mode, must strive to link up with ideas that promote and enable their existence, regardless of their truth or falsity.[42] Ideas exist in a kind of energetic field and express all of nature, human and nonhuman, rational and

---

42. Bennett also notes parenthetically that "ideas strive to enhance their power of activity." "The Force of Things," 353.

nonrational. For an idea to follow from the nature of a particular mode and thereby express its virtue, the mode must contain, literally, the premises of the conclusion embodied in the idea. Since each of us is but a tiny part of nature, we are affected above all by partial and confused ideas, ideas that follow from other natures, from larger constellations of ideas that may be hostile to our particular well-being, as the patriarchal family was for the children portrayed in the film. Moreover, nature itself, from whose infinite essence all ideas necessarily flow, is indifferent to human flourishing.

The incompatibilities between different finite modes, including those we call "human," prompts Spinoza to advocate "joining forces" (*E* IV p35s; cf. IV p18s). A project of joining might be especially important with respect to the forces of ideas. If ideology critique involves contradicting received ways of thinking, the politics of renaturalization acknowledges that challenging ideas are vulnerable, and require care, cultivation, and nourishment in order to grow enough for their virtues or vices to be revealed. As the film shows, one might need to experiment and try several times to find an environment suitable for an idea, however certain we are of its truth, in order for it to redetermine our and others' lives. Imagine our ideas as living, growing, and changing things that may also require revision, critique, or pruning. The project of ideology critique, from a renaturalist perspective, is not content to recognize pernicious or damaging ideas and affects circulating in one's environment. It requires an ongoing practice of sustenance and attention to new insights, promising ideas, and counterhypotheses, seeking amenable ambient forces that might allow them to take root and become adequate for increasingly many thinking powers. Spinoza's portrait of ideal existence encourages us to consider which practices, associations, and relationships might strengthen and care for emerging, fragile, and challenging ideas that will not immediately find fertile soil.

To affirm that, rather than thinking, one is "in thought" or "in Ideology" is to begin to ask the question, in Foucault's words, of what thought "silently thinks, and so enable it to think differently."[43] Before one can ask the question of what thought silently thinks, an accumulation of favorable encounters must take hold. Favorable ideas are those that enable a mind better to understand the conditions of its power and activity and thus to aid its perseverance. To ask the question of what thought "silently thinks" is not sufficient. One must gather the forces of ideas compatible with one's striving. This gathering involves a receptive power to be af-

---

43. Foucault, *The Use of Pleasure*, 9.

fected by enabling forces, which is subsequently converted into an active synergy. The renaturalization of ideology is constrained to work within the passionate agency proper to modal life. How does this work? What kind of politics follows from the renaturalization of ideology?

What Is to Be Done?

Althusser famously calls Ideology an "omni-historical" reality.[44] With Spinoza, we can affirm that the mind dwells in thought by nature, eternally and inescapably. It belongs to a power of nature that it can never transcend, encompass, or comprehend as a totality. Any mind remains subject to infinitely many other ideas; yet it is likewise a subject, an actor that, in an irreducible way, composes part of reality, or nature (*E* I p36).[45] To be a finite power of thinking, or a composite idea, is to be exposed to infinitely many other powers of thinking (II p9). At the same time, to be is to impact others, to enable and constrain their power. A *mens* is an agent and a patient at once, vulnerable to and responsible for the being of ideas. One is always in thought, as in Ideology, yet each ecosystem is dynamic and variable to the extent that its nature allows, while the totality of ecosystems (the divine mind) is infinitely malleable. This means that Ideology and thought are not only what we are *inside* by virtue of our finitude but also what we *do*, enact, and animate simply by existing as thinkers.

How do we think about mental acts, on my model? How do individual ideology critics and social movements join ideas to one another? First, I want to emphasize that the renaturalization of ideology does not entail ignoring bodily practices. When Montag notes that, with Althusser, ideology no longer concerns consciousness, he underscores the materiality of ideology, its existence in practices and institutions, its reproduction in corporeal habits, rituals, performances, and discipline.[46] I want to insist that even the most spiritual dimension of existence, thought itself, should be considered in terms of force relations. Thought, for Spinoza, is one way of describing nature, which has a precise corollary in extension. Thus, an analysis of ideology in and as thought cannot replace an analysis of the life of ideology in extension. Spinoza notes that ideas are moved, causally determined by other ideas. Likewise, ideas resist ideas and endeavor to preserve and enhance themselves. "The cause of one singular idea is

---

44. "Ideology and Ideological State Apparatuses," 161.
45. Cf. Smith, "What Kind of Democrat was Spinoza?" 13.
46. Montag, *Louis Althusser*, 56.

another idea, *or* God [nature], insofar as he is considered to be affected by another idea . . .], and so on, to infinity" (*E* II p9d). This proposition echoes his assertion that finite beings exist and act by virtue of the affections of other finite beings (I p28). He thereby underscores that ideas, too, are singular things that endeavor to exist and act, and succeed only insofar as they are in relationship to others of their kind. The existence of ideas is determined by and dependent upon the forces and strivings of other ideas, just like the being of bodies. This is why freedom and power depend upon caring for our minds as much as for our bodies.

Ideology as an "omni-historical" reality, or a universal ontological condition for finite beings, is a neutral understanding of ideology. It simply emphasizes mental finitude. Yet from this neutral claim follow implications of nonneutrality.[47] To be unable to transcend an infinite power indifferent to one's flourishing and to be surpassed by the aggregate force of infinitely many other modes means that one cannot avoid being subject to hostile forces. Therefore, a study of ideology is a critique of ideology. It is a struggle within thought to identify those forces contrary to our perseverance and to unite with those ideas amenable to our thriving. If the bad news is that a mind cannot be without being-against, the good news is that all particular ideologies are likewise finite. As Althusser puts it, any crystallization of ideas results from "aleatory encounters," encounters without any metaphysical guarantee. The encounter, as Vittorio Morfino suggests, "emerges out of and is founded on a triple abyss: [it] 1) can not be; 2) can be brief; [and] 3) can no longer be."[48] If patriarchy, for example, often appears as an omni-historical, transcultural reality, it still requires the constant nourishment and incessant reproduction of supporting forces in order to postpone its death. Patriarchy hangs over an abyss of contingency, like any other form of misery or joy.

The renaturalization of ideology begins with the affirmation that we are *in* thought, rather than its authors, in order to gain a critical perspective upon this inevitable aspect of our modal existence. The task is not to extirpate the imagination, those many conclusions without premises that populate our minds, but to develop an appreciation of its peculiar character. Renaturalization acknowledges the irreducibility of passivity by virtue of our finitude, but in order to take it up in a new way. Renaturalizing ideology involves bringing adequate ideas to bear on the imagination, but,

---

47. For an illuminating account of the centrality of conflict in Spinoza, see Del Lucchese, *Conflict, Power, and Multitude in Machiavelli and Spinoza.*

48. Morfino, "An Althusserian Lexicon."

as Moira Gatens notes, "understanding does not cancel out my imaginary relation" to the effects that bodies and minds have on me.[49] In the best circumstances, we find ways to be enabled by those external forces to which we cannot but be exposed (*E* V p3d).

Regarding Spinoza's "third kind of knowledge," a mode of nonillusory freedom, Althusser claims that

> we are never faced with a *new* object but simply a new form of appropriation (the word is Marx's) of an object that is *always already there* since the first kind of knowledge [imagination]: the 'world,' the *Lebenswelt* of the first kind, is elevated while remaining the same. . . . What changes is never the being itself of things . . . but the relation of appropriation that the human subject enters into with others.[50]

Although I must bracket an account of the third kind of knowledge, we might observe that the new relationship of appropriation underscores a notion of freedom as nontranscendence. The freedom yielded by the politics of renaturalization depends upon the lived, critical understanding that our conditions of activity are not entirely given but constructed, made out of the materials at hand.[51] Freedom is a recomposition and reappropriation of what is given by the shared reality of historical, social, and natural life. Recomposition represents not just a perspectival shift but a rearrangement of constituent corporeal relations and activities. If we affirm that thinking otherwise entails being otherwise, relating to ourselves, bodies, and ambient beings in new ways, we glimpse why ideology critique is so difficult.[52]

As I emphasize above, the reappropriation of images that are given to us in perception cannot be achieved by simply being presented with the correct conclusions. Even if we generate adequate ideas from our own internal resources, they are easily muted when they lack sufficient support from other ideas. The renaturalization of ideology is not exclusively a question of truth but is most importantly a question of power. My claim is not that truth is irrelevant to the renaturalization of ideology.[53] Rather,

---

49. Gatens, "The Politics of the Imagination," 200.
50. "The Only Materialist Tradition," 9.
51. Cf. Tosel, *Du matérialisme de Spinoza*.
52. That ways of knowing are also ways of being is a premise of a number of Spinoza interpreters in the French tradition, including Althusser, "The Only Materialist Tradition"; Deleuze, *Expressionism in Philosophy*; and Balibar, *Spinoza and Politics*.
53. Rorty takes me to task for underplaying the importance of truth and adequate ideas in an earlier version of this argument, in "The Politics of Spinoza's Vanishing Dichotomies."

my concern is that true ideas can be weak. "No affect can be restrained by the true knowledge of good and evil insofar as it is true, but only insofar as it is considered as an affect" (E IV p14). Adequate ideas in finite intellects may not be robust enough to stand up to the affects that contradict them. True ideas need reinforcement from institutions, joyful passions, and, above all, fellow thinking powers, or they will easily be overwhelmed, such that "often we see the better and follow the worse" (III p2s). Moreover, especially with respect to "social facts" that are so often the target of ideology critique, we can have ideas that adequately grasp a network of causal relations, ideas of what is the case that should nevertheless cease to be true. Renaturalizing ideology involves more than rational reconstruction of the causes that sustain and produce pernicious realities. More than denaturalizing an idea by offering a genealogy of hitherto unquestioned ideals—like masculinist images of autonomy, or patriarchal beauty standards—it must ascertain the affective power of ideas. The generation of adequate ideas and the production of rationality necessarily include joy for Spinoza, by virtue of expressing the mind's power to act (III p53), this counterjoy, to endure, must be stronger than the pleasure produced by the idea one opposes. Considerable pleasure attaches, for example, to imagining oneself to be entirely unencumbered, the sovereign author of one's own ideas and actions. Challenging the idea that we are "free as birds" entails not only revealing how, for example, capitalism requires this illusion to obscure the systematic production of wage servitude. Making sense of the systematic connections giving rise to ideologies of autonomy by performing critical genealogies of the material conditions, class interests, or masculine psychology helps us to engender adequate ideas of the widespread conviction that to be human is to be free from natural determination.[54] Yet our adequate ideas will not determine our action if they are weaker than counterattachments and contrary affects. Hence, Spinoza cites Ecclesiastes approvingly: "He who increases knowledge increases sorrow" (IV p17s).

Regard for the affective force of ideas, the relationship of ideas to other ideas, and the ecosystemic support of counterhegemonic ideas entails considering ideology on a horizontal plane. Ideology is not best understood as something that is produced by the powers that be and imposed upon the malleable crowd.[55] Rather, regardless of where they come from,

---

54. Feminist care theorists emphasize masculine psychological structures in the production of notions of autonomy. See, e.g., Gilligan, *In a Different Voice*, and Benjamin, *Bonds of Love*.

55. This is what Rorty refers to as ideology in her response. She refers to the myth-making function of sovereigns, religious leaders, and reformers. While I would include such mytholo-

ideas are powerful insofar as they occupy and flow from many minds. Powerful ideas, true or false, feed and are fed by the current arrangement of energetic resources. The question, then, is not only how to understand ideas in the causal network, but how to dismantle an oppressive or disabling constellation of ideas, regardless of its truth or falsity. As feminist and other social movements have shown, adequate, true ideas can be noxious for finite beings. In order for countertruths and their corresponding counterjoys to prevail against harmful and deeply rooted ideologies, they must be mobilized en masse. In such cases, true ideas must not be enveloped by the understanding but, once assessed, starved, resisted, and extinguished.

Consider an example. I have often heard women (on talk shows and in beauty magazines) remark that they desire plastic surgery because it bolsters their self-esteem. They deny that they are pursuing alteration of their bodies to please their male partners or to attract a mate. They claim that they are doing it entirely for themselves. Indeed, liposuction and breast augmentation may be sources of joy, indicating an increase in the power to persevere in being, on Spinoza's model. Empirical studies show that women who correspond to patriarchal standards of beauty are better remunerated and more likely to be encouraged in school and to receive regular expressions of affirmation from intimates as well as strangers. That a woman might enhance her power to persevere in existence by altering her body in conformity with community standards of beauty gets at a certain truth. A feminist, like myself, would suggest that an adequate idea of this phenomenon entails understanding the systematic connections that produce such community standards of beauty. With Marilyn Frye, she might conclude that most relationships to feminine beauty in a misogynist society produce a double bind. Beauty standards will be seen to be oppressive, because women are penalized either for being attractive (they are treated as objects and are seen to invite male aggression) or for failing to be attractive (reduced pay, less intellectual encouragement, and ridicule).[56] Forcibly altering one's body to conform to oppressive standards reinforces those standards, perpetuates misogyny, and harms women as a social group.

Denaturalizing the social requirements for self-esteem might not ren-

---

gies in the category of ideology, I use the term in a broader sense to refer to the way we imagine ourselves and our relations to the world in general. Moreover, for the purposes of my argument, it doesn't matter whether myths are perpetuated by the State or by the multitude (certainly, any very effective one will be nourished by both).

56. Frye, "Oppression."

der plastic surgery any less "rational" (in the calculative sense) as a strategy of well-being. In a sexist context, a woman may fare better if her body conforms to patriarchal standards. Moreover, even the feminist with a full grasp of the causal context that sustains patriarchal beauty standards will still be affected by the desire to be seen as attractive (even if that affect does not determine her actions), because being seen as beautiful, even in these terms hostile to her "nature" (singular essence), produces pleasure and power.[57] The transformation of the causal nexus upholding oppressive measures of beauty is one of the tasks of feminist action.[58] That surgical alteration of one's body is an appealing means to attenuate self-hatred must *cease to be true*. Feminists and antiracists collectively challenge beauty standards hostile to their thriving by proliferating counterimages of beauty, forming alternative communities in which nonconformists can find appreciation and assistance. The appropriate response to the idea that conforming to sexist community standards of beauty feels good is not *only* to understand the various forces that hold such standards in place. An enlargement of perspective by which one can come to regard such standards as misogynist and disabling for a large proportion of women is necessary but, in this case, has not disabled such a powerful and effective ideology in most societies. The tenacious desire to be looked upon by others with joy, or to be loved (*E* III p13s), too often overwhelms our ability to be loved in terms that better accord with our singular strivings.

Critical practice still involves truth-bound inquiry, but I am arguing for a primacy of what might be called "power-bound inquiry." The nature of such primacy, however, is not necessarily temporal. One *may* need adequate ideas in order to engage in certain oppositional activities effectively, but determining any such temporal priority is a futile exercise in the abstract. In renaturalizing ideology critique, my concern lies above all with social movements endeavoring to reorganize and transform hostile ideas that determine their actions and passions. The politics of renaturalization

---

57. Consider the case of the women's studies student who sold her virginity to the highest bidder as a perverse effect of denaturalization. Having learned that virginity was a "social construct," valuable only by virtue of misogynist cultural ideals, a women's studies student decides that she might as well profit from a system that is generally stacked against her. According to a narrow version of rational choice, her decision makes perfect sense. Renaturalization, likewise, does not promise a quick fix for social problems. I fear that there are only difficult battles and no easy answers for individuals suffering oppression.

58. Popular forms of "empowerment" feminism tend to affirm whatever makes women feel good about themselves, which often results in celebrating the uplifting effects of consumer goods. As understandable as the desire to celebrate women's pleasure and self-nurturing in any form is, we desperately need a more ambitious feminist movement. For a biting critique of popular feminism, see Power, *One-Dimensional Woman*.

affirms, with Foucault, that there is no truth without power (nor is there power without truth effects, for good and for ill), and such power is that of a multitude of natural forces rather than a sovereign, a philosopher king, or a wise legislator. Far from requiring a sage ruler, or ruling class, my interpretation of Spinoza's politics calls for the arduous and precarious process of engendering liberating conditions that will enable and constrain the passions of the entire body politic. My (overly ambitious) hope is that renaturalization may aid social movements in fortifying and organizing powerful minds and bodies.

Spinoza's account of the cultivation of reason and joyful affects in light of our radical finitude remains underdeveloped. The path toward the shared development of thinking power is marked only by abstract prescriptions. Spinoza insists that reason includes a desire to unite as many others as possible to one's intellectual striving (*E* IV pp18s, 36), but even if he declares that the rational person desires life in a state and cherishes friendship (IV p73), he is not clear about the precise practices, institutions, or environments that fortify thinking (although they apparently involve pleasant aromas, IV p45s). In the political writings, a clue lies in his frequent insistence upon the need for large deliberative assemblies. He claims that any state—monarchy, aristocracy, or democracy—is best served by instituting the most inclusive consulting process that its nature allows. He privileges democracy because it includes the totality of citizens and thereby approaches most closely absolute self-determination.[59] In the *Theological-Political Treatise*, he promotes democracy because it engenders the most enabling ideas: "there is less reason in a democracy to fear ridiculous proceedings. For it is almost impossible that the majority of a large assembly would agree on the same absurdity" (*TTP* 16.9). More forcefully, he claims in the *Political Treatise* that collective deliberation brings into being ideas that could never emerge from the meditations of a solitary leader, however sage.

> When all decisions are made by a few men who have only themselves to please, freedom and the common good are lost. The fact is that men's wits are too obtuse to get straight to the heart of every question, but by discussing, listening to others, and debating, their wits are sharpened, and by exploring every avenue they eventually discover what they are seeking,

---

59. The totality of citizens does not include, for Spinoza, women or servants. This is perplexing and disappointing for many reasons, which I cannot address now. For useful discussions see, Matheron, "Femmes et serviteurs dans la démocratie spinoziste" and Gullan-Whur, "Spinoza and the Equality of Women."

something that meets with general approval and that *no one had previously thought of.* (TP 9.14)

Spinoza does not insist that any particular topic be discussed, but decisions (which are nothing other than affects) ought to be made through discussion, debate, and experimentally "exploring every avenue." He does not advocate entrusting the freedom of the commonwealth to the few. He promotes deliberation as a conflictual but productive process that generates ideas to guide a collectivity in accordance with its peculiar requirements. He recommends large assemblies, I contend, because ideas need to be connected and their strivings joined to one another by actual proximity. Although Spinoza could not have anticipated cyberspace, or perhaps any form of genuinely mass media, something emerges with the actual co-presence of human bodies. Studies of the devastating effects of solitary confinement show that despite the ability to communicate by video, somatic co-presence activates us in ways that cannot be simulated.[60] On this account, isolation hurts minds for at least two reasons: First, it is the co-presence of many thinking powers that gives birth to emancipating ideas "that no one had previously thought of." Second, because true ideas cannot become powerful simply by virtue of being true, many thinking powers must pool their efforts to sustain enabling ideas. The fragility of any particular idea speaks to the difficulty not only of arriving at adequate and enabling ideas but of sustaining and strengthening them.

What is at stake in the survival and nourishment of good, adequate, and enabling ideas is nothing less than the perseverance of human and other natural beings. In other words, we should strive for robust, powerful ideas, ideas that include knowledge of their causes and thus know themselves, not because we value truth in itself, but because we *are* ideal assemblages. Not only is our thinking power an instrument that enables us to manipulate the world or direct our lives, but it is an important way in which we exist. As finite beings, we desire to exist as powerfully and joyfully as possible, which occurs only by coordinating our thinking power with ambient agencies. Since we depend upon, affect, and are affected by powers other than human, we should attend not only to social relations but to any and all relations. How to cultivate fortifying nonhuman relations receives little of Spinoza's attention. He notes that the life of wisdom includes pleasurable involvement with natural beauty, enjoyable smells,

---

60. Guenther, "How Does the Light Get In?"

decoration, and especially a diversity of food and drink (*E* IV p45s and IV appXXVII). He treats these nonhuman forces as necessary for the education and diversification of the body and mind. Today more than ever, nonhuman nature demands our thoughtful attention, as we continue to consider our vulnerability to and need of fellow humans.

The politics of renaturalization urges ideology critique to concern itself with the ecosystems that sustain ideas. Ideology critique often functions to determine that families of ideas disable those who internalize them. The renaturalization of ideal vitality exhorts us to develop counterforces that dissolve oppressive networks of ideas. We must aim not only to demystify hostile ideal formations through understanding their structural character but also to bring to life alternatives to force them out of existence or weaken them. Because ideology critique is above all a question of relations of power and force among ideas, the politics of renaturalization emphasizes, with Spinoza, that many, many humans thinking together is the key to living well. For Spinoza, reason asserts that all "should strive together, as far as they can, to preserve their being; and that all, together, should seek the common advantage of all" (*E* IV p18s). Although Spinoza was thinking primarily of gathering an assembly of masculine human beings, the politics of renaturalization takes even more seriously than he did the mutability of finite modes entailed by his ontology.

We are thereby called upon to engender and nourish counterideas amenable to our striving so that they may become true and powerful within our particular milieus. For Black to be beautiful, for fat to be fabulous, and for meat to be murder, oppositional groups have reconstructed the relationships and causal connections that organize their own mental-corporeal lives. These ideas became true, became adequate in certain causal contexts, by virtue of the actions and passions of many resistant thinking powers. We must, in addition to understanding them, displace, minimize, and starve certain hegemonic ideas. Reason is not an inoculation against affectively charged oppressive ideas. An adequate grasp of the causes and conditions that make oppression the case often emerges in the process of fighting it. The task of liberation entails rendering oppression no longer the case and destroying the truth-value of certain judgments through reorganizing the vital forces that have sustained them until now. The politics of renaturalization encourages an activist posture with respect to our mental environments. The ideas that are permitted to grow, expand, and take hold matter; they are a way in which we strive and thrive. Ideology critique is never merely a problem of false consciousness or an inadequate grasp of the structures and causes that make something the case. The renaturalization of ideology involves, from the point of view of finite powers of thinking, the production of new and better truths through the resistant reconstruction of our ideal environments. We might equally well describe oppressive forces in the language of bodies, but this portrait of the ecosystem of ideas shows just how much of a materialist, albeit a highly unconventional one, Spinoza really is.

3

Man's Utility to Man:
Reason and Its Place in Nature

> It is impossible to know anything about men except on the absolute precondition that the philosophical (theoretical) myth of man is reduced to ashes.
> —LOUIS ALTHUSSER

Even though Spinoza is widely celebrated as a critic of anthropocentrism, he has been accused of maintaining a robust notion of human privilege in his practical philosophy. Even if nature has no special place for man, Spinoza's "morality" is said to exclude meaningful concern for nonhuman beings.[1] I have argued that Spinoza's philosophy performs a radical renaturalization of human agency. His philosophy reinscribes what are often treated as the distinguishing marks of human existence within nature. Our affects, actions, passions, and thoughts do not elevate humanity above the order of cause and effect and operate according to the same laws as any other thing (*E* III pref). The previous chapters outline how thought, mind, and affect come to be seen as natural phenomena, predicable of all existents. Rather than being exclusive properties of humans (or angels, or God), thinking, perceiving, and feeling are forces of nature that are more

---

1. Lloyd, "Spinoza's Environmental Ethics," 294.

or less complex depending upon an individual's ability to be affected and disposed in a great many ways (II p13s).

What becomes, then, of Spinoza's ethical rationalism? Why is a life of reason to be preferred to any other? Why is nothing more useful to man than man? Why should we strive, above all, to know God, establish friendship with others, and educate as many as possible to share in the pleasures and powers of the mind? What are the ethical and political implications of Spinoza's renaturalization of humanity and mind?

If "man" has come to mean something different for Spinoza, we must determine what it means for his ethics to be "man-centered." Only once we have seriously considered his redefinition of man can we understand his claims about the supremacy of human association. Given that thought is a wholly natural force, we must reconsider what it means to be rational and to associate reason with humans in particular. The task of this chapter is to make sense of Spinoza's appeals to "human nature," his unequivocal valorization of human association and friendship, and his understanding of reason as the foundation of ethical practice.

Along with a number of other commentators, I interpret Spinoza's appeals to a universal "human nature" as rhetorical. Strictly speaking, there is no human essence; there are only singular essences of similar beings that are called "human." Although it is not an uncontroversial interpretation, several Spinoza scholars deny that he maintains any doctrine of universal essences. What is less recognized, however, is the local character of reason within Spinoza's thought. I argue that reason expresses the power (virtue) of situated minds. This has the result that rational ideas, even if grounded in universal properties of bodies (called "common notions"), are not necessarily shared by those who reason. If there are no features common to all humans as such, in distinction from any other being in nature, rational activity does not necessarily promise universal human fraternity. Rather, reason expresses particular compositions of power and correlates to acts that enhance the lives of those specific beings that have joined forces.

Nevertheless, Spinoza's ethics and politics emphatically concern "men." His entire philosophy aims to enable the most potent human community possible. The renaturalization of man, even as it deprives humanity of its quasi-divine status, belongs to a project of human power, pleasure, and sociability. Spinoza observes that in desperately seeking signs of superhumanity in their prophets and rulers, humans desire "things that are strange and alien to their own nature, and they despise their natural gifts" (*TTP* 1.2). The premise of the politics of renaturalization is that self-deification breeds self-contempt. We need to discover ways to affirm ourselves as we really are, as parts of nature, which entails, for Spinoza, a special regard for our own kind. We are better able to relate to ourselves and one another insofar as we avow our radical dependence upon other natural beings, especially those "similar" and potentially compatible beings we call "human." Does this special regard for our kind imply practical anthropocentrism? I explore Spinoza's remarks on animals in detail in chapter 6. This chapter confines itself to an investigation of the character of Spinoza's appeals to human nature, which seem to be in tension with his naturalism.

The Politics of Human Nature

To my assertion above that, strictly speaking, there is no human essence, one might reasonably respond: But doesn't Spinoza frequently use the phrase "human nature"? And yes, the notion of human nature and reference to its "laws" are in no way alien to Spinoza's writings. Indeed, I even agree with Filippo Del Lucchese's claim that Spinoza's "conception of human nature is crucial to his idea of politics."[2] But what *is* this idea of human nature, if humans must not be understood to be "an empire within an empire" (*E* III pref)? What are the "laws of human nature" such that they conform to the order of nature, like any other thing? Before embarking on a technical discussion of whether Spinoza can justifiably appeal to a human essence, I will outline what I call the "rhetorical functions" of the term "human nature" in Spinoza's writings. Although I will not establish that his use of the term serves as an exhortation rather than a rigorous definition until the following sections, a brief overview of his diverse deployments of the term will lend some prima facie plausibility to my contention.

Spinoza appears to say contradictory things about the nature of man. He mentions that "men are ... by nature enemies" (*TP* 2.14) and that "man is a God to man" (*E* IV p35s). Interpreters, rather than reconciling the two claims, tend to emphasize either our unsocial sociability or our perfectibility.[3] Spinoza uses the term "human nature" to serve at least three different functions, which may appear to be incompatible with one another. If we are careful not to import a spiritual understanding of rationality

---

2. Del Lucchese, *Conflict, Power, and Multitude in Machiavelli and Spinoza*, 74.
3. See Smith, *Spinoza, Liberalism and the Question of Jewish Identity*, and Levene, *Spinoza's Revelation*, respectively.

that reflects the eternal moral law, however, these distinct uses of the term are not as contradictory as it might seem. As long as human nature is understood as a description of generalities rather than as a definition of an eternal essence, Spinoza can consistently maintain that humans are characteristically antipathetic and that they are capable of unity. Nevertheless, just because his use of the term human nature can be understood to be consistent, it does not follow that it names a shared essence, as I hope to show in the following section. Presently, I confine myself to describing the rhetorical function of the term in his writings.

Although this taxonomy is not exhaustive, I suggest that Spinoza's statements about human nature serve three distinct functions.

1. A humbling function: Spinoza insists on the irreducibility of our subjection to passions and the consequent inevitability of conflict among us. These remarks are sometimes relatively neutral statements, like: "since all men everywhere, whether barbarian or civilized, enter into relationships with one another and set up some kind of civil order, one should not look for the causes and natural foundations of the state in the teachings of reason, but deduce them from the nature and condition of men in general" (*TP* 1.7). At other times, Spinoza underlines not only a universal susceptibility to be seduced by Sirens' songs (7.1), and thereby to act irrationally, but an ineradicable enmity that plagues our kind: "men are by nature enemies, and even when they are joined and bound together by laws, they still retain their nature" (8.12). In these cases, "their nature" is one of divergence and diffidence.

2. An admonishing function: Closely related to the first function of highlighting human finitude are several statements underlining, rather than the finitude of individual persons, the limits of sovereign power. The vast majority of Spinoza's descriptive remarks about human nature point to antipathy among humans aroused by jealousy and hatred and emphasize a lawlike impulse to resist coercion operating in the human heart. Most characteristic in this vein, Spinoza notes that "no one will ever be able to transfer his power and consequently his right to another person in such a way that he ceases to be a human being" (*TTP* 17.1). Del Lucchese suggests that this is tantamount to defining the human as the one who cannot but defend himself.[4] To be human is to resist being significantly weakened or destroyed. Such statements

---

4. Del Lucchese, *Conflict, Power, and Multitude in Machiavelli and Spinoza*, 54.

issue a warning: extreme repression, always in every circumstance, by virtue of the unchanging and unchangeable laws of human nature, will sound the death knell of the tyrant. Human nature marks a natural and therefore unsurpassable limit to repressive power and sovereign authority.

3. A unifying function: These statements characteristically present reason as what unifies humanity into a common project of enjoying together their common and greatest good, the intellectual love of God. "Insofar as men live according to the guidance of reason, they must do those things which are good for human nature, and hence, for each man" (*E* IV p35d). This is meant to show that even if the irrepressible tendency of each to pursue what is to his advantage so often results in conflict, when we properly understand our nature, our genuine interest, the pursuit of our desire will result not in a world of conflict over scarce resources but in one of plenitude and mutual love.

It might be tempting to note that the perfectionist moments heralding the unification of humanity with a view to enjoying knowledge of the infinite power of nature all appear in the *Ethics*, whereas the political writings, especially his final work postdating his own confrontation with mob violence,[5] underline hatred, violence, and antagonism. Yet a bifurcation of the ethical and political doctrines would be too easy. The *Political Treatise* outlines the conditions under which a commonwealth can be "guided as if by one mind" (3.5), such that legislators would share a perception of "what is honorable [*honestas*]" (8.6). Likewise, the *Ethics* repeatedly acknowledges that "men are naturally inclined to hate and envy" (III p55s). So how can both hatred and love, enmity and unity, express human nature? What is this polarized nature, characterized by such intense ambivalence?

For now, I can make some general indications. First, most properties attributed to human nature in these rhetorical appeals are not unique to humans. Rather, Spinoza's deductions from an understanding of "human nature as it really is" (*TP* 1.4) "follow from the most essential feature of human nature in whatever way it might be considered, namely, from the

---

[5]. In 1672 the leaders of the Dutch Republic, the brothers Cornelius and Johan de Witt, were torn to pieces in a terrible act of mob violence. Spinoza admired the brothers and the atmosphere of relative tolerance they promoted. Despite his well-known equanimity, this incident so inflamed him that he had to be prevented by his landlord from posting a plaque declaring the incident to be *ultimi barbarorum*, which would have put both of them at grave risk. See Nadler, *Spinoza: A Life*, chap. 11.

universal striving of all men to preserve themselves" (*TP* 3.18). In other words, he deduces the natural foundations of the commonwealth from the irreducibility of the *conatus*, the striving to persevere in being that defines any and all "singular things" in nature, be they animate or inanimate, human or nonhuman. Insofar as anything preserves a stable proportion of motion and rest, it can be presumed to exert force to maintain itself and to oppose anything that "takes its existence away" (*E* III p6d).

It is not by virtue of an affront to human dignity, then, that "human nature does not allow itself to be absolutely compelled." It is simply a law of the *conatus* that a being resists its diminution and destruction, opposing anything that threatens its perseverance.

> For while men are acting from fear alone, they are doing what they do not want to do; they have no reason of interest or necessity for doing what they do; they seek merely to avoid punishment or even execution. Indeed, they cannot help but rejoice when their ruler suffers pain or loss . . . they cannot help but wish him every calamity and inflict it when they can. (*TTP* 5.8)

Spinoza thus admonishes tyrants that the common people are no different from themselves, "all men share in one and the same nature" (*TP* 7.27), and no one tolerates being coerced or mutilated beyond certain limits. When someone appears to threaten to take a multitude's existence away, "they *cannot help* but wish him every calamity and *inflict it* when they can." Natural beings as such are invested in their survival and the particular shape of their existence. Humans fight their diminution not because they are spiritual beings, unable to endure the indignity of oppression, but because to be is to resist.[6] The notion of human nature is crucial to Spinoza's politics not because it is human per se but because it is in the nature of anything to desire only what it perceives to be conducive to its survival and flourishing.

Similarly, it is not our humanity that renders us susceptible to passions but simply our finitude. Being but parts of nature, we cannot eradicate determination by external causes, and thus we find ourselves opposed to one another and ourselves (*E* IV pp33–34). Because we are never absolutely autonomous, we are subject to the play of passions and vulnerable to the vicissitudes of fortune. This is as true for a human as for a greyhound un-

---

6. This formulation is indebted to Bove, though he is exclusively concerned with human resistance to sovereign authority. *La Stratégie du conatus*.

able to avoid chasing a rabbit without a protracted reeducation. To be finite is to be stimulated, constrained, and enabled by ambient forces, to be dependent and connected, unable to rise above one's environment. We are creatures of affect, necessarily affecting and being affected by others. The complexity of our bodies and the impossibility of total self-inoculation against external forces prompt those all too frequent akratic moments when, even equipped with knowledge that, for example, cooperation will best enable us to meet our needs, we are overcome with greed or hatred.

These are features of human nature, Spinoza's refrains suggest, that must be kept in mind in order to build an effective and enabling commonwealth. Forget our weaknesses, our finitude, and our tendency to quarrel, and we will lack any political art. Try to eradicate troublesome passions through draconian laws and you will found a desert rather than a polity (*TP* 5.4). Spinoza's remarks about human nature, even as they apply universally to any and all natural things, advocate democracy. Democracy is "the most natural state" (*TTP* 16.11), not because it accords with some special feature of human existence, but because the combination of *conatus* and finitude we share with every finite mode makes it so. Our desire to persevere in being, our opposition to those who threaten it, and our inability to survive alone make combination into the largest possible body the most enabling way of life. Moreover, because conflict among finite beings is inevitable, only the form of government that allows differentiation and even encourages disagreement will have a chance at stability, albeit a kind of stability that is always, like nature itself, in motion. Thus, Spinoza likens democratic association to the family. He notes that there are more quarrels between parents and children than between masters and slaves, and thus democracies appear to be less stable than tyrannies in which no one dares to question authority. Nevertheless, arguments among people who are bound to one another by affection and common interests can engender genuine peace, which "consists not in the absence of war but in the union or harmony of minds" (*TP* 6.4). Peace as a harmony of minds is linked directly to "quarrels," albeit "family quarrels," rather than to rational consensus.

What then of the unifying use of the term human nature? Spinoza suggests in the political as well as the ethical writings that "human life . . . is characterized not just by the circulation of the blood and other features common to animals, but especially by reason, the true virtue and life of the mind" (*TP* 5.5). Even if human nature names a tendency toward antipathy and agonism, it also points toward the possibility of unity and pleasure in shared knowledge and love of God. Indeed, love of nature is the greatest good, common to all, and can be enjoyed by all equally, because we seek only understanding, an infinite resource, insofar as we are guided by reason (*E* IV p36).

> It is not by accident that man's greatest good is common to all; rather it arises from the very nature of reason, because it is deduced from the very essence of man, insofar as [that essence] is defined by reason, and because man could neither be nor be conceived if he did not have the power to enjoy this greatest good. (*E* IV p36s)

This text poses the greatest challenge to my reading. We should first note two textual details, however. Owing to the lack of articles in Latin, we could justifiably render this "a man's greatest good" and insist that the "all" to which being in God is common includes all of nature (I p15). Second, the greatest good, the blossoming of the mind's greatest powers, is deduced from the essence of (a?) man only insofar as reason defines that essence. A human's essence is defined not exclusively by reason, but also by inadequate ideas and corporeal affections (*E* III p9d), which are certainly not universal. Thus "human nature," or a man's nature, cannot be confined to reason.

Are humans, then, those bearers of the most radical contradiction between finitude and infinitude, a contradiction that nothing natural could withstand, as Hegel contends?[7] Is it the case that insofar as we are finite, we come into conflict with our (true) selves and our fellows, while insofar as we understand, we share in the divine intellect and live in accord with the natural order? If this were so, Spinoza's understanding of man would echo the notion of the rational animal, the sole being who suffers as animal but glories as rational. Yet, on my interpretation, reason as the virtue of the mind, as "the power of bringing about certain things, which can be understood through the laws of [a man's] nature alone" (*E* IV def8), is not identical in every man. Or, more precisely, what is brought about by this power is necessarily different in diverse humans, even if the "foundations of reason" (common notions) are shared. The activity of reason, the production of adequate ideas from "the laws of one's nature," expresses particular rather than generic natures. As a result, human nature in the unifying sense does not name an essence that we might discover and thereby actualize by uniting into a single body (cf. *E* IV p18s). Rather, human nature, insofar as it is defined by reason, is aspirational. The uni-

---

7. Hegel, *Philosophy of Right*, §35E; cf. Descartes, *Med* IV.

fication of humankind by virtue of acting under the guidance of reason is constructed rather than found. Even in its perfectionist strain, then, the term human nature is political, not metaphysical. To make the case for my interpretation, we must examine further Spinoza's understanding of essences and rationality.

Reason and the Human Essence

The strongest claim Spinoza makes for the unifying power of human nature is perhaps the following: "Insofar as men live according to the guidance of reason, they must do only those things which are good for human nature, and hence, for each man, that is (by p31c), those things which agree with the nature of each man" (*E* IV p35d). "Human nature" appears here to be predicable of each man, and insofar as we act rationally, we do those things that are good for human nature and we thereby "agree" (*convenire*) fundamentally with one another. Spinoza adds the corollary, "When each man most seeks his own advantage [*utile*] for himself, then men are most useful [*utiles*] to one another." We are the kinds of beings, on this account, that agree with one another *insofar* as we seek our advantage (*utile*) under the guidance of reason. Insofar as we know what is genuinely good for us, we will not conflict with one another. A natural interpretation of this claim is that the same thing is genuinely to the advantage of each of us, and we enjoy harmonious relations insofar as we recognize this identical good. Spinoza asserts that our greatest good and genuine interest is to know and love nature, or God. Yet this knowledge is not an identical object but the universal power of God or nature, which manifests in infinitely many distinct ways. It is universal because "whatever is, is in God, and nothing can be or be conceived without God" (I p15). Each thing we know allows us to enjoy this good. But we may share this unlimited good without necessarily knowing the same things. How pursuing our advantage (*utile*) makes us most useful to one another will be the topic of the following section. Let us look more closely at the notion of reason and its guidance.

Reason seems to belong to the essence of the human mind, and so an interrogation of this mind's character seems to be in order. Yet Spinoza's only remark on this matter consists in the declaration of a rather open principle.

> And so to determine what is the difference between the human mind and the others, and how it surpasses them, it is necessary for us, as we

have said, to know the nature of its object, the human body. I cannot explain this here, nor is it necessary for the things I wish to demonstrate. Nevertheless, I say this in general, that in proportion as a body is more capable than others of doing many things at once, or being acted on in many ways at once, so its mind is more capable than others of perceiving many things at once. (*E* II p13s)

Spinoza never distinguishes the "nature of the human body" fundamentally from other composite bodies and thus never establishes anything absolutely peculiar to the human mind. Moreover, this principle does not guarantee the rationality of human minds. Yet this principle remains operative through the conclusion of the *Ethics* in relation to the highest expression of knowledge, the "intellectual love of God." "He who has a body capable of a great many things has a mind whose greatest part is eternal" (V p39).

This postulate, according to Matheron, not only fails to make a distinction between humans and animals, "it doesn't give us any principle by which we *could* make this distinction and specify the superiority" of the human.[8] The ability of a body to do many things and be acted on in many ways applies as much to many animals as it does to humans. Are not many animal bodies capable of a great many things, often greater than our own? The bodies of human infants are far less capable than those of many animals. Thus, Spinoza avers that "we strive especially that an infant's body may (as much as its nature allows and assists) change into another, capable of a great many things" (*E* V p39s). Being capable of a great many things is an uncertain achievement of some bodies, not all of them human.

Today, one might suggest that the human brain is the bodily part sufficiently capable of a great many things to engender reason. Had Spinoza been equipped with the knowledge of contemporary science, one might speculate that he would have recognized the brain, rather than generic corporeal properties, as the foundation of reason. We should be wary of how we understand the brain, however, in these speculations. As Antonio Damasio points out, Spinoza astutely saw that rationality cannot be isolated from a whole range of emotions. Only the "feeling brain" can act; only with the resources of the affects can one determine one's genuine needs.[9] As Spinoza's remarks on human nature emphasize, reason does not just contemplate eternal essences, it "brings things about." Reason is

---

8. Matheron, "L'anthropologie spinoziste?" 177.
9. See Damasio, *Descartes' Error* and *Looking for Spinoza*.

practical. If an idea is virtuous (powerful) by following from an individual's nature (essence), it is because it allows and encourages that individual to persevere. Adequate ideas express the virtue and power of the mind at least partly by looking out for the "good" (*utile*) of the individual who exercises it. Before clarifying the character of the advantage that reason pursues, let us look more closely at what a rational idea is. What is this power? And how does it express corporeal and affective multiplicity?

Spinoza defines "true ideas," which may be engendered by reason or intuitive science, as "adequate ideas." "By adequate idea, I understand an idea, which insofar as it is considered in itself, without relation to an object, has all the properties, *or* intrinsic denominations, of a true idea" (*E* II def4).[10] An adequate idea has the properties of a true idea but is true not by virtue of corresponding with its object. Truth as correspondence occurs only in the infinite intellect, while adequate ideas of finite minds have the intrinsic denominations of truth by virtue of enveloping their causes. Rather than its relationship to the "external world," the measure of an idea's adequacy is its ability to include a notion of its own genesis, its emergence from interactions amongst ideas. An adequate, true idea is one that, proportionally, follows more from one's own "nature" (essence) than from external causes. An adequate idea thus expresses the virtue or the power of an individual (IV def8). Spinoza also refers to reason as the "internal determination" of ideas (II p29s). Insofar as the mind causes ideas from amidst its "internal resources" more than from external causes, it generates adequate ideas (cf. III def1), expressing its particular striving to persevere in being. Imagination, the most basic form of knowledge, expresses an "external determination," but reason sees things "from the inside."[11]

Reason's "internal view" follows from a mode's nature, or essence, which is its unique place in the causal nexus. For one to understand an idea "through one's nature alone" is for that idea to follow from one's unique causal history and singular ratio of motion and rest. Nevertheless, we should guard against understanding the uniqueness of an individual on an atomistic model, since two humans, for example, might combine "to compose an individual twice as powerful as each one" and engender

---

10. The ontologies of rational and adequate ideas are slightly different. Reason is grounded in the "common notions," which I will discuss below, while intuition follows from the attributes or divine essences. The precise technical difference does not matter for my purposes here, since intuition "arises from" reason (*E* V p28). Spinoza's doctrine of intuition is rather elusive and controversial. For my interpretation, see "'*Nemo non videt*.'"

11. Deleuze, *Expressionism in Philosophy*, 278.

adequate ideas from their synergized mental power.[12] Likewise, a commonwealth directed "as if by one mind and one body" might be said to generate ideas in accordance with its nature, or what augments its power. Adequate ideas follow from distinctive mental compositions and express the particular strivings of the individuals that produce them. They follow from the ideas that compose a mind at a particular time and place and are thereby singular ideas, following from a part rather than the whole of nature.

As a consequence, the renaturalization of reason challenges rationalism understood as the recognition of a set of innate ideas with which the mind is originally endowed.[13] For better or worse, reason renaturalized is not necessarily universal in content and thereby does not automatically entail a harmony of minds. Reason is the power of a particular mind to generate ideas from its idiosyncratic, singular nature. Reason expresses a mind's virtue, rather than housing a set of stable, objective, eternal ideas. It could thus be the case that we are guided overwhelmingly by reason and still, like parents and children, quarrel. We can reasonably disagree, to use more contemporary parlance, since what supports my nature, what enables me to continue to be, is not necessarily what supports your being.

It often seems, however, that Spinoza says the opposite. Insofar as we are rational, we agree. Insofar as we are passionate, we disagree. Moreover, the common notions, the "foundations of our reasoning," seem to be identical in all who perceive them. Indeed, for Spinoza, the fundamental properties of bodies are perceived adequately by all. Universal properties of nature are the most fundamental common notions: "Those things which are common to all, and which are equally in the part and in the whole, can only be conceived adequately" (*E* II p38). For Spinoza, "the mind does not know itself except insofar as it perceives affections of the body" (II p29c). When a body encounters other bodies with properties identical to its own, it perceives them, in itself and in others, clearly and distinctly. Spinoza thus concludes that "there are certain ideas, *or* notions common to all men. For (by L2) all bodies agree in certain things, which must be perceived adequately, *or* clearly and distinctly, by all" (II p38c). This corollary refers to the second lemma of proposition 13, which holds that all bodies

---

12. Barbone denies that two individuals can combine because two natures, being singular, could never completely agree ("What Counts as an Individual for Spinoza?" 101). Yet Spinoza states explicitly that the natures of Adam and Eve agree perfectly (*E* IV p68s). I hope to clarify below how essences can be singular and yet agree perfectly.

13. Curley, therefore, argues that it is "wildly" inaccurate to call Spinoza a rationalist; "Experience in Spinoza's Theory of Knowledge."

are extended. Extension, thus, is a "common notion." Other examples of common notions are "motion and rest" and perhaps the idea that bodies fall downward. From this, we can affirm that all men have a perception of bodies extended in space and of other very basic features of nature. These generalities, which can loosely be called "laws of nature," enable us to engender adequate ideas.

These foundations of reason are not located only in human bodies. All bodies are extended, and it seems that even a stone should have this common notion. Spinoza thus lays the groundwork for a very expansive understanding of rationality. Absolutely no "man" is without these foundations of reason, Spinoza notes, yet it is not clear why any being would be without them. While Spinoza indicates no belief in animal rationality, Matheron concludes that the doctrine of the common notions must admit "many animals" as rational.[14] Yet the common notions name the foundations of reason, which may be necessary but not sufficient for rationality. Perhaps the adequate *perception* of motion and rest does not guarantee an adequate conception of ideas following these perceptions? Even though this doctrine does not commit Spinoza to an idea of nonhuman rationality, it does not seem far-fetched to surmise that many animals have accurate ideas that follow from their (necessarily adequate) ideas of extension, space, and movement. Two points are important for my argument: first, reason *follows from* universal ideas of ontologically general properties, properties inhering in each and every body, but is not necessarily *about* those properties; second, these foundations of reason do not, in themselves, imply human distinctiveness, since, by definition, they refer to properties that are not exclusive to human bodies.

Yet, beyond the most general "common notions," there are other adequate perceptions resulting from commonalities between two or more bodies, representing more local relationships of agreement. "If something is common to, and peculiar to, the human body and certain external bodies by which the human body is usually affected, and is equally in the part and in the whole of each of them, its idea will also be adequate in the mind" (*E* II p39). "From this it follows that the mind is more capable of perceiving things adequately as its body has many things in common with other bodies" (II p39c). Perhaps there is some property common to human bodies but not present in any other bodies that might account for a universally shared idea unique to human minds? Yet Spinoza refers only to "certain external bodies by which the human body is usually affected,"

---

14. Matheron, "L'anthropologie spinoziste?" 180.

which does not obviously constrain these more specific properties to any kind of external body.

Perhaps the idea of God, however, is a uniquely human common notion? Indeed, Spinoza claims that "God's infinite essence and his eternity are known to all." Yet he notes that this is so only because we perceive ourselves, our minds and bodies, as actually existing (*E* II p47). Since the attributes of thought and extension are defined as "what the intellect perceives of substance as constituting its essence" (I def4), this idea of God's essence could be nothing other than the perception of thought or extension as infinite and eternal. Such an idea, however understood, hardly seems to unify humanity into a seamless whole. Moreover, Spinoza acknowledges that even if we all have an idea of God, we do not necessarily recognize it as such or allow it to guide our actions. Indeed, the politics of renaturalization would hardly be arduous if this idea of God's eternal and infinite essence were so vivid and instructive.

Spinoza's claim about these local common notions implies that because our bodies can be affected in a great many ways, humans can *generate* increasingly many common ideas by way of contact. The foundations of human reason are not confined to what is given by the perception of universal properties like space, motion, and gravity. Diverse bodies are capable of a great many things, because they share more properties with more different kinds of bodies and thus have the power to know more parts of nature. The more complex a body is, the more it is replete with sites of accord and differentiation with respect to other bodies, and thus reason can do its characteristic work of grasping "agreements and differences" (*E* II p29s). As we cultivate diversity in our bodies, we will have more in common with diverse others.

We can conclude that difference, for Spinoza, is the basis of commonality.[15] We can share only because we contain, as Whitman heralds, multitudes. We might speculate that language is a good example of bodily diversification that begins in (relatively) passive experience and evolves into an increasingly adept power of connection to others. The more languages one learns, the more auditory and lingual dispositions one's body is capable of, and thus the more one can communicate and share. Likewise, those who have regular contact with companion animals or other nonhuman beings will come to be and to know themselves differently. The richness of the human body consists in the diversity of its components, which enable us

---

15. Cf. Timmermans, "Descartes et Spinoza."

to relate to a great variety of other beings.[16] The diversity of our components comes from our affects and habits as much as from our physiology. We can derive a kind of practical imperative from these claims about the physical basis of reason: Diversify your body so as to generate agreements (*convenientia*) with other bodies and become increasingly rational.

Spinoza's word for agreement is *convenientia*, from *convenio* in Latin. It indicates, not sameness or identity, but a meeting, a coming together, or an assembly. Although Spinoza often speaks as though reason harmonizes all human beings into an "agreement" (*convenientia*), no special feature of humanity sets us apart from other beings to furnish an exclusive agreement. When Spinoza exclaims that "men who are governed by reason—that is, men who, from the guidance of reason, seek their own advantage—want nothing for themselves which they do not desire for other men" (*E* IV p18s), recall that what rational men want is simply greater power to think (know God, or nature) and act. Rational desires might involve general precepts, such as to cultivate our capacities as modes of thought and extension through self-diversification, but what contributes to self-enhancement and the content of self-knowledge is not identical for each and every human being. Each of us does not become a greater power of thinking and a body capable of a great many things by knowing the same things about nature, even if a universal power of nature (thought) makes such knowing possible. The renaturalization of humanity reveals that what is most in our interest is knowledge and love of nature (IV p36), which is a nonrivalrous good attainable only by combining with many other natural forces, human and nonhuman. That the intellectual love of God is our greatest good means only that because we are thinking beings, we by necessity strive to think as powerfully and effectively as we can. This good is linked to love because to be a body is to seek as much vitalizing joy as possible. Spinoza believes that the maximization of our powers depends, first and foremost, on "joining forces" with other humans (IV p37s). We need and enjoy one another more than any other "thing" in nature (IV appIX). Only with one another can we come to enjoy the greatest good, the knowledge of ourselves united with all of nature. The radical renaturalization of humanity allows us to act in light of what we really are, parts of nature, modes of thought and extension that yearn to actualize their powers as our essences allow. There is no evidence that this energizing self-appreciation involves knowing ourselves *as humans* united

---

16. Pierre-François Moreau, *Spinoza, l'expérience et l'éternité*, 449, 454. A similar point is made by Matheron, *Individu et communauté chez Spinoza*, 74.

to nature. Rather, a cursory glance at *Ethics* V suggests that knowledge of ourselves united to nature is most robust insofar as we regard ourselves to be singular beings. Specific knowledge of ourselves and the constituent forces that make us what we are delivers the greatest good.

We can conclude, with Matheron, that Spinoza offers no theoretical definition of man. As Lee Rice similarly observes, "Spinoza neither has nor wants a univocal concept of human nature."[17] One implication I draw from this analysis is that precisely *because* there is no such thing as man, adhering to the character of ourselves as natural beings is all the more important.[18] "Human nature," for the politics of renaturalization, is neither a *fait à découvrir* nor a *fait accompli* but a *fait à accomplir*. If reason is produced but never guaranteed by fruitful encounters, the art of constructing the conditions under which as many diverse natures as possible can combine forces may be all the more "difficult and rare" (*E* V p42s). If Spinoza's ethics aims to *produce* acts of reason and foster the conditions for rational human association, the problem of "joining forces" effectively becomes all the more urgent. Thus, the question arises again, even if "man" is political rather than metaphysical, is Spinoza's ethics anthropocentric? Even if Spinoza's system does not entail a universally shared human essence that guarantees our superiority to other beings in nature, might his philosophy remain man-centered on practical grounds? In particular, does his doctrine of utility, according to which "nothing is more useful to man than man," signal a pragmatic imperative to distinguish humans from all others?

Man's Utility to Man

"Peter must, as is necessary, conform to the idea of Peter, and not to the idea of man" (*KV* I 6). While there is no biological or spiritual basis for human distinctiveness, Spinoza prefers human association by virtue of our relative "similarity" (*E* III p27) and our greater power to enjoy one another (IV appIX). The more similar a being is to me, he claims, the more "useful" it is. Thus, Matheron has suggested that rather than a universalist ethics, Spinoza's is an "ethics of similitude."[19] In a pluralist world, those who reject a universalist ethics might not find an ethics of similitude ap-

---

17. Rice, "*Tamquam naturae humanae exemplar*: Spinoza on Human Nature," 299.
18. Cf. Matheron, "L'anthropologie spinoziste?" 182.
19. Ibid., 182.

pealing. But let us examine the character of this similitude and the ethical practice it involves.

Even if there is not one single property that unites us and excludes all other beings, the relative similarity of our bodies makes for the greatest possible agreement (*convenientia*) among us. Nevertheless, each of us has a singular essence (or nature), a unique ratio of motion and rest and a distinctive striving to persevere in being (*conatus*) (*E* III p6). Desire is "the very essence of [a] man" (III p9s), and "the desire of each individual differs from the desire of another as much as the nature, *or* essence, of the one differs from the other" (III p57d). Spinoza notes the essential differences between a human and a horse but also between a drunk and a philosopher (he says nothing of the drunk philosopher, however). When distinct desires come into contact with one another, they will accord more or less with one another. Each of us desires to produce effects that enhance and preserve our natures, such that those with similar natures tend to amplify each other's power.[20] "Things which are said to agree in nature are understood to agree in power" (IV p32d). Adequate shelter and heat in Montreal during the winter, for example, preserve my being, along with that of my child, cats, electronics, and books. What maintains our being overlaps to various extents. What we do in the shared space of my apartment fortify our minds and bodies in complementary ways.

Human needs tend to be more complicated than protection from the elements, of course, and (albeit technically correct) it is only so helpful to think of my iPod as striving for shelter. *Conatus*, in the most general sense, refers to a particular composition of energy persisting in a relatively stable state. My child and cats clearly exhibit a *desire* to exist in determinate ways (*E* III p9s). They aim not only to avoid death but to enjoy their characteristic pleasures and cultivate their distinctive powers. All of the small animals in my home enjoin me to develop skills of communication, nurturing, and play. My son skillfully solicits me to develop new powers (rather relentlessly!), just as my interest in stimulating laughter and affection in him (which enables me to further love myself) encourages him to grow and thrive. We are, I dare say, mutually useful to one another. My cats and I likewise mutually support each other's vitality. Studies suggest that people who have regular contact with companion animals live longer.[21] As much as we abuse and instrumentalize animals, there are many

---

20. Matheron, "Spinoza and Sexuality," 95–96.
21. See Wilson and Turner, *Companion Animals in Human Health*.

indications that they enjoy our company, such as the meow by which cats address humans (but rarely one another), communicating their desires for food, play, and affection.

Although the suggestion that my child and I are involved in a relation of reciprocal utility is perhaps not an edifying notion, we should take note of Spinoza's peculiar definition of utility.

> Whatever so disposes the human body that it can be affected in a great many ways, or renders it capable of affecting external bodies in a great many ways, is useful [*utile*] to man; the more it renders the body capable of being affected in a great many ways, or of affecting other bodies, the more useful [*utile*] it is; on the other hand, what renders the body less capable of these things is harmful [*noxium*]. (*E* IV p38)

Spinozan utility is not, therefore, the "utilitarian" notion it is often taken to be. The notion of utility does not imply that other people are the most effective instruments for satisfying our preferences. Useful phenomena, encounters, experiences, and beings are those that "dispose" the body so as to make it more receptive and, thereby, more active. Utility names a kind of corporeal involvement that renders affected beings increasingly open to the world and thereby increasingly able to affect others. According to Spinoza, the most useful relationship in my house is between my adult partner and me, since we can nourish and stimulate one another's minds and bodies in the greatest diversity of ways.

The notion of *utile* echoes Spinoza's principle establishing the relative superiority of human minds. "The human mind is capable of perceiving a great many things, and is the more capable, the more its body can be disposed in a great many ways" (*E* II p14). Utility points to the affective conditions of perception. It names the sensuous receptivity and connectivity required in order to think and act under the guidance of reason. The same word designates "interest" or "advantage," because it describes the source of our activity as finite beings, ineluctably bound to one another.

Recall that Spinoza's doctrine of common notions maintains that we can perceive most clearly those properties that are shared by our bodies and those that we encounter most frequently. The more we have in common, the more we come to know our own bodies and those things they share with others. When our bodies "agree," or convene, we have increasingly many resources for generating adequate ideas, and we can better preserve and enhance our existence. Acting from these agreements, from our common resources, benefits others insofar as they are "like us," insofar as they have similar needs, pleasures, and powers.

Yet the extent to which individuals cannot make their desires compatible is the extent to which their essences differ. It is exceedingly rare for any of us to encounter another who "agrees entirely" with our nature, such that we would have exactly the same requirements or strivings.[22] But the more we have in common with one another, the more our striving will yield mutually beneficial effects. Rice points out that Spinoza says only that humans *can* agree (*convenire possunt*) in essence (*E* I p17s), not that they do.[23] Indeed, humans tend *not* to agree in power. Spinoza frequently laments that "insofar as men are subject to passions, they cannot be said to agree in nature" (IV p32). And since we can never bring it about that we are not subject to passions (IV p4c), for any given individual there will be many called "human" who do not accord with her nature (essence). There are always likely to be many humans who diminish or even extinguish each other's strivings. From the point of view of a particular nature, there will be useless people who reduce one's global capacity to be affected and to affect others, sometimes to the point of death. Learning to detect a global decrease in power is not always easy. Love, for example, may be harmful, especially if it fixates the imagination to the exclusion of anything else (IV p44s). There are obviously many ways in which we humans can be "contrary to one another" (IV p34).

It is not impossible, however, for human natures to agree perfectly (*E* IV p68s). Spinoza notes that "if, for example, two individuals of entirely the same nature are joined to one another, they compose an individual twice as powerful as each one." He proceeds to exhort his readers with an image of all of humanity united into a single whole, thinking and acting with a single mind and body.

> To man, then, there is nothing more useful than man. Man, I say, can wish for nothing more helpful to the preservation of his being than that all should so agree in all things that the minds and bodies of all would compose, as it were, one mind and one body; that all should strive together, as far as they can to preserve their being; and that all, together, should seek for themselves the common advantage [*utile*] of man.

---

22. Spinoza offers two examples: Adam and Eve prior to the Fall (*E* IV p68s) and a man who foresaw his son's death (*Ep* 17).

23. Rice, "*Tamquam naturae humanae exemplar*: Spinoza on Human Nature," 300.

From this it follows that men who are governed by reason—that is, men who, from the guidance of reason, seek their own advantage [*utile*]— want nothing for themselves which they do not desire for other men. (*E* IV p18s)

The ethics of similitude and utility provokes a rational "wish," a hope for a shared project of power. Similitude is not identity but compatibility (*convenientia*), such that our desires become mutually beneficial. Realizing my most ardent wishes, if they are aroused by knowledge of my true advantage (*utile*), will bring about what most benefits others. Although this image suggests that we might discover a universal common good and form a rational community composed of all of humanity, I do not think that we must know and love the same things in nature in order to so assemble.

Even though Spinoza's notion of utility relaxes the requirements for unity by pluralizing them, he still qualifies his appeals to unity with a lament about the irreducibility of passions and our tendency toward enmity. Without a notion of a stable common good discoverable in each human heart, the convenience of diverse natures remains precarious and arduous. If a synergy of rational powers is an achievement rather than a recognition of an underlying sameness, the form of this achievement is in no way prescribed by the politics of renaturalization. Rationality is not everywhere the same and reflects a local grasp of nature's infinite power. What is rational for one human individual, polity, institution, or family is not necessarily rational for another, because what follows from one finite nature does not necessarily follow from another.

As Spinoza says, music may be "good for the melancholy, bad for the one who is mourning, and neither good nor bad to one who is deaf" (*E* IV pref). Music may or may not enhance one's striving. Melancholics, perhaps, would do well to combine with musicians, since music will be conducive to the intensification of each of their powers of activity (if the particular musician appreciates an audience). Even if a "wise man" ought to enjoy life with "pleasant food and drink, with scents, with the beauty of green plants, with decoration, music, sports" (IV p45s), some will not be enhanced by music, sports, or drink. The same things are not good for all "wise men," and, as obvious and banal as this claim is with respect to physical health, there is no reason not to extend this principle to ideas. Certain concepts and idioms do not engender adequate ideas in some individuals but will be exhilarating and emancipating to others. Spinoza suggests that most humans exhibit corporeal complexity such that, given a favorable affective milieu replete with occasions for joy, they can generate adequate ideas reliably, even if they will always also suffer passions. If adequate ideas follow from our singular natures, reason will be expressed in irreducibly diverse ways. A reasonable life is an achievement contingent on effectively combining energies and coordinating strivings. Rather than the given needs of the human species, the contours of a common agreement will be determined by the requirements of a particular composition of natures. Reasonable agreements will vary from commonwealth to commonwealth, not only because we cannot escape our passions, but owing to the very nature of reason. What a particular composite body needs to flourish reflects the concrete disposition of its corporeal and mental powers, which, because they are natural, are local.

If there is no underlying universal human essence accessible by reason, why should our unions be governed by the species boundary? If we come to see, "from the inside," our particular compositions and their structures, might we discover nonhuman relations as essential to our thriving, on par with our families, teachers, and community leaders? Spinoza, it must be admitted, has a normative vision of total human community when he announces that "man is a God to man" (E IV p35s) and urges all to combine into "one mind and one body" (IV p18s). Yet this vision of radical cooperation and collective striving to know and love nature becomes possible only upon the development of common notions through contact and affective exchange.

The history of human conflict shows that developing overlapping understandings of our good is incredibly arduous and, in many of its expressions, misguided. The politics of renaturalization rejects a stable human essence in favor of an exhortation to form indefinitely expansive and variable forms of human association. While no natural being is infinitely malleable—indeed, there are limits proper to any "nature" (E IV pref)—the lack of content to Spinoza's notions of the human and its good may be what renders our fellows supremely "useful." Because nobody knows what a human can do, of what affects it is capable, we are encouraged to experiment with forms of association to discover new joys and powers. Because utility is defined by receptivity and variability, its contours are not defined in advance.

Nevertheless, Spinoza uses the term "human nature" and refers to its inexorable laws as part of an effort to treat humanity as a unity. He appeals to the desirability of an image of man to guide our striving toward greater perfection (E IV pref). It is interesting to note that in the *Ethics*, his most precise and systematic philosophical text, the term "human nature" and his appeal to our yearning for an exemplar of man appear only in the fourth part, "On human servitude." This is no accident in my view. Our need for such ideas, and for the paradigms that inevitably accompany them, is an expression of our finitude. The model of man springs from our desire to persevere in being because reason in its pure form views things *sub specie æternitatis* and cannot thereby tell us how to act in this moment and context. Practical reason always involves a robust imaginative aspect. Yet practical reason, aware of itself as a partial expression of nature, cultivates awareness of its own limits and treats the idea of human nature as a useful fiction.

Spinoza's asserts that we "desire a *model* [*exemplar*] of human nature" immediately after defining "models" as imaginative notions that we use to judge things to be more or less complete (*E* IV pref). While everything is perfect (finished, complete) from an absolute point of view, finite beings, striving in time (duration), must appeal to models to make things more or less "perfect," more or less conducive to our striving.[24] Our model of man is no different from our idea of a house. A model allows us more or less effectively to act with a view to an end we set before ourselves. Spinoza's critique of finalism posits that nature has no ends toward which it strives (I app). Likewise, there is no perfect actualization of human existence toward which history ought to tend. Nevertheless, as finite, changeable beings, we strive toward particular goals we imagine to be desirable.

The particular shape of this model matters, as feminists and race theorists have persuasively shown. Is this man to whom we look above all self-sufficient? Is he implicitly or explicitly European, white, and property owning? Does his property include servants, slaves, and women? Or do we think of humans as fragile, dependent animals, always in need of mothering persons? Do we think of ourselves as potentially or actually those mothering persons? Do we think of humans as closely bound to nonhuman nature, animal, plant, and mineral? Do we see how we are constituted by our machines and technology? Who is man?

Many of these questions were invisible to Spinoza. Spinoza's renaturalization of man is concerned to show above all that our action is necessarily constrained and that we should not expect anyone, including our leaders, philosophers, and neighbors, to be in command of him- or herself in most circumstances. Indeed, no one is ever entirely in command, in the sense of being independent of the causal forces in one's environment. His idea of man also warns political authorities against doing whatever

---

24. For a more in-depth analysis of exemplarity as a bridge between objective and subjective value, see Rosenthal, "Why Spinoza Chose the Hebrews."

they please, establishing the natural limits to any exercise of coercion. The ineliminable diversity of natural beings suggests that a commonwealth approximates nature by cultivating a relationship of family quarreling. To be citizens whose natural character cannot be extirpated is to be, like a family, in it together while remaining different from one another. And finally, he wants to show that the more our bodies can be disposed in a great many ways, the more useful we are to one another. He outlines a portrait of reason and utility that underscores sensuous receptivity as the condition of possibility for agency. Together, insofar as we are guided by a grasp of our genuine good, we can become more resilient and capable thinkers and actors.

The question that arises today is: Do we still need this paradigm of human nature? What do we do with our ideas of man, men, and the human? And is humanity sufficiently different from our animal cousins to justify their exclusion from our ethical community? What of the myriad other nonhuman dependencies in nature? Is Spinoza's renaturalized man nevertheless still, first and foremost, a *man*, looking out for his own kind? In the final section, I will detour away from the technical discussion of reason and offer some thoughts about the implications of renaturalizing humanity.

Nonhuman Utility

Our epoch is ideologically humanist. Even if neoliberalism has narrowed humanity to the figure of *homo œconomicus*, the sentient calculator, political philosophy is still concerned, above all, with "the freedom of the individual, the respect for legality, the dignity of the person."[25] Even if dignified person includes corporations and excludes the extraordinarily dependent and cognitively disabled, most theorists remain trained upon the problem of "the human." Essentialism is out. The human no longer has a self-same, stable, and eternal essence. Indeed, for liberals and radical democrats alike, the human is a "postmetaphysical" term of contest, subject to constant challenge and revision, a normative promise rather than a description of what unifies our kind. The human is, for someone like Judith Butler, explicitly imaginary. The human is a horizon of aspiration. It performs a normative function toward which we can endeavor to adopt an ever more critical stance. Spinoza anticipates an embrace of "man" as a strategic rather than a descriptive figure. In this "desire for a model of

---

25. Althusser, "Marxism and Humanism," 221.

man," today we can find both promise and danger. The second half of this study will ask whether the time has come for a politics without man, the human, or even woman. In this section, I return briefly to the question of whether Spinoza's conception of humanity is anthropocentric. Do his notions of humanity and rationality exclude meaningful considerations of nonhuman nature?

Spinoza clearly holds that "to man . . . there is nothing more useful than man" (E IV p18s). Humans dispose one another's bodies to become increasingly complex and affectively rich. This relationship of "use" is not a relationship of exploitation. Rather than a mercenary account whereby other humans are mere means to my acquisition of more and more power (as if power were possessed rather than exercised), I interpret Spinoza's renaturalized notion of utility to have greater affinity with a feminist ethics of care. It is by virtue of the arts and capacities we develop in relationship to one another that we become capable. Rational autonomy, on this model, is understood not as an absence of constraint but as an affective, local knowledge of how to respond effectively within a constellation of relationships.[26] Care ethics also concerns primarily human relations. Are they the only relevant relationships for Spinoza, as most critics find? If the celebration of fellow humans as supremely useful is not an exhortation to mutual exploitation, can the same be said for Spinoza's remarks on nonhuman nature?

Descartes is often "credited" with articulating the still dominant worldview in which humans are "masters and possessors of nature."[27] Within this worldview, reason is an instrument by which we can progressively control the natural world and manipulate our own bodies, subordinating all matter to the requirements of spirit. Some feminists, critical theorists, and ecologists appreciate Spinoza's alternative portrait of reason, in which human rationality is not a power separate from nature.[28] Spinoza's reason is not a spiritual tool that might "work on," improve, and cultivate nature.[29] Rather, reason is an effect of complex relations among natural beings. Reason is what composite, complex ideas do by their very nature and by virtue of ambient natural forces. Reason does not imply a kind of special (moral) lawfulness, applicable only to spiritual beings.

Deep ecologists find in Spinoza's rationalism the possibility of harmony

---

26. Cf. Armstrong, "Autonomy and the Relational Individual."
27. Cf. Plumwood, *Feminism and the Mastery of Nature*.
28. See, e.g., Lloyd, *Man of Reason* and *Part of Nature*.
29. Cf. Locke, *Second Treatise on Government*, chap. 5, and Hegel, *Phenomenology of Spirit*, chap. 4.

with nonhuman nature. Arne Naess declares, "No great philosopher has so much to offer in the way of clarification and articulation of basic ecological attitudes as Baruch Spinoza."[30] Naess claims that despite Spinoza's highly technical vocabulary, ecologists can find inspiration in his assertions that nature is a vital creative unity that is and must be infinitely diverse. Naess and other deep ecologists are attracted to Spinoza's doctrine of *conatus* (striving), which contends that each and every thing, organic or inorganic, strives to persevere in being and enhance its existence to the extent that its character allows. Recognition that each and every thing aims at "self-realization," according to the ecological interpretation, fosters an appreciation of other beings' efforts that might restrain human exploitation. Indeed, Spinoza condemns certain expressions of anthropocentrism, the view that the nonhuman world exists exclusively for the use and pleasure of human beings. Spinoza criticizes the all too common tendency of each man to imagine "that God might love him above all the rest, and direct the whole of Nature according to the needs of their blind desire and insatiable greed" (*E* I app).

Deep ecological interpretations of Spinoza have been met with criticism by a number of theorists, most prominently Genevieve Lloyd.[31] Lloyd notes that while Spinoza adduces a nonanthropocentric metaphysics, his "morality" is entirely "man-centered" and excludes any moral consideration of nonhuman beings. Spinoza finds that "other species can be ruthlessly exploited for human ends."[32] Her criticism centers on Spinoza's assertion that "a law against killing animals is based more on empty superstition and womanish compassion than sound reason. The rational principle of seeking our advantage teaches us to establish a bond with men, but not with beasts, or with things whose nature is different from human nature" (*E* IV p37s). Spinoza's view that humans should establish bonds only with one another does not appear to promise a profound ecological sensibility.

Deep ecological interpretations of Spinoza emphasize his general metaphysical picture. They praise the portrait of all beings united within nature, sustained by an infinite network of interlocking, dynamic life "systems," sometimes referred to as "selves."[33] Deep ecologists acknowledge Spinoza's repugnant anthropocentric attitude (they do not mention his misogyny) but deny that such remarks taint the fundamental insights

30. Naess, "Spinoza and Ecology," 54.
31. See also de Jonge, *Spinoza and Deep Ecology*.
32. Lloyd, "Spinoza's Environmental Ethics," 294.
33. Mathews, *The Ecological Self*.

his system provides.[34] Karen Houle, in her review of the debate around Spinoza's "ecosophy," helpfully points out that proponents of the green Spinoza reinsert human/nature dualism and treat nature as something "out there," separate from human practice and community.[35] Houle notes the frequent elision of the fact that Spinoza means by nature *absolutely everything*, including synthetic phenomena like toxic waste and robots.

The virtues of Naess's rebuttal to Lloyd, however, are generally unrecognized by Spinoza scholars. Naess points out that Spinoza never uses the term "moral" in the *Ethics*. Naess exclaims that Spinoza may be "one of the greatest opponents of moralism that ever lived."[36] He insists that Lloyd misleads her readers when implying a uniquely human moral community that enjoys special "rights" separate from "natural right." Naess notes that the "rights" a community institutes by law are simply means to engage in self-realization that humans happen to have within their power. Such forms of association are different in character but not in kind from those of a pack of wolves, a hive of bees, or a field of flowers. Although Spinoza cannot support a program of animal *rights*, his views allow nonhuman animals, according to Naess, to be "members of *life communities* on par with babies, lunatics, and others who do not cooperate as citizens, but are cared for in part for their own sake."[37]

Naess argues that Spinoza's notions of *civil right* ought not to be understood as "moral." He does not indicate precisely what he means by morality, or why it has no place in Spinoza's system. Nonetheless, on my reading, antimoralism follows directly from anti-anthropocentrism. Moral judgment is often precisely what is supposed to elevate humans out of nature. A central underpinning of humanism is that we are uniquely capable of moral judgment, conceived as the ability to act in accordance with a principle, maxim, or rule disclosed by transcendental reason. For Spinoza, however, since humans are different only in degree from other natural beings, they do not act in accordance with special laws that might be called "moral." If all beings are bound by the same causal network and follow the same "laws," there is no a priori reason to consider the human community in antagonistic opposition to nonhuman nature. Indeed, we seem to be discovering all too slowly that we may not survive without extending our sense of those beings whose flourishing we must seek to secure. Naess's

---

34. See Sessions, "Spinoza and Jeffers on Man in Nature."
35. Houle, "Spinoza and Ecology Revisited."
36. Naess, "Environmental Ethics and Spinoza's Ethics: Comments on Genevieve Lloyd's Article," 315.
37. Naess, "Environmental Ethics and Spinoza's Ethics," 319.

insistence on the pragmatic boundaries of communities upheld by right might effectively link Spinoza to ecological projects.

Nevertheless, Lloyd indicates a fundamental ambiguity in ecological thought. She notes that while ecological thought aims above all to undermine anthropocentrism, it often does so by "humanizing the nonhuman."[38] She notes that within ecological discourse, nonhumans are seen to exhibit "preferences," bear "intrinsic value," and merit "rights." The universe is described as a great "Self," suggesting a personal God rather than an impersonal natural power. Lloyd observes that anthropocentrism is not weakened by affirming that all beings are like us, extending the umbrella of selfhood to include mountains and rivers. Rather than expanding human categories to foster respect and care for nonhuman life, Spinoza's philosophy suggests that we renaturalize humans as thoroughly as possible. This does not mean, however, that we ought to view humans primarily as biological beings.[39] Neither does it mean that people are better understood as wild animals or impersonal spiritual flows. Spinoza encourages us to see that we are defined by our actions and passions. Moreover, we act only by virtue of the many diverse natural powers, human and nonhuman, upon which we depend.

But if Spinoza's is an "ethics of similitude," as Matheron argues, what are the consequences for those who do not appear to be "like us"? Is Spinoza consistent with his view of our radical interdependence when he asserts that "we may take for our own use, and use in any way, whatever there is which we judge to be good, *or* useful for preserving our being and enjoying a rational life" (*E* IV appVIII)? When he claims that we may kill animals because they have a "different nature," the notion of use (*utile*) appears to have a different application with respect to nonhuman beings. Has anthropocentrism been smuggled back in precisely in the name of "enjoying a rational life"? Is Lloyd correct to affirm that however egalitarian Spinoza's ontological picture may be, his "morality" is irredeemably anthropocentric? Or might we write off Spinoza's remarks as a "blind spot," as Matheron and Rice have done?[40]

Although I agree with Rice that it would be a mistake to try and draw any conclusions about "animal nature" from Spinoza's offhand remarks on "beasts," as I argue in chapter 6, we miss the point if we think that his discourse on animals has anything to do with them. A systematic study

---

38. Lloyd, "Spinoza's Environmental Ethics," 307.
39. Houle, "Spinoza and Ecology Revisited," 423.
40. Matheron, "L'anthropologie spinoziste?" 183; Rice, *"Tamquam naturae humanae exemplar:* Spinoza on Human Nature," 302.

of his comments on animals reveals that his concern is only with the normative force of the figure of the animal. The question for Spinoza is not that of animal rights, or even of human behavior *toward* animals. Rather, these remarks exclusively concern human self-understanding, an understanding that forms the basis of the politics of renaturalization. For my purposes here, however, I want only to make a few observations about the question of nonhuman utility.

Granting Naess's rejoinder about the absence of any morality that implies human transcendence in Spinoza's system, Lloyd correctly notes that Spinoza cannot easily be made to support an ethos predicated upon human self-restraint in view of other beings' flourishing. Spinoza dismisses any concern for the striving of nonhuman animals to persevere in being and chastises the feminine *pathos* he detects in such concern. Yet his discussions of reason and human nature suggest that any model of the human is strategic and revisable, within certain limits. Although the *conatus* is irreducible in each natural being, our idea of human nature and its distinctive requirements is only a more or less enabling imaginative projection. As Matheron notes, "man" is simply whatever we are in the habit of imagining him to be.[41] Indeed, Spinoza explicitly says as much (*E* II p40s).

Spinoza's images of man are wildly varied. He represents us to be "natural enemies" (*E* III p55s), Gods to one another (IV p35s), and united into a single mind and body (IV p18). He represents the nature of beasts to be alien to humanity, even hostile to freedom and rationality (IV p68s). Yet given the strategic place of human nature in Spinoza's thought, *our* notions of human nature must be assessed for their utility. To what extent does a notion of human nature as not-animal-nature amplify our striving? A habit of imagining ourselves as not-animal may not be useful today. Not all of Spinoza's images, drawn as they are from his perception of human requirements, are suited to our striving. Obviously, democracy is undermined by his image of citizen as "man," an exclusionary image that Spinoza explicitly defends with his last breaths (*TP* 11.4) Given that democratic association is one of the key features of a rational life for Spinoza, we must insist that his exemplary free men are no longer as "useful for preserving our being and enjoying a rational life." We must displace Spinoza's figures of freedom if we are to realize a project of shared power, pleasure, and knowledge.

Posthumanism suggests that even the gender-neutral "human" marks a barrier to our freedom and self-understanding. Many today challenge

---

41. Matheron, "L'anthropologie spinoziste?" 182.

the extent of the difference between human and animal natures. The intimate history of our coevolution with our animal companions and workers prompts Donna Haraway to assert that "we have never been human."[42] Famously, her political myth of the cyborg also calls into question the boundaries of our humanity. The cyborg calls our attention not only to the permeability of organic beings with respect to one another but to our machinic powers and pleasures.[43] From various directions, posthumanists argue that we fail to know ourselves under the description "human." Perhaps the term human has become overly resistant to renaturalization. In order for Spinoza's ethics to be practiced today, we might explore alternative exemplars. Rather than becoming the man who desires nothing for himself that he does not desire for other men, the realization of Spinoza's ethical vision might depend upon our becoming something far stranger. The second part of this book explores the possibilities for the politics of renaturalization beyond the image of man.

---

42. Haraway, *When Species Meet*.
43. Haraway, "A Cyborg Manifesto."

PART II

Beyond the Image of Man

4

Desire for Recognition?
Butler, Hegel, and Spinoza

> All authentic reading is in its own way violent, or it is nothing but the complaisance of a paraphrase.
> —PIERRE MACHEREY

Hegel and Spinoza have come to represent two possible alternatives to the mainstream liberal tradition springing from figures like Hobbes, Locke, and Kant. If contemporary liberalism presumes the reality of individual freedom in each of us that must be safeguarded, Hegel and Spinoza call into question the possibility of either individuality or liberty outside of a network of substantial relationships. If liberalism is concerned first with the rational justification of public authority, Hegel and Spinoza ascertain the processes by which desire for particular forms of authority is constituted. Thinkers turn to Hegel and Spinoza seeking a more richly affective and relational account of freedom and selfhood than the more narrowly juridical models drawn from classical liberalism. Yet, for many, it is not possible to seek resources in both Hegel and Spinoza. To look to Spinoza is to regard desire as an irrepressible affirmation of life and joy, which inspires a vital politics of collective self-organization.[1] For Deleuze

---

1. Hardt and Negri, *Empire* and *Multitude*.

and those he inspires, "Spinoza's is a philosophy of pure affirmation."[2] Spinoza's self may be driven by self-preservation, but the desire for preservation is not, for these thinkers, poised for a battle to the death, but overflowing with a feeling of vitality. Hegel, in contrast, is viewed as one for whom desire is, in essence, destructive and violent. Although Hegel envisions overcoming the annihilating aspect of desire, the irreducibility of the negative moment renders his psychology unacceptable to many Spinozists. As Deleuze puts it, Hegel portrays self-consciousness as the bearer of "that internal death, the universal sadomasochism of the tyrant-slave."[3] The two approaches appear to many to be antagonistic. In looking for a fresh philosophical perspective on politics, there is a choice: Hegel *or* Spinoza.[4]

Feminist theory inherits the standoff between Hegel and Spinoza. Rosi Braidotti, for example, contends that Judith Butler's work is constrained by her "negative" notion of desire drawn from Hegel, which ought to be supplanted by a more "affirmative" principle found in Spinoza.[5] Butler's reliance upon Hegel, albeit a reconstructed version, is explicit and well-known.[6] Like Hegel, Butler is criticized for a negative picture of desire, allied with lack, violence, and destruction.[7] For her critics, Butler's inheritance of Hegelian desire implicates feminine subjects in an inescapable spiral of servitude and self-mortification, a master-slave dialectic without any promise of redemption. "A signifier for the unreachable sign of loss and destitution, a recipe for despair, Butler's feminine is reduced to a pathetic effort at simulating signification on the road to nowhere."[8] Braidotti proposes Spinozism as an alternative for feminist theory:

> Desire does play a role in Butler's thought, but it is a negative, mournful theory of desire, which understates the impact of pleasure on the constitution of the subject . . . what if the "fixer" of the psychic landscape were the over-flowing plenitude of pleasure, rather than the melancholy dis-

---

2. Deleuze, *Expressionism in Philosophy*, 60.
3. Deleuze, *Spinoza: Practical Philosophy*, 12–13.
4. The portrait of Hegel and Spinoza as two competing alternatives to liberalism has its roots in mid-twentieth-century French philosophy. See Althusser, "On Spinoza," and Macherey *Hegel ou Spinoza*.
5. Braidotti, *Metamorphoses*. Negri also claims that Hegelian dialectics poses an obstacle to Butler's critique of patriarchy, in Casarino and Negri, *In Praise of the Common*, 381 n. 15.
6. See Butler, *Subjects of Desire*.
7. See, e.g., Allen, "Dependency, Subordination, and Recognition," and Oliver, *Witnessing*.
8. Braidotti, *Metamorphoses*, 50.

course of debt and loss? I think the *more Spinozist* option has a great deal to offer.⁹

Spinozan desire, for Braidotti, signals an exhortation to a feminist politics of joy and a salutary response to feminism's long history of focusing on violation and victimization. Taking a cue from Deleuze, Braidotti exclaims, "I actively yearn for a more joyful and empowering concept of desire and for a political economy that foregrounds positivity, not gloom."¹⁰

Butler claims, however, that her considerations of desire take their bearings not from Hegel alone but from Spinoza and Hegel together. In response to Braidotti's criticism, Butler claims that "the Spinozan *conatus* remains at the core of my work."¹¹ Indeed, Butler mentions Spinoza in her earliest work,¹² and she invokes his principle of *conatus* throughout her corpus. Refusing their opposition, Butler's references to Spinoza are often immediately followed by the suggestion that his notions of *conatus* and *cupiditas* prefigure Hegelian desire. Butler lauds Spinoza's view in which desire, the human expression of *conatus*, expresses the desire to persevere in being, yet she insists that human desire can be understood only in terms of the Hegelian paradigm of recognition. Hegel reveals that "to persist in one's being is only possible on the condition that we are engaged in receiving and offering recognition."¹³ Butler maintains a continuity and complementarity between the two thinkers, such that each corrects the other. While Hegel adds the dimension of intersubjective recognition to Spinoza's framework, Spinoza's *conatus* "underwrites recognition," such that the refusal of recognition implies a threat to the fundamental effort to survive.¹⁴ Butler's fusion of Hegel and Spinoza produces the following thesis: "If certain lives do not qualify as lives or are, from the start, not conceivable as lives within certain epistemological frames, then these lives are never lived nor lost in the full sense."¹⁵ Denied recognition, one presents a "living figure" without "a life." A life is human only by virtue of the collective recognition of one's death as an irrecuperable loss that must be mourned. Butler frames her philosophy and politics with Spinoza's *co-*

9. Ibid., 53.
10. Ibid., 57.
11. Butler, *Undoing Gender*, 198.
12. *Subjects of Desire*, for example, 4, 12.
13. Butler, *Undoing Gender*, 31.
14. Butler, *Giving an Account of Oneself*, 44.
15. Butler, *Frames of War*, 1.

natus, but rather than an essential striving predicable of all natural beings, she understands it to indicate human fragility. *Conatus* names the fraught character of bodily persistence given over to "a network of hands."[16] She infuses Spinoza's core ontological principle with Hegel's insight about desire as an intersubjective striving for recognition, and she adds a Foucauldian dimension to reveal how power relations adumbrate recognition to confer the status of humanity on some while foreclosing it for others.[17]

Butler's alliance of the two thinkers violates the narrative of a number of theorists writing under the banner of Spinoza. Rather than identifying Spinoza as a radical, materialist alternative to the Hegelian tradition, Butler locates him squarely within it. Spinoza, far from opening a way beyond an ethics and politics of specifically human (inter)subjectivity, inaugurates the line of thinking that culminates in a post-Hegelian politics of recognition. As Butler increasingly heralds the need to speak of "the human," she insists all the more upon her debt to Spinoza.[18] The Spinozan desire to live is useful to her only when it is construed as the desire of a social (and, emphatically, not natural) subject seeking the recognition of other social subjects, negotiated within the constraints of formal and informal institutional structures. She thus enlists Spinoza in a radically antinaturalist tradition of social criticism that highlights the fragile contours of our psychic landscape.

In the following, I ascertain the roots of this antagonism among feminist theorists and continental philosophers by interrogating the basis of Butler's heretical alliance between Hegel and Spinoza. I argue that the binarism of affirmation and negation fails to capture what is at stake in posing Spinoza and Hegel as alternative foundations for social and political theory. The opposition between the negative and positive approaches to desire is Hegel's own. By invoking this dichotomy, Spinozists reproduce Hegel's division between his thought and Spinoza's. Hegel thought Spinoza was confined within an "Oriental" perspective, blind to the majestic labor of the negative.[19] Spinozists have inverted the value implication of his judgment, without challenging his terms. They thus accuse Hegel of dwelling in the darkness of negativity, unable to affirm the plenitude

---

16. Ibid., 14.
17. Butler, *Undoing Gender*, 31–32. I bracket discussion of Foucault for this analysis, but Butler's connection of Spinoza to Foucault is anticipated by Macherey's analysis in "Towards a Natural History of Norms."
18. See especially *Undoing Gender*, but also *Giving an Account of Oneself. Gender Trouble* is written in the wake of "antihumanism" but does not mention Spinoza.
19. Hegel, *Lectures on the History of Philosophy*, 477.

of life. Yet this opposition between them, if not wrong, does not explain why Hegel and Spinoza offer competing alternatives to mainstream political thought. They continue to nurture counterperspectives, in my view, because they are both profound thinkers of relationality. To identify the differences between the politics of recognition and the politics of renaturalization, we need to understand their models of relationality. To see how their respective paths lead away from liberalism but in different directions, let us examine the place of desire within their ontologies. We will find that their distinct conceptions of power, agency, and politics follow not, first and foremost, from an emphasis on negation versus affirmation. Rather, their politics differ because Hegel is concerned above all with relationships of representation, while Spinoza examines relationships of composition among human and nonhuman forces.

Butler and others are correct to treat Spinoza and Hegel as vibrant alternatives to mainstream liberalism, which remains guided by Hobbesian understandings of desire and methodological individualism. As fruitful as Butler's juxtaposition of Spinoza and Hegel is for her own theory, she underestimates Spinoza's challenge to any politics grounded in the representation of humanity and personhood. Butler's ultimate reduction of politics to a problematic of recognition and representation detracts from the resilience of Spinoza's conception of *conatus*. Her emphasis, with Hobbes and Hegel, on vulnerability to death inflates the power of the social to the detriment of natural determination. The idea that we live only insofar as we are recognized as human is anathema to the politics of renaturalization. The politics of renaturalization begins with the denial of human exceptionalism. We live better insofar as we view humans in terms of the same laws as anything else in nature. This chapter restages the contrast between Hegel and Spinoza to clarify the difference between a humanist program of recognition and the politics of renaturalization.

Spinoza in Hegel

In his lectures on the history of philosophy, Hegel declares that "thought must begin by placing itself at the standpoint of Spinozism; to be a follower of Spinoza is the essential commencement of all Philosophy."[20] Spinoza founds all true thinking, on Hegel's account, since he views being as a single totality. Mind is not alienated from God, nature, or body but is one with the true universal. Particularity is banished and thought is

---

20. Ibid., 482.

liberated to absolute status: all is thought and thought is all. Without an idea of the unity of being and the reconciliation of opposites, like mind and body, thought falters. For Hegel, "what constitutes the grandeur of Spinoza's manner of thought is that he is able to renounce all that is determinate and particular, and restrict himself to the One, giving heed to this alone."[21]

Spinoza is only the beginning of thought, which must be overcome for thought to develop. Spinoza's single substance, for Hegel, is motionless. Determinacy and individuality disappear in the One. Spinoza is the first to truly grasp the infinite, but at the cost of the finite. Because all is God and God alone, finitude "has no truth whatever."[22] Indeed, "with him there is too much God."[23] Spinoza speaks of particularity, but he assumes it without justification. Finite modes have no independence from substance and cannot thereby confirm their individuality.

> The moment of negativity is what is lacking to this rigid motionlessness, whose single form of activity is this, to divest itself of their determination and particularity and cast them back into the one absolute substance, wherein they are simply swallowed up and all life in itself is utterly destroyed.[24]

Even if Spinoza recognizes the link between determination and negation (*Ep* 32), negation remains external. Indeed, Spinoza notes that it is not in the essence of any being to destroy itself (*E* III p4). Negation is a limit or a privation imposed by external causes. It is not something internal to a being's desire to persevere in existence. For Hegel, the absence of internal negativity robs agents of the motor of self-transformation. Change comes from the outside. In essence, one strives to remain the same, but external pressures induce alterations and adaptations. Moreover, for the infinite being, there is no real change, and thus finite beings are mere appearances, deprived of the reality that negation and, even more importantly, the negation of the negation make possible.[25] As Macherey points out, Hegel does not insist on the negative for its own sake. Rather,

---

21. Ibid., 483.
22. Ibid., 506.
23. Ibid., 507.
24. Ibid., 513. Cf. *Science of Logic*.
25. Melamed confirms Hegel's judgment that finite modes are ultimately illusory for Spinoza, in "Acosmism or Weak Individuals?"

negation is necessary for true positivity, for self-determination through self-correction. Without the negative, there is no dialectic.[26]

Hegel judges Spinoza to mark the beginning of philosophy, because he articulates the first moment most audaciously: Being. Spinoza affirms the positivity of being as the absolute power to exist. Yet he lacks a true account of negativity by which negativity can be overcome. He grasps negativity as an externality but not as transformation. As a result, determinacy, particularity, and individuality are not real. They are resolved into substance, God, or nature, their immanent cause and thus their truth. Any difference between the finite and the infinite is denied by their formal identity.[27]

Deleuze and his readers concur with Hegel's diagnosis of the difference between himself and Spinoza. Spinoza is a philosopher of unequivocal affirmation, while Hegel is the most profound thinker of negation. Echoing Hegel but inverting his evaluation, Deleuze notes that "[a]nimals at least teach us the irreducibly external character of death. They do not carry it within, although they can necessarily bring it to each other."[28] If you read these words adumbrated with contempt rather than approbation, they could be Hegel's own. Animals are not self-conscious because they cannot will their own absolute negation; their deaths come from the outside. It is only humans who are infinite, because we can will self-annihilation.[29] Yet, for Deleuze,

> [i]n the reproach Hegel will make to Spinoza, that he ignored the negative and its power, lies the glory and innocence of Spinoza, his own discovery. In a world consumed by the negative, he has enough confidence in life, in the power of life, to challenge death, the murderous appetite of men, the rules of good and evil, and the just and unjust. Enough confidence in life to denounce all the phantoms of the negative.[30]

The negative is the specter of death and the positive implies the irrepressibility of life. For many Deleuzians, philosophers either tarry with death in the company of Hegel or praise life with Spinoza.

Whatever truth lies in this opposition, the terms are Hegel's. Yet, for

---

26. *Hegel ou Spinoza*, 149.
27. Ibid., 173.
28. *Spinoza: Practical Philosophy*, 12.
29. *Philosophy of Right*, §35A.
30. *Spinoza: Practical Philosophy*, 13.

Hegel, Spinoza's affirmation is of life that is not really life at all. If our existence is a pure given, it is not truly self-constituted. If individuals have no reality outside of the absolute, if they cannot die their own deaths, they do not live their own lives. To be subject to a death that is external, imposed from the outside, is to remain an animal, a natural rather than a spiritual being. Insisting that humans remain animals in death, for Deleuze on the other hand, testifies to Spinoza's courageous refusal of murder and self-annihilation as signs of virtue, testaments to conscience, or monuments to humanity. Spinoza's refusal of dialectics was perspicaciously *avant la lettre*. Deleuze's interpretation clearly intervenes in French and German mid-twentieth-century thought. Spinoza as a figure of pure affirmation is a provocative alternative to Hegel's psychophysiology of violence. Yet Hegel's opposition does not tell us why Spinoza and Hegel, together, point toward alternative political horizons.

To see the fresh perspective either affords on problems inherited from classical liberalism, Butler's focus on desire proves instructive. Hegel's appreciative yet sharp criticism of Spinoza in his lectures and his *Science of Logic* is based only on the first set of definitions in the *Ethics* and his use of the geometrical method. Surprisingly, Hegel ignores Spinoza's *conatus* and thus overlooks an important dimension of finitude. In ascertaining their respective understandings of desire, we can put a finer point on the politics of renaturalization. In particular, we can see how, although Spinoza and Hegel share a rich conception of relationships as sources of freedom and individuality, the politics of renaturalization combines uneasily with a politics of recognition.

Desire in Hegel

Hobbes and Spinoza depart from ancient and medieval treatments of the affects. For both, desire, the basic impulse to live, constitutes the primary affect, whereas love is the exalted affect among Christian medieval philosophers. Love for Aquinas, for example, is that by which we apprehend the good.[31] Characteristic of the seventeenth century, in contrast, is the view that the good is not discovered objectively in the cosmos, external to the self. Rather, in the words of Spinoza, "we judge something to be good because we strive for it, will it, want it, and desire it" (*E* III p9). Desire, Matheron suggests, is the concept that prompts moderns to reject value objectivity. Values come to be viewed as reflections of particular selves, and

---

31. Matheron, *Individu et communauté chez Spinoza*, 84–85.

desire displaces love as the index of good or bad, beneficial or harmful.[32] In the modern period desire appears coextensive with the self; it ceases to be "alien," beyond, or outside of the self: "my desire is desire of the self, and this desire of the self is me, in all of my richness and complexity."[33] For Spinoza, the essence of each being, human or nonhuman, is its *conatus*, or striving to persevere in existence (III p7). The fundamental urge to be, characteristic of all singular, finite beings, is named "desire" insofar as one is conscious of it. Thus, "[d]esire is [a] man's very essence" (III def affI), the impulse by which each strives to persevere and enhance his life.

Hegel inherits the modern innovation that views desire as the basis of self-experience. For Hegel, desire is key to understanding the unique character of self-conscious or spiritual existence. In Hobbes and Spinoza, conscious desire is only a complicated expression of an ontologically universal "endeavor" proper to all existent beings. And while Hegel acknowledges a drive for self-preservation belonging to animals, he claims that genuinely human desire, in pursuing life, seeks more. Here we see the roots of Butler's distinction between mere living, mere endurance, and the desire to live "a life." The desire for life, rather than mere organic continuity, finds "satisfaction" only in the intersubjective affirmation of its own freedom. As Axel Honneth shows, Hegel endows Hobbes's rivalrous struggle for self-preservation with a moral valence. The endeavor to preserve oneself is not brute biological instinct but a desire for others to recognize the value of one's existence and thus one's right to live. In order to become a right and not merely a shared endeavor (which animal communities experience), the desire to live must be underwritten by public acknowledgment of one's "personhood," or moral agency. Competition for honor ceases to be merely an instrumental accumulation of power, where power names the ability to influence others' actions to facilitate one's survival and comfort.[34] Battles for prestige, "in truth," express the desire for "an affirmative relation-to-self," achievable only by socially conferred appreciation of one's individual character and acknowledgment of one's universality, or "personhood."[35]

For Hegel, Hobbes observes a particular manifestation of desire as the determination to live, but fails to see its truth, the seed within it striving

---

32. I don't think Matheron's portrait is generalizable to the whole period. Descartes is perhaps a cusp figure since he places love before desire in the order of the affects (*PS* a. 69), yet the good/God is discovered by way of introspection into the self (*Med* V).

33. Matheron, *Individu et communauté chez Spinoza*, 89.

34. Hobbes, *Leviathan*, chap. 10.

35. Honneth, *The Struggle for Recognition*, 22.

to blossom into a more mature form. Hobbes correctly treats desire as the heart of the self, the motor of what Hegel will call "subjectivity." But desire is not yet "essentially" the desire for recognition. Desire appears in the *Phenomenology of Spirit* in the well-known section entitled "the truth of self-certainty," which marks the transition from consciousness to self-consciousness. "With self-consciousness," Hegel remarks, "we have entered the native realm of truth," and "self-consciousness is *desire* in general."[36] Hegel understands truth as a correspondence between subject and object. What is the case internally, or in the realm of representation, in order to be true, must also be the case externally, in the objective world, outside of a particular consciousness. Yet Hegel's is a developmental or "historical" notion of truth, meaning that the subject and object in question come, in time, to correspond with one another. Being is not automatically and exhaustively represented in a divine intellect. Rather, being comes to be reflected as becoming, as dynamic and living truth, especially through the transformative activities of self-conscious beings.

Self-consciousness, as the term suggests, concerns the representation of oneself to oneself. The subject and the object, for self-consciousness, are the same. The question is how subjective self-apprehension can be objectively verified. What is the process of development by which the subject and the object arrive at correspondence? According to Hegel, self-consciousness begins with the point of view of "self-certainty," or "the identity of itself with itself."[37] Of what precisely are we, as self-conscious beings, certain? What does it mean to be identical with oneself? In his lectures, Hegel asserts that "I have the certainty of the truth of my identity with myself in contrast to the appearance that I am dependent."[38] As in Descartes's *cogito*, I know that I am self-identical or self-sufficient. I know that my awareness depends only on me, even if my corporeality implies that I depend on external things in order to exist. Unlike Descartes, however, I cannot arrive at this self-understanding through immediate introspection. I must, in actuality, overcome my dependence on others, through expanding and complicating my self-understanding as an ethical (rather than a substantial) individual.

To galvanize a more complex self-understanding, subjective self-certainty is falsified. Paradigmatically for Hegel, just as for Descartes, physical need belies one's self-certainty. The conviction that I am free,

---

36. Hegel, *Phenomenology of Spirit*, §167.
37. Ibid.
38. *Lectures on the Philosophy of Spirit 1827–1828*, 184.

independent, self-sufficient, and one with myself is contradicted by my feeling that I need to live, by my attachment to biological life. Specifically, I need others to live. Sustaining my body requires other beings. Hegel, unlike Descartes, does not dismiss this requirement of others as contingent or inessential.[39] Food is Hegel's primary example of the need for external things. His example refers to adults, but nourishment first comes directly from another person, the mother or, albeit controversially in Hegel's time, a wet nurse.[40] For Hegel, "[c]onsciousness is the drive to suspend this appearance of its relation to an other, and to posit this other in identity with itself, to know itself as that in relation to which this object is no longer an other, but is suspended in self-consciousness and united with it."[41] Human being, either as an individual or as a "spiritual" (*geistige*) community, is driven by the desire for its self-representation to have objective validity. The first motive of desire, then, is to annul indications of its dependence. Only when this response to natural dependency fails does self-consciousness discover the need for enduring monuments to its independence. An enduring objective reality for one's freedom is necessary for the truth of self-certainty to cease to be abstract. Each of us must actively establish a correspondence between subject and object by way of a dialectic between dependence and independence, slavery and domination.

In Hegel's well-known narrative, the self-conscious being discovers that the desire to live is not attached to mere life, since consumption and negation remain "unsatisfying." At least two experiences prompt the discovery that one desires more than life. First, desire is not satisfied by its power to annihilate external objects that testify to its dependence. This fails because "self-consciousness, by its negative relation to the object, is unable to supersede it; it is really because of this relation that it produces the object again, and the desire as well."[42] One needs to be able to negate one's dependence, but one also needs evidence of that negation to endure, to take place in the world.

Second, in rivalrous struggle, not only over physical necessities but

---

39. The representation of the Cartesian self as exclusively mental has been challenged recently by a number of commentators, but I am working with Hegel's understanding for the purposes of this presentation. For an appeal to nuance the received view, see Deborah J. Brown, *Descartes and the Passionate Mind*. For an outright rejection, see Wilkin, "Descartes, Individualism, and the Fetal Subject."

40. Benjamin treats the drama of the master and slave in relation to the original mother-child dyad in *Bonds of Love*, chap. 2. On wet nurses during Hegel's time, see Brace, "The Tragedy of the Freelance Hustler."

41. *Lectures on the Philosophy of Spirit 1827–1828*, 184.

42. Hegel, *Phenomenology of Spirit*, §175.

over prestige, consciousness learns that it is willing to lose life in order to acquire something higher, something spiritual. The famous struggle between the bondsman and the lord dramatizes the lesson that desire aims at "a life," an enduring self-representation in another self-consciousness. In order for the conviction that one is free to exist subjectively as well as objectively, one requires another structurally identical being, another "negative" (free) being, to house one's self-certainty. Not just any object can testify to one's freedom. In Hegel's words, "Self-consciousness achieves its satisfaction only in another self-consciousness."[43] This, of course, inaugurates the struggle for recognition.

Other scholars insist that the master-slave dialectic is far from the whole story of recognition.[44] First, it is an example of failed recognition: the lord does not satisfy his yearning for recognition as long as the bondsman remains enslaved. The lord's freedom needs to be confirmed by a subject whose freedom he likewise respects. Recognition, to be complete, must be both mutual and freely given. The negative moment of mutual destruction must be resolved into positive, mutual affirmation: the negation must be negated. Finally, mutual recognition cannot occur in the isolated dyad. It comes to fruition only in the ethical community whose institutions allow the particularity of each to find reflection in the universal self-representation of the legal person. Only by virtue of just institutions can spirit find fulfillment in the "'I' that is 'We' and the 'We' that is 'I.'" All I aim to confirm here, in fleshing out Butler's argument, is that the desire to live, for Hegel, has as its "truth" the desire for recognition. What one experiences "immediately" as the urge to persist becomes through the mediation of self-consciousness the desire for reflection in another self-consciousness.

Importantly, Hegel does not simply deny that the desire for self-preservation is fundamental to subjectivity. He remains "modern" in this respect. The dialectic of dependence and independence, master and slave, includes the lesson that we cannot get what we want without life. We desire something more than biological endurance, and yet, unsurprisingly, we do not find satisfaction in death. Nevertheless, in order to affirm that desire is not for mere life, self-consciousness must have a "serious" encounter with death, genuinely confront it, and thereby witness the profoundly unstable character of reality through experiencing the absolute

---

43. Ibid., §175.
44. See, e.g., Robert Williams, *Hegel's Ethics of Recognition*.

fear of the Lord.[45] Historically, humans establish institutions—religion, the state, and work—that foster and stabilize this experience of fear and trembling before a mighty power. According to Hegel, such institutions, as unpleasant as they seem, perform a necessary developmental function. They teach us about human existence and being itself. Fear and work reveal reality as something that comes into being and passes away. They are the conditions for a fully embodied apprehension of becoming as the truth of being. Perhaps most important, from the point of view of political theory, is that the human willingness to tolerate and embrace institutions of domination, even at great cost to oneself, reveals human existence as "the contradiction" between supranatural values and attachment to life. Developmentally, establishing servitude as a cultural relationship allows humans to overcome (and yet preserve in a new form) their enslavement to biological life.[46] Coercive institutions are often justified, promoted, and tolerated on the grounds that they preserve life (security), yet they do not, for Hegel, treat life as an absolute value. They are the means by which humans live on their own terms. Through institutions, people transmute a relationship to nature into a relationship to culture. The desire to live is thereby overcome (*aufgehoben*) rather than negated.

Spinoza famously asked why people "will fight for their servitude as if for salvation" (*TTP* 0.7). Hegel offered the deceptively simple answer that they would rather live than die. Put otherwise, people usually accept the terms of inclusion, however mutilating, offered by their culture in place of total destitution.[47] Institutions of domination are empirical manifestations that reveal desire as pointing beyond life and yet requiring the medium of life for its actualization. Hegel contends that the desire to live is implicitly the desire for recognition, and thus desire can be understood only as the desire for recognition. While it is sometimes ambiguous in the work of Butler, the force of the "ought" for Hegel is not merely descriptive or phenomenological. Hegel's philosophy does more than provide an etiology of domination; it justifies it. Hegel does not justify domination as a permanent and irrevocable condition of human affairs, as Hobbes arguably does. Many institutional forms of domination ought to be resisted and replaced with increasingly universal equality and more satisfying relations of recognition. Nevertheless, master-slave relations are a *neces-*

---

45. Hegel, *Phenomenology of Spirit*, §194.
46. Hyppolite, *Genesis and Structure in Hegel's* Phenomenology of Spirit, 169.
47. We see much higher instances of suicide among native Americans and nonheterosexuals, suggesting that not everyone conforms to the terms of social inclusion.

sary and *just* aspect of individual and social development. Institutionalized relationships of domination, for Hegel, belong to a historical process of "humanization" whereby desire becomes increasingly "socialized."[48] In his account of self-consciousness in the *Philosophy of Spirit*, Hegel avows the necessity of oppression and force proper to an education in genuine, human freedom.

> All states have originated in force, and this subjugation, domination . . . is thoroughly necessary, legitimate, and just. This struggle must take place because self-consciousness must be for another self-consciousness, and the individual must come into relation with another. This has been called a social drive, but in fact it is reason, the unity of self-consciousness.[49]

He further asserts that "peoples must first pass through a great oppression until they acquire sufficient power and ability to free themselves. Then they know they are inherently free." Peoples, like children, require a long training in obedience in order to transform their immediate "arbitrary will of self-seeking particularity."[50]

In order for desire to become genuinely human and actualize freedom, the suffering of "great oppression" imposed by "force" is both necessary and justified. For desire to overcome its naturalness, its immediacy, its absolute bondage to the body, it must be educated by stable, enduring institutions of domination, embodied, as in the schema of Hegel's *Philosophy of Right*, in the spheres of the family, the state, and labor. Nature must become culture, animality must be transubstantiated into humanity, in order for desire to find genuine satisfaction. Desire is human only when it can be referred to a drive for self-knowledge. Humans do not desire prestige for merely instrumental purposes. We accept domination, paradoxically, because we want to know ourselves as free and, ultimately, as structurally similar to existence itself (i.e., infinite and absolute). In Jean Hyppolite's terms, each wants to be with himself, not in the dumb way that substantial nature appears to be, but as the "disquiet" of the self, the perpetually self-transformative fire that existence truly is.[51] Structures of

---

48. The interpretation of the master-slave dialectic as a process of "humanization" is often attributed to Kojève, but that aspect of his interpretation is far from extravagant. See *Introduction to the Reading of Hegel*.

49. Hegel, *Lectures on the Philosophy of Spirit 1827–1828*, 190.

50. Ibid., 193.

51. Hyppolite, *Genesis and Structure in Hegel's* Phenomenology of Spirit, 167.

domination and submission are the condition of possibility for knowledge of ourselves as free and essentially spiritual beings.

Self-consciousness learns through a process of immanent self-correction that human freedom is won through a historical establishment of the conditions by which each can be-with-oneself-in-another.[52] Hegelian freedom names both a relationship to oneself (the relation of being "with oneself") and a relation to others (the relation of being "in another"). This other in which one enjoys freedom includes the family, the ethical community, the state, and other self-consciousnesses. Recognition is the paradigmatic mode by which one can be "in others." Freedom is a matter of being represented appropriately by others, which is made possible through just constellations of laws, traditions, and practices that comprise ethical life (*Sittlichkeit*). Recognition is freedom as being-with-oneself-in-another. If, for Hegel, spirit is not at home with itself in Spinoza,[53] it is because there are no true others, no real differences within the totality of being.

In asserting that Hegel aims not only to describe but to justify desire's necessary education through institutions of domination, I do not mean to indict his political philosophy. All I mean to establish is that Hegel's account of desire has an important justificatory function. Even if Hegel's philosophy is much more richly descriptive than contemporary liberalism, it is ultimately a normative political philosophy that functions to affirm the necessity and justice of relationships of domination, even as it also advocates overcoming them. It is no coincidence that he develops his notion of desire through critical reflection on Hobbes rather than Spinoza. If speculative philosophy begins by affirming and then negating Spinoza's view that all is One, political philosophy commences by affirming and negating the Hobbesian view of man as desire for self-preservation. Spinoza takes the principle of *conatus* from Hobbes, but it is Hobbes who deduces from our desiring essence the necessity of absolute sovereignty. Hegel pursues the route from desire to domination as the basis of politics rather than the route from desire to God or nature. As is well known, for Hobbes there is "a general inclination of all mankind, a perpetual and restless desire of power after power, that ceaseth only in death,"[54] which entails that "men have no pleasure, but on the contrary a great deal of grief, in keeping company where there is no power to overawe them."[55] Hobbesian

---

52. See Neuhouser, *Foundations of Hegel's Social Theory*, for an illuminating analysis of Hegel's formulation from *Philosophy of Right*, §7A.
53. Hegel, *Lectures on the Philosophy of History*, 513.
54. Hobbes, *Leviathan*, 159.
55. Ibid., 170.

desire produces the necessity of a master-and-slave relationship between individuals and the state. This is Hegel's starting point, and, as Matheron observes, recognition structured by ethical life provides a means to supersede (raise up, cancel, and preserve) the state as great Leviathan, an "artificial eternity" of domination.[56]

Spinoza's philosophy, as Hegel laments, finds in desire the immanent determination of the infinite force of nature. His politics takes the *conatus* as its starting point, but it does not function to justify any particular arrangement of political power. As many commentators have observed, Spinoza's is not a normative political philosophy in the juridical sense.[57] Spinoza's account of desire leads to a contextually sensitive politics in which the form of government must be determined by the particular horizon of a multitude's imagination, even if the link between our "advantage" and collective life implies that it is always in our interest to democratize our institutions, be they monarchical or republican.[58] The question that remains, however, is whether Spinoza's notion of desire is enriched by placing it within a trajectory that leads to a politics of recognition, as Butler does.

Conatus and *Cupiditas* in Spinoza

Whereas Hegel's *Phenomenology of Spirit* concerns spiritual (*geistige*), human beings, Spinoza's *Ethics* begins with a treatment of existence as a whole. Based upon a characterization of substance (nature or God), its attributes, and their modifications, Spinoza makes specific claims about human life. Human phenomena, problems, and experiences must be examined within a general portrait of nature. Desire is no different. Like Hegelian desire, Spinozan desire exists within a relational field and is fully actualized only with favorable relations. Yet Spinoza maintains a different understanding of the relationships that contour desire and power, which results in a broader view of the forces and connections essential to agency. Assimilating Spinoza to a neo-Hegelian political program mutes the fundamental insight of the politics of renaturalization: human striving is undermined insofar as we apprehend ourselves as different in kind from the rest of nature.

The striving to persevere in being is the "essence" or "nature" of each

---

56. Matheron, *Individu et communauté chez Spinoza*, 164.
57. This is a primary contention of Den Uyl's study, *Power, State, and Freedom*.
58. See, especially *TP*, but also *TTP*, chap. 17.

and every singular thing. "Each thing, as far as it can by its own power, strives to persevere in its being [*in suo esse persevere conatur*]" (*E* III p6). A singular thing might be an idea, an artifact, or an organism. Each being aims not to exist *simpliciter* but to persevere in *its* determinate way. To strive to be, even as a table, is to exert some kind of effort to be *this* table. A table does not yearn to approximate tableness but rather perseveres by virtue of a unique arrangement among its parts that effectively preserves its integrity amidst the many other ambient bodies. *Conatus*, Spinoza's notion of essence (III p7), names the singularity of beings, a force of existence unique to each thing, which accounts for the infinite diversity of finite things in nature. Such striving should not be understood, as Matheron contends, as an abstract concept of bodily motion.[59] *Conatus* is not simply a mechanical, inertial movement that stops only when contradicted by an opposing force (*Ep* 81). *Conatus* names a power of self-organization, self-maintenance, and striving to preserve one's distinctness amidst infinitely many other singular beings. It is the principle of *conatus* that endows Spinoza's metaphysics with a vitalistic element and makes it irreducible to simple mechanism. One's *conatus* constitutes an intrinsic determination, which is not communicated from the outside by external, finite beings. Conative striving in living organisms is a desire for life, yet Spinoza asserts that it is not reducible to a biological function (*TP* 5.5). Each strives to be in a singular rather than a generic way. Thus, we strive not simply to be alive but to be alive as a distinctive power of mind and body.

Nevertheless, within Spinoza's relational ontology, the singularity of each essence does not entail that the *conatus* is the exclusive cause of a being's perseverance. To remain this table or this body, one must maintain a constant flow of exchanges with myriad ambient beings (*E* III p13postIV). One must perpetually mutate in order to remain what one is. Moreover, Spinoza notes that "the power [*potentia*] of each thing, *or* the striving [*conatus*] by which it (*either alone or with others*) does anything, or strives to do anything . . . is nothing but the . . . actual essence of the thing" (*E* III p7d; emphasis added). Beings act and strive "either alone or with others." Our most fundamental power to be cannot ultimately be separated from the concurrent forces of other beings. It is for this reason that the concept of "transindividuality," described in chapter 1, is particularly apt for Spinoza. We are complex singular beings whose agency is not ultimately isolable. The striving of a given being is irreducible to that of any other and yet would not exist without infinitely many others. Rather than designating

---

59. Matheron, *Individu et communauté chez Spinoza*, 88.

a solitary agency, *conatus* indicates a basic power of individuation that remains ineluctably situated within a relational field.[60] A thing, for Spinoza, always perseveres in being and maintains its integrity amidst and *by virtue of* many other beings.

As mentioned above, *conatus* implies that a thing cannot be self-opposed in essence: "No thing can be destroyed except through an external cause" (*E* III p4). Thus, commentators have called the *conatus* a force of "self-affirmation."[61] Spinoza notes that "while we attend only to the thing itself, and not to external causes, we shall not be able to find anything in it which can destroy it" (III p4d). Pace Hegel and Freud, negation is "fundamentally extrinsic to the nature of things."[62] We are not creatures of *thanatos* who must come to terms with our impulse toward death and nothingness. Ostensibly self-annihilating behavior like suicide, anorexia, and self-abuse must be explained by external causes overwhelming the impulse of self-affirmation that belongs essentially to each and every being.

For Hegel and Freud, being riven by *eros* and *thanatos* makes us special kinds of beings, but human *eros* (*cupiditas* in Latin) does not have its own laws for Spinoza. Only after offering an account of *conatus* as it applies to any and every singular thing in nature does Spinoza describe its typical human manifestation.

> When this striving is related only to the mind, it is called will; but when it is related to the mind and body together, it is called appetite. This appetite, therefore, is nothing but the very essence of [a] man, from whose nature there necessarily follow those things that promote his preservation. And so [a] man is determined to do those things.
>
> Between appetite and desire there is no difference, except that desire is generally related to men insofar as they are conscious of their appetite. So *desire* can be defined as *appetite together with consciousness of the appetite*. (*E* III p9s)

Desire does not exhaust the human essence but describes a particular relationship to one's striving typical of those beings called "human." In contrast to Hegel, nothing obviously distinguishes human and animal desire for Spinoza, since many animals exhibit awareness of their appetites.

---

60. Cf. Simondon, "The Position of the Problem of Ontogenesis."
61. Bove, *La stratégie du conatus*; Negri, *The Savage Anomaly*.
62. Macherey, *Introduction à l'Ethique de Spinoza*, 3:72.

Rational or true knowledge of appetite is not necessary in order to be conscious of it. Spinoza's definition of desire as (a?) man's essence follows a proposition asserting that *conatus* issues from both adequate and inadequate ideas. Desire reflects appetites regardless of whether their causes are understood. In most cases, our ideas about what we desire are inadequate, prompted by the aleas of imagination.

Deleuze argues that, for Spinoza, "consciousness is inseparable from the triple illusion that *constitutes* it, the illusion of finality, the illusion of freedom, and the theological illusion."[63] Far from being the seat of truth, consciousness invokes the most problematic aspects of human psychology. The triple illusion that Deleuze identifies belongs to a fantasy of human exceptionalism. Consciousness of one's desire, especially as it is described in the appendix to part I of the *Ethics*, includes a notion of reality designed for human use and enjoyment (finalist illusion) by a God who can offer or withhold love (theological illusion) from an individual who can freely earn or fail to be worthy of salvation (freedom illusion). Like Hegel's, Spinoza's desire prompts the spontaneous conviction that one is free, in the sense of being unconstrained by external causes. Spinoza links desire to an illusory conviction of freedom that must be overcome in order to enjoy genuine freedom. In contrast to Hegel, however, the human *conatus* is not governed by a *telos*, driven to confirm its self-certainty. For Spinoza, *conatus* does not guarantee any passage from the illusory negative freedom to the positive freedom afforded by enabling forms of association. For a Hegelian, Spinoza's aimless desire might indicate the system's lack of internal development or history.

Yet the "triple illusion" that Deleuze describes seems to be historically specific. Rather than constituting consciousness as such, it aptly describes what might loosely be called Christian psychology. It is the psychology of those who believe that we are divine creations, endowed with free will, who may or may not use this will to earn salvation. Nevertheless, this phenomenon cannot be reduced to "culture," since everything is equally nature for Spinoza. The psychology Spinoza describes is based in the structure of complex, finite bodies, typical of humans.

> I take as a foundation what everyone must acknowledge: that all men are born ignorant of the causes of things, and that they all want to seek their own advantage, and are conscious of this appetite. From these [premises] it follows, *first*, that men think themselves free, because they are con-

---

63. Deleuze, *Spinoza: Practical Philosophy*, 20.

scious of their volitions and their appetite, and do not think, even in their dreams, of the causes by which they are disposed to wanting and willing. (*E* I app)

Consciousness of the appetite to seek one's own advantage prompts the belief that we are free, while we remain unaware of the causes that determine what Hegel would call "self-seeking."

For Hegel, Spinoza's notion of desire is vulnerable to the same criticism leveled against Hobbes. Desire appears as a rather impoverished portrait of human motivation, reflecting primarily the physical urge for self-preservation. The freedom that we seek to enlarge is merely the freedom to satisfy our immediate appetites. Yet here Spinoza portrays a confused relationship to desire. Spinoza begins with the premise that we desire and pursue our advantage, convinced that our desire signals our freedom. We typically perceive something as desirable and believe that we pursue it by virtue of a self-originating appetite. Hegel begins his story of desire similarly, but the drive to consume leaves the subject unsatisfied and prompts him to find another human to challenge. Spinoza's scene, however, does not proceed to describe an intersubjective encounter between human beings. Desire is not thwarted by an Other who refuses to be the object of our self-satisfaction, demanding his own self-satisfaction. Rather, from the pursuit of self-preservation, Spinoza describes God as a kind of narcissistic self-projection.[64] In order to grasp our true freedom, we must cease to see God as more perfect versions of ourselves, be that image a wise father, an awe-inspiring king, a human-centered design, or Tyler Durden in a feather boa.

The tendency to imagine God as a power that arranges things purposefully for human pleasure is prompted by our experience of the excellent design of our bodies and things that meet our basic needs. In Spinoza's words, "they find—both in themselves and outside themselves—many means that are very helpful in seeking their advantage, for example, eyes for seeing, teeth for chewing, plants and animals for food, the sun for light, the sea for supporting fish" (*E* I app). Contra Hegel, Spinoza maintains that neither the body nor the world fails to satisfy desire. Desire is not driven to develop by encountering obstacles. Rather, the pleasures of food, visible beauty, and the sun's warmth please humans all too well and prompt us to infer that there must be a "ruler of Nature" who arranged everything to suit us. The body does not indicate our dependence

---

64. One that is developed by Feuerbach in *The Essence of Christianity*.

but testifies to our fitness and justifies the instrumentalization of nature. Bodily experience and its pleasure in the world inspire the notion of "man in Nature as a dominion within a dominion" (III pref). Consciousness of corporeal experience prompts an erroneous conviction of human transcendence. His interpretation of bodily experience is the precise opposite of the phenomenological tradition, of which Hegel is a founding figure.[65] Far from being a prison of immanence, the body's desire, its hunger and its satisfaction, animate the illusions of consciousness.

From the belief that their actions are prompted by self-generated goals, humans tend to be falsely convinced that God, too, acts with an end in view, that end being, simply, humanity. Yet nature does not always provide, and while the successful pursuit of self-satisfaction generates the notion that pleasant things exist for the sole purpose of enriching human life, unpleasant things are seen to reflect human vice. Misfortune incites superstition and fear of divine punishment but does not interrupt the narcissistic notion that good or bad events, pleasant or repugnant things, point to oneself as a member of God's most beloved creation, humanity. Insofar as we are trapped within the triple illusion of (Christian) consciousness, we are convinced that the external world, no less than our bodies, exists for us, and, the more we find ourselves to be favored, the more we are convinced that God recognizes, validates, and rewards us. As Spinoza puts it, "So it has happened that each of them thought up from his own temperament different ways of worshipping God, so that God might love him above all the rest, and direct the whole of Nature according to the needs of their blind desire and insatiable greed" (*E* I app). In accord with a certain worldview that arguably persists today, our desire prompts a portrait of God and nature as instruments of self-satisfaction, not unlike the initial perception of the Other encountered by self-consciousness in the *Phenomenology of Spirit*.

In Hegel's narrative, desire's originary notion of freedom must undergo a process of correction in order to enjoy an authentic experience of freedom. For Hegel, we remain unfree as long as desire takes the form of undisciplined self-seeking. Immediate desire is that of the willful child or the hungry animal. Self-conscious desire evolves from an animalistic expression to an increasingly spiritual (social) one. Desire, through education (fear) and work, yields freedom in its distinctively human form. Desire must be "socialized" in order to find its satisfaction in the mutual recogni-

---

65. On the body as immanence and conscious freedom as transcendence, see Beauvoir, *The Second Sex*.

tion of a fully developed ethical community.[66] Corporeal, animal desire is replaced with the desire for a particular relationship to oneself, possible only by virtue of satisfying relationships of recognition. Genuine freedom, for Hegel, is freedom-in-relationship. The liberating relationship is essentially an intersubjective, spiritual, or human one. Only minded equals can mirror our freedom for us. We require a system of ethical life in order to produce the concrete equality that engenders such mutual regard. Hegel's is an ambitious and, in many ways, admirable program for the institution of real freedom.

For Spinoza, desire is also liberated by establishing a distinctive kind of relationship to oneself and others. Spontaneous desire is less free insofar as we persist in the belief that desire is not constrained, provoked, and oriented by a complex history of causal determinations. We remain servile as long as we do not see ourselves as relational beings. Rather than socializing desire, however, we must naturalize it. We must come to act in light of being but a tiny "part of nature," one singularity submerged within an acentric force field of powers and counterpowers.

Spinoza's ethical transformation of freedom, nevertheless, has a similar trajectory to Hegel's. For Hegel, desire goes from a Hobbesian notion of freedom as absence of constraint to an understanding of freedom as an arduously achieved form of relationship. For Spinoza, desire also begins with an idea of freedom as lack of determination by external causes and comes to view freedom as a coordination of strength and vitality in relationship to others. Yet the liberating relationship is not achieved through establishing relationships with other self-consciousnesses in which we *represent* one another in more satisfying ways. The politics of renaturalization is not a politics of representation. Or, rather, representations are not immediately revisable for Spinoza. We must act, first and foremost, on our affects, many of which remain unconscious. The representation of ourselves as unique kinds of beings, elevated out of nature, is a key aspect of Hegel's political philosophy. The politics of renaturalization demands that we first transform our relationship not to human others but to God or nature itself. God, or nature, unlike the other subjects in Hegel's account, is not structurally identical to oneself. Nature is absolute and self-caused, but freedom requires that we cease to see ourselves as independent in the same way as God. We will not find our freedom mirrored, at least not in a symmetrical way, in God's freedom. Human freedom is won only by coming to terms with our lack of freedom. We come to act

---

66. See Bernstein, "From Self-Consciousness to Community."

effectively only when we appreciate that our agency is infinitely surpassed by the totality of other natural beings (*E* IV p3).

As I argue in the following section, the initial desire to be affirmed or loved by God above all others as a unique and irreplaceable being must be surrendered. The politics of renaturalization denies the possibility of mutual recognition between God and humanity, the Other and the self. Nevertheless, our power, or agency, is identical to the power of God, or nature, but in its finite form. We are not each spiritual wholes. We are singular expressions of the power of infinite nature, knowledge of which Spinoza calls beatitude or glory. Glory in ourselves as God (i.e., parts of nature) is not primarily a relationship of representation. It is the liberation of desire through a new relationship to dependency. Rather than personal salvation or recognition, freedom involves a kind of depersonalization. The irrecoverable loss of oneself in God is precisely what Hegel rejected in Spinoza's system, yet, in an epoch where the risk of too much man is arguably greater than the risk of too much nature, let us see whether we might find resources for a posthumanist view of agency in Spinoza's account.

From Interpersonal Recognition to Impersonal Glory

Conatus prompts all beings to pursue their "advantage" (*utile*) and fortify their "selves," yet the self that one seeks to fortify and the advantage one pursues take different forms, depending upon the affects that animate one's striving. Like a number of early moderns, Spinoza views ambition and a desire for glory to be powerful motivators. The centrality of ambition to Spinoza's political psychology supports Hegel's argument that what appears to be a desire for enduring (biological) life is properly understood as a social desire, a yearning to be esteemed by fellow subjects. Of course, Spinoza denies any distinction between nature and culture. Nevertheless, with his notion of affective imitation he provides a rich analysis of what might be called "sociality," albeit not an exclusively human sociality as we also imitate the affects of beasts (*E* IV p68). The imitation of the affects gives rise to striving toward similitude, which may seem to anticipate the Hegelian scene in which two structurally similar beings struggle for an exchange of recognition. However, close attention to Spinoza's distinction between ambition and glory indicates his alternative to the dialectic of recognition.

Spinoza describes a dynamic of mutual affection among beings who consider one another to be "similar." Humans tend to love what provokes joy in our beloveds, and hate what causes sadness for them (*E* III p22).

Since love describes an increase in power (III p13s), according to Spinoza, we are enabled both by the persons we love and by whatever contributes to the perseverance and power of our beloveds. The individuals we love implicate us in a constellation of attachments and alienations, attractions and aversions that have bearing on our *conatus*. The automatic corporeal communication produces a spontaneous libidinal economy, where we affect each other with our desires as we are affected by the desires of ambient others. This economy operates, moreover, not only between lovers and friends, but among anyone whom we imagine to be similar to us. "If we imagine a thing like us [*nobis similem*], toward which we have had no affect, to be affected with some affect, we are thereby affected with a like affect" (III p27). Spinoza does not elaborate on the conditions of our perception of similitude. Is there a particular property that we perceive? A behavior? A structural compatibility? Spinoza points out many cases of lack of sympathy among human beings (e.g., III p46; *TTP* 17.24), which demonstrates, as if it were necessary, that the relative similarity of our bodies and minds is no guarantee that we will regard one another as similar. The principle of the imitation of the affects points only to a tendency for affects to circulate among those who perceive one another to be similar, however unconsciously and by whatever criteria. Moreover, a "thing like us" is not necessarily human (e.g., *E* IV p68s). We communicate affects with any body, or any kind of body, that seems to have a strong affinity with ours. Automatic affective involvement serves as the basis of an account of both social conflict and powerful affective bonds between humans and significant others that are not human.[67]

Given that sympathy and emulation depend upon the perception of similitude, imitation of the affects arouses a striving toward similarity, perhaps a kind of equality, which resonates with the Hegelian scene of desire for recognition. For Hegel, each subject aims to be seen as free by the other, but Spinoza's notion of affective imitation has less content. It names only the flow of enabling and disabling feelings amongst corporeally similar beings and the imaginings that accompany them. Our power to persevere in being includes an irresistible tendency to identify with others, which is an effect rather than a cause of corporeal confluences, the structural convenience of our physical efforts with those of others (*E* IV p31). For Spinoza, ambition is related to a basic urge "to do also whatever we imagine men to look on with joy, and on the other hand, we shall be averse to doing what we imagine men are averse to" (III p29).

---

67. Chapter 6 discusses in detail nonhuman animal affects.

Prompted by our more or less accurate notions of the joys and aversions of our fellows, we aim to please them, which, by definition, comprises an effort to be a source of power for them. If we succeed in generating joy, we contribute to the perfection of others and are in turn enabled by (and experience love for) them. Thus, according to Spinoza, the very effort to empower oneself is objectively inextricable from enabling others, even if one's subjective purpose is often quite different. Finitude is such that one cannot be powerful without fortifying others as well.

Yet sociality is highly complicated. Depending on the degree to which the strivings and pleasures of those who appear to be "similar" to us nourish and support our singular essence, the effort to be seen with joy might involve enabling or diminishing activities. In the best-case scenario, the activities through which one is able to experience oneself as an object of others' love amplify one's capacities. When my activities give others joy (i.e., power by way of an external cause, *E* III p11s) and strengthen my mind and body, ambition contributes to a circuit of mutual empowerment. We might, perhaps hubristically, imagine that teaching philosophy is precisely the kind of activity that strengthens us through enhancing the mental and corporeal capacities of others. In striving to articulate ideas and communicate them to a diverse group of students, I come to understand the ideas and their causes better along with the students. Students' questions and challenges force me to link the ideas to still other images and signs, develop different idioms and connections to daily life, and thereby produce a more adequate understanding of philosophical ideas. Similarly, political organizing, in the right circumstances, sharpens the powers of organizers as they engender enabling relationships, improve civic institutions, and galvanize collective projects. Done well, it strengthens oneself through empowering others. Ambition follows from a salutary drive to cause joy (to engender power) in one's imagined community of "men" as part of an impulse to love oneself and enhance one's life. Moreover, this drive serves as a motor encouraging people to "join forces" and imagine that "man is a God to man" (IV p35s). Is ambition best understood as the inchoate ideal of an ethical community of mutual recognition?

All too often, the desire to be seen with joy entails risks to an individual's striving. Although Spinoza only indirectly addresses such issues, these risks are graver if someone belongs to a devalued group or is not regarded to be "similar." How one's actions will be received depends upon how one is perceived and how effectively one gauges the pleasures of others. Regardless of how hospitable the social environment is, however, Spinoza contends that ambition affects us all. "*The striving to do something (and also to omit doing something) solely to please men* is called *ambition*, especially when we strive so eagerly to please the people that we do or omit certain things to our own injury, or another's" (*E* III p29s). The general drive for approval gets the less flattering name "ambition" when it accompanies a willingness to harm oneself or others. The distorting effects of striving to please others are more pronounced insofar as one does not resemble the majority. When one's striving does not agree (come together) with the activities favored in a certain context, the effort to be seen with joy can result in self-mutilation. Striving to be an object of love within a hostile community of onlookers is one way that our passions render us opposed to ourselves. A college student allergic to alcohol, for example, might find it very difficult in certain social situations to find approval. Young women in engineering might find it more challenging to submit to the misogynist hazing rituals perpetrated on new students at some universities. Feminists and theorists of racism offer many persuasive analyses of the asymmetrical costs of social validation.

Ambitious desire to please others both forges community and encourages conformity at the expense of singular essences and minority groups. When one thinks *only* of "what pleases men," but does not consider what strengthens oneself or produces a resilient social body, Spinoza holds that the desire to be seen with joy tends to be injurious. In other words, when one considers only one side of the affective economy—the recipients of joy, who are also the potential purveyors of admiration—rather than the ensemble of transformations that the joy will engender in everyone involved, injury often results. In fact, Spinoza considers someone driven exclusively by ambition to suffer from a "species of madness," for such an individual's *conatus* is transfixed by a particular source of power, remaining blind both to the complexity of its causal environment and to the "great many other ways" in which it might enlarge its power of thinking and acting. When the mind is "possessed," captured, or occupied by a single source of joy or pleasure, neglecting everything in the world that does not point to one's preoccupation, one is properly called "mad" (*E* IV p44s).

Nevertheless, ambition is not liable to become a species of madness because Spinoza does not consider the desire to please others to be misguided. Indeed, when acting to secure others' pleasure doesn't involve injury to ourselves or others, it is called *humanitas*, or "human kindness" (*E* III p29s). Ambition has a negative connotation only because it characteristically consists in exclusive attention to one side of the affective economy. One pursues the desire to be imagined favorably and praised by others without reflecting on the costs to one's singular constitution or to the constitution of the social body to which one's actions contribute.[68] Ambition wears blinders trained upon the dominant regime of representation. If the dominant imaginary likes keg stands or silicone breasts, ambition delivers them. In the best-case scenario, conforming to the expectations of others will indirectly promote self-esteem and mutual understanding. All too often, however, dominant values and images fail to provide avenues for the amplification of one's multifarious capacities.

The solution for many political theorists in the tradition of the politics of recognition is to expand and diversify the terms of acceptance for the category "person." Prompted by Hegel, they understand ambition to be, in truth, a desire to be esteemed rather than a will to dominate and expropriate. They understand peace and social order not merely in terms of the distribution of goods, and thus not contingent exclusively on economic justice. Rather, the ambitious pursuit of goods or coercive power is properly understood as an essentially human need to be seen as human.[69] For theorists of recognition, we cannot but strive to be loved, admired, and recognized as free persons. Society, then, needs to be forced to develop increasingly universal standards that allow as many as possible to be recognized as lovable, valuable, and worthy of personal dignity.[70] Ethical life must be challenged to accommodate the demands of spiritual beings to be recognized as free in each of the domains of selfhood: we want to be recognized in our capacities as an intimate, a worker, and a citizen.

Spinoza acknowledges the nearly irresistible desire to engender such a world. Indeed, the theological imagination that he describes in the *Ethics* presents a failed effort at the constitution of a world in which each is free, lovable, and valued as a unique individual by God. He stipulates that no commonwealth endures without recognizing the irrepressibility of human ambition and desire for equality (*TP* 7.5, 7.20). Ambition, he observes, "can hardly be overcome" (*E* III def affXLIV). Yet the rub lies in the fact that, as long as ambition includes the desire to be seen as a unique kind of being, it cannot be fulfilled. So building a society to meet the universal desire for recognition is going to be a frustrating effort. Rather than fulfilling the ambition to be seen as a multidimensional free being, as appealing and humane as that goal may be, the politics of renaturalization channels ambition away from personal recognition and toward glory in nature's infinite power.

---

68. Cf. Bove, *La stratégie du conatus*, 80.
69. See Honneth, *The Struggle for Recognition*.
70. Cornell and Murphy, "Anti-racism, Multiculturalism, and an Ethics of Identification."

The same affect that nearly guarantees ambition, the desire to please others, can also be directed toward a more salutary feeling of glory. Glory, like ambition, belongs to the impulse of self-love. Ambition and glory follow from the fact that most humans, most beings "like us," "strive to do whatever we imagine men to look on with joy, and on the other hand, we shall be averse to doing whatever we imagine men are averse to" (*E* III p29). "Ambition is a desire by which all of the other affects are encouraged and strengthened (by p27 and p31); so this affect can hardly be overcome. For as long as man is bound by any desire, he must at the same time be bound by this one." Spinoza, in the definitions of the affects, conflates glory and ambition: "As Cicero says, *Every man is led by glory, and the more so, the better he is. Even the philosophers who write books on how glory is to be disdained put their names on these works*" (III def affXLIV). Conative striving determines us to want to please others, which underscores that we cannot avoid being affected by others. Ambition and glory encourage all affects, forming a social-psychological basis, because they animate an inescapable yearning to be enabled by others.

Yet while both glory and ambition flow from the same psychophysical foundation, glory attends to the other side of the affective economy. Defined as "joy accompanied by the idea of an internal cause," glory is directed at one's own joy and power, rather than at one's representation of the imaginations of others. This joy can be entirely delusional, since "it can easily happen that one who exults at being esteemed is proud and imagines himself to be pleasing to all, when he is really burdensome to all" (*E* III p30s). Glory can become indistinguishable from pride (*superbia*) and produce the same injuries as ambition. Yet glory also names the most enabling and virtuous affect. Glory is "the very love by which God loves himself, . . . insofar as he can be explained by the human essence" (V p36), or desire. What transforms the fool's glory, which is indistinguishable from pride, into glory that yields "acquiescentia" (IV p52, V p27), that greatest of joys following from considering one's power of action?

Rather than being an exclusive focus upon engendering a positive representation of oneself in the minds of others (ambition), glory accompanies the image of one's own agency. Glory denotes the experience of one's power achieved through pleasing others. Thus, like ambition, glory acknowledges, even if often implicitly, that one requires others and is nourished by their joy (power). Both affects indicate the pursuit of socially conferred pleasure, often in the form of praise, a positive reaction, such as appreciative laughter, or public approbation, like a diploma or election to political office. Glory affirms one's own power as a dynamic between one's activity and the passive experience of the others' joy. Glory and ambition can prompt the beginning, then, of an escape from one of the illusions of consciousness, the phantasm of purely self-generated desire and power. Yet the approbation of others and their perceptions do not define glory. Glory is defined by one's own power, that is, "joy accompanied by the idea of an internal cause" (*E* III p30s).

Ambition too often fails to escape the illusions of consciousness, since it tends only to invert the fantasy of self-endowed freedom.[71] In particular, ambition projects the theological illusion, which imagines God observing and judging all of our actions, onto the social body. One's fellows become the vigilant and observant Other, and the self is the object of universal evaluation. Like the superstitious person who imagines that her fate is revealed in the patterns of the flight of birds, the ambitious person anxiously reads the responses of her community as an index of her worth. Ambition fails to correct the illusions of consciousness when it evolves, as it too easily does, into a narcissistically motivated yet abject dependence on others. Ambition tends to imagine that the social imaginary is one's personal reflection and that well-being is thereby an effect of external or transcendent causes. Ambition does not properly grasp power as a transindividual phenomenon, where one is both produced by and productive of the social world. The root of ambition's potential for failure, paradoxically, lies in its lack of self-regard. Even though ambition is often represented as a tyrannical drive to dominate others, it remains trained exclusively on the imagined desires of others, with insufficient attention to the singularity of one's own desire or essence. As the old adage goes, no one is more enslaved to opinion than a tyrant. Ambition is convertible, however, into glory, which can become the most enabling affect.

Spinoza presents a program for converting any passion into an action. The program begins by relating a given affect to "more and different causes" and thereby affirming its immersion within a complex nexus of causal community (*E* V p9). Since glory consists in an idea of one's own power and the idea of oneself as a cause of joy, the activation of glory's salutary features entails relating one's power to an increasing multiplicity

---

71. Julie Cooper urged me to consider how Spinoza allows ambition to take on a distinctly positive valence with both *humanitas* (*E* III p29s) and *modestia* (IV appXXV). Indeed, all affects have their "correct use" and none are, in themselves, problematic for Spinoza (V p10s). Even if it risks simplifying Spinoza's account, it is nevertheless fair to say that when he defines ambition as "the striving to do something solely to please men," Spinoza implies a negative association. In contrast, while *gloria* is also double-edged, its beneficial and injurious faces preserve the same name. I appreciate that Julie called upon me to nuance my contrast of the terms.

of causes. With an adequate understanding of glory, one's agency ceases to be understood as a direct effect of an isolated act, quality, or aspect of oneself. The better one understands the glory one enjoys, the less one will feel that a single deed determines one's fate. Social imaginaries come to be seen as irreducibly complex and conflicted by nature and not susceptible to human design. The process by which certain values predominate reveals glory to be less exclusive and personal. Rather than revealing values—good and evil, white and black, beautiful and ugly—to be the exclusive product of human agents, we can see them as crystallizations of human and nonhuman power that cannot simply be willed away by good intentions or enlightened minds. A vast network of causes, in any given situation, renders some people powerful, glorious, and praiseworthy in contrast to others. The impersonality of such a network of causes is not, however, a reason to avoid reorganizing one's milieu to support a greater diversity of agents and, in particular, to enable one's own efforts to affirm and enhance one's life. Indeed, the ambition to amplify one's power "can hardly be overcome," as long as we live. Well directed, this ambition is equivalent to "courtesy" (*modestia*) and is nothing but good. Yet the politics of renaturalization is less sanguine about the resources of the human will than the politics of recognition. As Antonio Negri puts it, reversing the Gramscian formula, Spinozism maintains an "optimism of the intellect and pessimism of the will."[72] It is only by surrendering the hope of ordering the world in accordance with the requirements of spirit that one can hope to find power and satisfaction as a finite part of nature.

Glory reaches its height by understanding oneself, along with as many diverse things in nature as possible, with the third kind of knowledge, intuition. Intuition is notoriously complex in Spinoza's philosophy, and a full account is beyond the scope of this chapter.[73] Most generally, intuition names the single apprehension of what is concretely universal in all beings and, concomitantly, what distinguishes them from everything else. It is the idea of something as universal and singular at once, an idea of the intrinsic power by which a being strives to persevere in existence, expressing, in its determinate way, the infinite power of nature. Glory in its active form is the joyful apprehension of oneself as a finite singularity infused with the infinite power of nature. "The greatest satisfaction of mind [*mentis acquiescentia*] there can be arises from this third kind of knowledge" (*E* V p27). "He who knows things by this kind of knowledge

---

72. Negri, *Subversive Spinoza*, 41.
73. For my interpretation of intuition, see Sharp, "'*Nemo non videt*.'"

passes to the greatest human perfection, and consequently (by def affII), is affected with the greatest Joy, accompanied (by II p43) by the idea of himself and his virtue" (V p27d), or power (IV def8).

Pace Hegel, "the greatest human perfection" follows from relinquishing the conviction that humans are a "dominion within a dominion," elevated out of nature by any unique virtues and moral powers, making them the special object of God's love. For Spinoza, the highest form of self-knowledge that accompanies intuition involves the intellectual love of God (nature), which is decidedly not mutual. "He who loves God cannot strive that God should love him in return" (*E* V p19). The lack of mutuality is two-sided. God does not create humans in order to be loved and glory in his almighty power. Humans are not God's self-image, the vehicles of his glorious self-representation. God is en entirely impersonal natural force that is not oriented around humanity. Loving nature or God is nothing other than the active joy by which we love ourselves, not as exemplars of human goodness, but as absolutely unique instances of nature's power. Love is not between God and man. The intellectual love of God does not follow from a mutually satisfying correspondence of representations between two structurally identical beings; it is not a relationship of recognition. God does not seek a satisfying portrait of singular beings. The divine intellect always already contains ideas of every existing thing. Humans never arrive at a comprehensive representation of God, or nature as a totality. Rather, the "more we know singular things, the more we understand God" (V p24). Beatitude, freedom, glory, or "the greatest human perfection" is not an exchange of representations but "the very love by which God loves himself" as finite (V p36).[74] Love is power (III p13s). Intellectual love of God is a force of self-determination that follows from being a force of nature, in both senses of the genitive.

The highest and most empowering form of self-love emerges from understanding oneself as a tiny part of nature, immersed within the infinite but nevertheless constituting part of it definitively. The glory that we experience by virtue of social relations initiates the understanding of ourselves as both singular strivings and constituents of a "global *conatus*."[75] If this glory becomes active, it ceases to be a personal yearning for a positive self-reflection in one's social milieu and becomes the self-love of nature itself. One thereby knows oneself as an agent, an active constituent of

---

74. Spinoza equates this self-love with "God's love for men," but there is no duality or correspondence between subject and object in the intellectual love of God, as we have with the dialectic of recognition.

75. Bove, *La stratégie du conatus*, 80.

nature's power, who acts by virtue of an intrinsic striving, irreducible to that of any other natural force, and the determinations of infinitely many other beings, human and nonhuman. Spinoza claims that the glorious self-love that follows from intuition is "much more powerful" and "can accomplish" so much more than rational or imaginative knowledge. While rational knowledge is as true as intuitive science, it "does not *affect* our mind as much" (*E* V p36s). Glory, when it includes intuitive knowledge of oneself as a cause of joy, becomes the highest affect because it is the most powerful, accomplishes the most, and involves the greatest intensity of affect. Glory is not the liberation from turbulent affect into the calm of knowledge but rather liberation by way of affect, following from the determinate grasp of one's constituent dependence on nature. Hegel and many others view the intellectual love of God as a form of self-obliteration,[76] but the intensification of feeling suggests that this love singularizes rather than vaporizes the self. Greater feeling of self delivers knowledge of the precise contours of one's power as part of nature.

Moreover, dependence on nature is not self-surrender to an infinite and amorphous totality. Natural dependence cannot finally be distinguished from dependence on human and nonhuman powers.[77] For Spinoza, we are clearly mimetic creatures, automatically absorbing and communicating the affects of similar bodies. Human social relations appear in the *Ethics* as the privileged medium in which we develop our powers and coordinate agencies. The politics of renaturalization demands that we appreciate how *conatus* entails our need of one another. Like Hegel, we understand ourselves best and enjoy the greatest measure of freedom when we apprehend ourselves as individual constituents of a larger universality and affirm that universality as the ground of our individual freedom. Although Spinoza's and Hegel's accounts of desire and its liberation both depend upon affirming the self as a radically relational being, Spinoza understands relationships less in terms of intersubjectivity and representation and more in terms of the communication of activating affects.[78] Rather than positive representations, Spinoza emphasizes the concrete

---

76. As Feuer so colorfully characterizes the intellectual love of God: "Can we love it without hating ourselves, offering ourselves in masochistic self-immolation to the God who does not love us?" *Spinoza and the Rise of Liberalism*, 229.

77. For a more detailed argument about the connections between intuitive science and politics, see Del Lucchese, "Democracy, Multitudo and the Third Kind of Knowledge in the Works of Spinoza," and Sharp, "Feeling Justice."

78. Balibar makes this point with respect to Leibniz, but I think the same follows with respect to Hegel. See Balibar, *Spinoza: From Individuality to Transindividuality*, 33.

coordination of powers, the linking of agencies, and the composition of enabling assemblages. Most important, his treatment of the affects suggests that preoccupation with experiencing satisfying representations in the social imagination, although to some degree inescapable, will be self-undermining as long as it involves a need to be seen as a free, transcendent being: a man. The trajectory of Spinoza's *Ethics* implies a politics that, without ignoring a tendency toward ambition, depersonalizes agency and emphasizes our immersion in nature. In contemporary terms, this means that the regulatory norms requiring scrutiny include the symbolic, but we deny our natures by insisting on being persons, uniquely free beings within an otherwise determined field of natural forces. Because nature does not love us back, freedom emerges not from intersubjective mutuality but from the transformation of the pernicious elements of personal ambition into impersonal glory. What this suggests for political action is the subject of chapter 5. Let me conclude by returning briefly to Butler's enlistment of Spinoza in a "post-Hegelian politics of recognition."

Judith Butler's Post-Hegelian Politics of Recognition

Butler's suggestion that Spinoza's *conatus* prefigures Hegel's desire for recognition inspired this analysis. Yet it is important to note that her adoption of the ethics and politics of recognition is not an uncritical assumption of the Hegelian model. Even in her early treatment of Hegel, she asserts that "Hegel's subject can no longer be entertained, even in an imaginary domain, apart from the thesis of its very impossibility."[79] What has ceased to be viable in the Hegelian model is the notion that recognition promises to deliver humanity from an intolerable dependence on alterity to the comfort of self-sameness, to freedom understood as being at home with oneself. Butler consistently interprets Hegel to attenuate the "Aristophanic" image of self-loss that resolves itself in wholeness,[80] but she argues that the Hegelian model of subjectivity should not be adopted completely. "To revise recognition as an ethical project, we will need to see it as, in principle, unsatisfiable."[81] Butler, in fact, presupposes precisely what I have argued that Spinoza reveals: fully satisfying social relationships are not achievable. For Butler, however, the problem is not the notion of a transcendent (antinatural) human subject but the program to ne-

79. Butler, *Subjects of Desire*, 231.
80. Butler, *Undoing Gender*, 150.
81. Butler, *Giving an Account of Oneself*, 43.

gate the distinctiveness of other people. In order to remain ethical, on her account, the desire for recognition must extirpate the desire to suppress the Other that is its condition of possibility. The politics of recognition must acknowledge that the terms of recognition are necessarily exclusionary; it therefore must remain tentative, provisional, and revisable.[82] One can never hope to reside in the fully actualized ethical community (*Sittlichkeit*) that Hegel envisions. For Butler, not every subject will find her freedom and humanity reflected in the social world. As soon as a community believes it has succeeded in embracing everyone, it fails to respond to the inchoate and future challenges of its constituent others.

The figure of Spinoza, for her, offers an important corrective to the Hegelian narrative. Although Butler criticizes precisely Spinoza's naturalism, he functions in her thinking to highlight the centrality of viability, vulnerability, and the struggle to negotiate survival, especially within a hostile symbolic order. For Butler, Spinoza provides a perspective on "the fragility of the *conatus*"[83] and thereby reveals that "forms of recognition or, indeed, forms of judgment that seek to relinquish or destroy the desire to persist, the desire for life itself, undercut the very preconditions of recognition."[84] In contrast to most contemporary Spinoza commentators, she finds in his philosophy an emphasis on finitude and physical vulnerability in relationship to desiring subjectivity.

In "The Desire to Live, Spinoza's *Ethics* under Pressure," Butler interprets Spinoza's *conatus* to foreground (a) its sociality, (b) its opacity with respect to individual self-consciousness, and (c) an intrinsic possibility of self-negation. Most commentators in the continental tradition agree with her emphasis on relationality and unconsciousness with respect to *conatus*. It is only the third aspect of her interpretation that is contentious. Butler acknowledges that she must read Spinoza against the grain of his own principles in order to locate the possibility of self-destruction in the self rather than in external causes (cf. *E* IV p20s). While I do not find Butler's creative rendering of Spinoza's *conatus* as a prefiguration of the death drive convincing,[85] her attention to the fragility and vulnerability in Spinoza is far from misplaced. Spinoza acknowledges the threats proper to being a tiny part of nature (*E* IV ax1), especially when immersed within a hostile social environment (IV appIV; *TP* 2.14). Yet Spinoza has

82. This point is reiterated several times in *Undoing Gender*.
83. This phrase is Hull's, "Spinoza in a Fabulous Red Scarf."
84. Butler, *Giving an Account of Oneself*, 44.
85. I discuss her interpretation in greater detail in "Melancholy, Anxious, and *Ek-static* Selves."

a programmatic commitment to overcoming negative affects that accompany a philosophical preoccupation with death and destruction, which I think necessary in today's philosophical and political climate. Nevertheless, while it is not surprising that Spinozists, like myself, resist Butler's (neo-Hobbesian) emphasis on vulnerability to death and her portrait of sociality as, above all, a condition of risk,[86] I do think Spinoza offers resources for considering life's precariousness. Moreover, I have no interest in barring creative uses of Spinoza's thought. Neither feminist nor queer theory would exist if they were not able to mine philosophers for ideas hostile to their original aims.

It is tempting to object to Butler's effort to infuse Spinoza with an element of fundamental negativity and thereby reconcile Spinoza with Hegel. In a perfect reversal of Deleuze's assessment that Spinoza had the courage to be a purely affirmative thinker refusing Hegelianism and the death drive *avant la lettre*, Butler notes that Hegel failed to see the negative at work in Spinoza's *conatus*. Perhaps Hegel himself would have noticed had be paid more attention to their shared focus on desire and striving rather than the relationship between infinite substance and finite modes. Yet, for my purposes, focusing on the question of affirmation versus negation concedes too much ground in advance to Hegel. We remain confined to Hegel's orbit when interrogating whether Spinoza's subject can truly harbor the power of negation. Moreover, the Manichean opposition between Hegel and Spinoza overlooks their common ground, from which differences arise more relevant to the politics of renaturalization.

In short, Butler's appropriation demonstrates that even in its revised form, the politics of recognition is necessarily humanist. Although Hegel and Spinoza both condition individuality and liberty upon social networks, Butler continues to treat these networks as distinctively human and thus supernatural. Fundamental to Butler's approach is the conviction that ethics and politics follow from a particular conception of the subject. To cite just one formulation of hers, "one must ask how the formation of the subject implies a framework for understanding ethical response and a theory of responsibility."[87] This perspective is fundamentally Hegelian. Desiring self-consciousness drives social conflict and subtends various forms of political organization.

The politics of renaturalization neither begins nor ends with human subjectivity. It grounds a view of relationality distinct from the Hegelian

---

86. See, for example, Butler, *The Psychic Life of Power*, 27–28.
87. *Giving an Account of Oneself*, 135.

one. Spinoza and Hegel both present desire as situated within relational ontologies and oppose an understanding of freedom as the property of an isolated individual. For Hegel, however, the relationality to be grasped in order better to actualize human freedom is essentially intersubjective. His is a politics of recognition because what is at stake is ultimately how we represent each other and ourselves, and how these representations are embodied in institutions. Freedom follows from finding oneself adequately reflected in formal and informal institutions, the symbolic order, and interpersonal relationships. The condition of enjoying such freedom is reflecting others back to them in a way that both preserves their differences (particularity) and avows their humanity (universality). In contrast, Balibar claims that Spinoza's ontology of relation should be understood in terms of "transindividuality," which is "mainly a question of actions and passions" rather than one of a "correspondence between *representative contents*."[88] Put otherwise, what is at stake for Spinoza is the communication of powers among bodies and minds that exceeds human consciousness. Moreover, greater consciousness of one's affective milieu and the network of causal relationships that shapes one's agency is an effect rather than a cause of enabling encounters. Consciousness is not the motor of development in Spinoza's system. It is not a phenomenology of spirit or mind. Desire and psychic life elude our understanding as long as they are not viewed as natural.

The politics of renaturalization must be something other than the conscious and unconscious effort to satisfy the fundamental structure of subjectivity, as it is on the Hegelian (and Hobbesian) model. Politics is not an art of satisfying self-consciousness. Although Butler insists on the impossibility of the Hegelian project, and, for her, social life implies an unsurpassable lack of satiety for desiring subjects, her ethics and politics remain an expression of the basic structures of human subjectivity. Moreover, by insisting on the impossibility of the Hegelian project, she resigns herself to a melancholy project of perpetual dissatisfaction. The paradox she asks her readers to confront is that one cannot be said to have lived without the conferral of a mutual recognition that is nevertheless unachievable. Human life becomes a perpetual and unrealizable project of seeking to find ourselves within the dominant schema of representation. Butler's is, in my view, an improvement on the Hegelian paradigm, since her politics demands perpetual contest and resists the notion that human community

---

88. Balibar, *Spinoza: From Individuality to Transindividuality*, 33.

can be perfected. Yet the terms of aspiration, the desire for recognition and inclusion, remain tied to an antinatural concept of the human.

For the politics of renaturalization, struggle is a question of the conditions under which desires for perseverance, human and nonhuman, combine and form enabling or disabling assemblages. These assemblages include air, sound, and water quality, the organization of space, and the character of relations with nonhuman animals. These forces exist and act whether we recognize them or not. Moreover, to appreciate our immersion in nature is to cease to see our life-worlds as exclusively human products, as artifacts of the will, however historical and anonymous. How do we reorient our ambition toward glory, however, if ambition cannot be overcome? How do we devise a politics that refuses human transcendence, that illusion that inevitably animates our desire? This book only begins to imagine what a politics under a banner other than the human might look like. The following chapter pursues the alternative suggested by feminist champion of renaturalization Elizabeth Grosz.

5

The Impersonal Is Political:
Spinoza and a Feminist Politics of Imperceptibility

"Who taught you to hate yourself from the top of your head to the soles of your feet?" Malcolm X asks his black audience in 1962.[1] The once "new social movements," including feminists, queers, and antiracist activists, name self-hatred as a primary injury of oppression. A spokesman for the black consciousness movement in South Africa fighting apartheid, Biko, characterizes the fundamental challenge of his struggle thus: "the only vehicle for change are these people who have lost their personality."[2] The dehumanization carried out under oppression deprives the oppressed of self-respect and self-love. Hatred is animated in the oppressed not only toward their abusers but toward themselves. They cannot avoid entertaining the possibility that they, by virtue of deed or intrinsic property, merit systematic degradation. As W. E. B. Du Bois famously put it, "It is a peculiar sensation, this double-consciousness, this sense of always looking at one's self through the eyes of others, of measuring one's soul by the tape of a world that looks on in amused contempt and pity."[3] Sandra Bartky similarly characterizes feminist consciousness as that anguish that occurs upon recognizing that one has internalized the "intimations

1. Malcolm X, speech given in Los Angeles, May 22, 1962.
2. Biko, "We Blacks," 29.
3. Du Bois, "Of Our Spiritual Strivings," 45.

of inferiority"[4] more and less subtly communicated in misogynist environments. Women often consume themselves with self-punishment since so many of society's messages convey that we are simply not good enough the way we are. The rigors of feminine hygiene become so many quotidian exercises of self-abuse, until we come to feel that painful contradiction that ignites feminist consciousness: the belief that one is and is not inferior.[5]

Leaders of political movements often formulate the act of resistance as necessary, not only to convince, as if by rational argument, those in power that they are wrong, but to engender a sense of self-worth in the oppressed. To contradict systematic and pervasive acts of shaming and humiliation, queers declare their pride in themselves and their communities in annual festivals all over the world. This is not only a message to those in power ("we're here, we're queer, get used to it!") but an act that produces a feeling of one's own power ("we *are* here, we exist, our presence will endure"). Thus, Martin Luther King Jr. hails "the Negro revolution" as a transformation internal to the Negro soul. What matters first of all is not affecting the oppressors but transforming defeated beings into self-valorizing persons. By virtue of resistance, the oppressed shows himself that "he was *somebody*."[6] The task of so many movements for liberation is heralded as a decolonization of the imagination, an exorcism of the master from the bodies and souls of slaves.[7] Many borrow from the powerful imagery of Hegel to pose the question of how to develop an autonomous point of view by which to love oneself anew. The art of resistance and revolt reroutes the circulation of hatred that prompts the oppressed themselves to imitate the affects of their oppressors, becoming occupied by the contemptuous gaze of the master and thereby hating themselves.

Seizing on Hegel's portrait of violent struggle as an effort to secure dignity and equality, many activists and theorists invoke, albeit often ambivalently, the politics of recognition. Within this tradition inspired by Hegel, the struggle against oppression belongs to a process of "anthropogenesis," of becoming men by winning the respect of the Other. For the politics of recognition, the goal is to establish mutuality among masters and slaves such that they regard one another as belonging to the same universal category. To be recognized is to uphold the imperative of

---

4. Here Bartky alludes to Fanon's description of black experience in *Black Skin, White Masks*.
5. Bartky, "On Psychological Oppression," 32.
6. King, "The Sword That Heals," 16.
7. Cf. Fanon, "The Negro and Recognition," in *Black Skin, White Masks*, 210–21.

abstract right: "be a person and treat others as persons."[8] Struggle is conceived as the confrontation of two rationalities transmuting particular points of view into universal ones. Through transforming the content of universal categories defining the human person, those seeking recognition win their personality and gain their dignity in struggle with the oppressor. Without struggle, personality is empty and abstract. If freedom is granted by the master to the slave, Frantz Fanon contends that it only confirms the master's magnanimity and thus his superiority.[9] The slave must act to transubstantiate himself and his world. His is a struggle not only with the external other but with the internal other who denies his core humanity.

Yet, for good reason, many theorists and activists, like Fanon, question whether white, masculine universality can be expanded to include Black, feminine particularity, without reestablishing the status quo. The possibility of mutuality and reciprocity that animates the politics of recognition is called into question by postcolonial theorists, even as they invoke the master-slave dialectic as a paradigm for overcoming self-contempt.[10] Thus, although many movement leaders and theorists link the struggles of the oppressed to a need to overcome self-hatred, there is disagreement about the conditions necessary for winning a new form of self-regard. The question of whether freedom is to be gained by throwing off the shackles of the master "by any means necessary," including putting down the dog that bites you,[11] is only the best-known controversy within black liberation. The debate about racial or sexual separation, to take another example, implies a disagreement about how to address hatred. Should the strategy lie in appealing to the ideals of universal personhood and humanity in order to establish genuine fraternity? Or ought we to cultivate an autonomous perspective amongst ourselves, in some measure of isolation from the dominant culture?

A feminist and queer theorist, Elizabeth Grosz, makes a novel and perhaps perplexing suggestion that avoids either universalism or separatism. She seeks to abandon the master-slave dialectic, the ambition of confronting the other either without or within, by rejecting the goal of anthropogenesis. She urges that we cease to seek to become human, which, for

---

8. Hegel, *The Philosophy of Right*, §36.
9. Fanon, "The Negro and Recognition," *Black Skin, White Masks*, 222.
10. Cf. Sekyi-Otu, *Fanon's Dialectic of Experience*.
11. Malcolm X, "The Ballot or the Bullet," 33.

her, can only mean becoming "men."[12] Rather than denaturalizing constructions of blacks, browns, queers, and women as essentially inferior and seeking to confirm ourselves as spiritual beings, she prescribes renaturalizing ourselves as corporeal forces striving to actualize our power within nature. Grosz urges gender and race theorists to abandon the "regime of recognition," which, she contends, cannot escape an investment in a humanistic politics of identity.[13] Rather than mobilize for visibility, intersubjective affirmation, and cross-cultural, mutual understanding, she advocates "a politics of imperceptibility" grounded in an "inhuman" ontology of forces.

In this chapter, I outline the problems Grosz identifies with a politics of recognition and examine her exhortation to "imperceptibility" and "impersonality." I propose that Grosz's idiom of force, nature, and impersonality grounds her effort to produce a political vocabulary entirely alien to humanism. I understand humanism in politics to include any vision of justice derived from a special feature of existence that is not exhibited by nonhuman beings but is held to be universally shared by humans. A politics grounded in the recognition of shared rationality, the universal ability to formulate one's life plan or vision of the good, or the capacity to assume reciprocal obligations would be included. Grosz is concerned, however, not with any and all political theory but specifically with feminist, queer, and antiracist thought. She is concerned with movements among the oppressed to constitute alternative ways of life, not defined by their oppressors. The politics of recognition often appears more congenial to gender and race theorists than either liberal individualism, which disavows the constitutive role of relationships and radical human dependency in shaping autonomy and selfhood,[14] or an unmodified communitarianism, which lacks a sufficient analysis of power relationships internal to communities.[15] Understandably, these thinkers and actors appreciate the emphasis in the politics of recognition upon the arduous and antagonistic intersubjective processes of establishing relationships of respect, equality, and sympathy among people with distinct languages, cultures, and histories. The politics of recognition, importantly, aims to heal the profound damage caused by

---

12. The exhortation to fight oppression by becoming men is everywhere in the language of the "new social movements," from Fanon to King to Biko. It is also to be found in "old social" workers' movements.
13. Grosz, "A Politics of Imperceptibility" and *Time Travels*.
14. Kittay, *Love's Labor*.
15. Frazer and Lacey, *The Politics of Community*.

oppressive sociosymbolic regimes that promote "crippling self-hatred."[16] The affective damage of oppression is, at best, inadequately addressed by mainstream liberal and egalitarian politics, which focuses on the rights owed to individuals and the just distribution of goods, respectively. Grosz rejects the politics of recognition, however, on the grounds that the desire to be known, seen, and valued by the Other is an inevitably submissive acquiescence to a humanism that can never fail to be masculine.

In an effort to develop her alternative "politics of imperceptibility," I turn to Spinoza's critique of anthropocentrism. In support of Grosz's suggestive remarks, I contend that a posthumanist politics of renaturalization might better address some of the needs a politics of recognition identifies. Indeed, the politics of renaturalization I derive from Spinoza is, perhaps first and foremost, a strategy of antihatred. Spinoza frequently identifies his naturalism as a response to the psychic and corporeal damage entailed by the proliferation of hatred, which can be extended to misogyny and cultural imperialism. The politics of recognition rightly aims to respond to this damage, but renaturalization maintains that the cure for dehumanization cannot be the achievement of "personhood," as long as personhood depends upon regarding one another as uniquely capable of transcending nature. Grosz's call for an experimental politics animated by a desire for joyful affects and the enhancement of bodily pleasures, practices, and powers offers a contemporary idiom and application for the politics of renaturalization. In linking our projects, I hope to show that Spinoza's philosophy speaks to gender and racial oppression, even if Spinoza sometimes exhibits a dim view of women's capacities (TP 6.37, 11.4). In particular, the politics of renaturalization offers an alternative remedy for the sad affects provoked by misrecognition. Moreover, it includes affective criteria for measuring the successes and failures of political practice that do not imply an opposition between humanity and nature. In both Grosz and Spinoza, we discover the need for a practical wisdom of renaturalization by which we affirm that the impersonal is political.

The Politics of Recognition

The politics of recognition has come under suspicion recently,[17] even as it arguably remains a predominant way of conceiving political struggle in North American and western European multicultural democracies. Many

---

16. Taylor, "The Politics of Recognition," 226.
17. For example, Markell, *Bound by Recognition*, and Oliver, *Witnessing*.

are likely familiar with the debates about whether the terrain of politics has shifted entirely toward recognition and away from redistribution,[18] but the various parties tend to concede Charles Taylor's claim that recognition is "a vital human need" and that the misrecognition of identities is an appropriate way of understanding oppression and injustice in late capitalism. Present-day theories of recognition are diverse and rather vague as to what precisely the desire for recognition is, what aspect of the self or group requires and is owed recognition, by whom, and toward what end. As Patchen Markell points out, it is often unclear whether the politics of recognition aims to re-cognize the already existing truths of intact identities, or whether the dynamics of recognition are meant to bring into being and enable the very subjectivities to whom recognition is due. In other words, Markell asks whether the politics of recognition is meant to know or to make social subjects.[19] The Hegelian paradigm allows doing and knowing to be understood as dynamic, co-constitutive processes, yet the metaphysical and epistemological tension between becoming and recognizing suggests that the satisfaction of a desire for recognition is an awkward yardstick for justice. If the construction of individual and group identity is an ongoing, responsive, and intersubjective process, how can moral demands for recognition be met? Can Spirit ever be satisfied that an act of recognition has succeeded? From the perspective of practice, can we codify the recognition of identities in institutions, laws, or procedures?

Although ambiguities lurk within the politics of recognition, we can identify its fundamental animating principles. Most basically, the model of recognition aims to replace the monadic model of liberal individualism with a dyadic (intersubjective) model of social subjectivity derived from Hegel's early Jena writings as well as his famous master-slave dialectic, from which the phrase "the struggle for recognition" acquired its renown.[20] Theorists in this somewhat diverse neo-Hegelian tradition develop moral and political theories that regard freedom as an achievement dependent upon social relationships and institutional conditions conducive to the development of "an intact identity" and a positive relationship to oneself.[21] The framework of recognition articulates a thoroughly social understanding of human psychology, which entails attention to the less

---

18. Fraser, "From Redistribution to Recognition?"
19. Markell, "The Recognition of Politics," 496.
20. Theorists of recognition in the French tradition rely heavily on Kojève and Hegel's *Phenomenology of Spirit*, whereas those in the German tradition, following Habermas, emphasize Hegel's earlier writings. I thank Cristian Lo Iocano for this point.
21. Honneth and Fraser, *Redistribution or Recognition?*

measurable forms of injustice inflicted by pervasive symbolic depreciation of particular identities. The politics of recognition takes into account how systematic social invisibility, misrepresentation, and distortion genuinely harm individuals and groups. Clearly, the damage produced by histories of conquest, genocide, slavery, colonialism, cultural and linguistic imperialism, and millennia of patriarchy is not healed by formal equality, greater access to jobs, housing, and social services alone. In the words of Charles Taylor, "misrecognition shows not just a lack of due respect. It can inflict a grievous wound, saddling its victims with crippling self-hatred. Due recognition is not just a courtesy we owe people. It is a vital human need."[22] Whether and how this vital need is met through political practice and institutions animates important divisions within political thought today.[23]

The neo-Hegelian paradigm is attractive in that it takes seriously a continuity, in feminist terms, between the "personal" and the "political." Feminists typically regard the personal and the political, the private and the public, to be co-constitutive. The same power relationships that function in the public domain of institutional life affect the ostensibly private realm of the home. For example, feminists call attention to how domestic violence and rape are systematic problems suffered disproportionately by women, especially women of color and Indigenous women.[24] Marxist feminists contend that the public roles typically played by men are contingent upon the invisible work (e.g., affective labor involved in sexuality, moral discipline, and childcare) of women in the home.[25] The public realm, then, is parasitic upon the private, its unacknowledged foundation, and constitutive of personal experiences and identities.

Hegelian politics accommodates considerations of "the personal" better than mainstream liberalism. For Hegel, in the home as much as in the domains of civil society and the state, we struggle to be recognized as free beings.[26] Because we are social beings, relations of domination and submission pervade our lives, and freedom emerges from a complex system of relationship between various spheres of "ethical life." Hegel's thought acknowledges the family as a site in which human freedom is brokered and produced. Although not a technical term when used in the feminist slogan "the personal is political," "person" implies a legal and moral iden-

22. Taylor, "The Politics of Recognition," 26
23. See the responses to Taylor's original essay in Gutmann, *Multiculturalism*.
24. See Crenshaw, "Mapping the Margins."
25. See Dalla Costa and James, *The Power of Women and the Subversion of the Community*.
26. Beauvoir extends Hegel's framework into domains of women's life, in *The Second Sex*.

tity rather than a natural property of humanity. It originally referred not to our private lives but to our public *personae*, the various masks we bear as social actors playing distinct roles. "Person" refers to how we represent ourselves and how we are represented by others.[27] It is an index of how a juridical sensibility has infused our quotidian sense of who we are that, in feminist politics and colloquial discourse, "person" names how we want to be seen: we are persons rather than things. Moral discourse, feminist and otherwise, conveys a yearning to be regarded as self-defining beings with a moral sensibility and an interior life. The personal is political, for feminists, in this sense, too. From a Hegelian perspective, whether women are visible as moral agents, capable of making free choices, depends upon "ethical life."[28] Feminism is, at least in part, a struggle for women to be regarded as persons.[29]

For Hegel, "person" is an ambiguous term. "What is highest for a human being is to be a person, but nevertheless the bare abstraction 'person' is something contemptible in its very expression." Because considering ourselves to be "persons" involves understanding ourselves as radically free wills, undetermined by bodily impulse or sensuous circumstance, "personality" is our greatest achievement. Nonetheless, being an abstract, universal term predicable of each and every rational being is unsatisfying and even insulting.

> The person is thus at once what is high and what could not be lower; there lies within it the infinite and the simply finite, or the determinate and the thoroughly limitless. What can sustain this contradiction, which nothing natural has within itself or could bear, is the majesty of the person.[30]

Its inability to say anything about who I am makes it contemptuous, and yet "personhood" is an indispensable form of freedom in modern life. Individuals and peoples transcend their natural condition of arbitrary particularity and achieve the universal status of person only by virtue of those other domains in which freedom is concretely constituted: the loving space of the family home; the competitive realm of civil society; and

---

27. See Poole, "On Being a Person," 45.
28. This is not her language, but I am thinking of Gilligan's now classic work, *In a Different Voice*, as well as the tradition it inspired.
29. See, e.g., Bordo, "Are Mothers Persons?"
30. Hegel, *Philosophy of Right*, §35.

civic institutions.³¹ Persons, from a Hegelian perspective, are not "transcendental conditions" of morality and law but products of social practices and institutions. Through a historical process of anthropogenesis, we cease to be things and become persons. To be a person is to be more than a human-animal. It is to be a creature of dignity, a bearer of reason, capable of moral relations with one's fellows.³² The politics of recognition is friendly to feminism insofar as it acknowledges that "personhood" is not given but achieved in relationship to others. It gives rise to a politics that explicitly acknowledges, not only the formal requirements of equality and freedom, but the essential roles of, in Honneth's terms, love and solidarity.³³ Of course, this is precisely where recognition risks becoming overly substantive for liberalism and threatens to encroach upon individual liberties.

It is beyond the scope of this chapter to address the complex set of debates surrounding the politics of recognition in political theory as a whole.³⁴ Grosz addresses her critique of recognition to gender and postcolonial theorists. She thereby targets those who write as the misrecognized, those who may be, according to Taylor, enduring "grievous wound[s]" and suffering "crippling self-hatred." In particular, Grosz responds to recognition theorists Drucilla Cornell, Sara Murphy, and Judith Butler. Grosz engages these particular theorists by virtue of sympathy for their overall political impulses and a shared desire to fight cultural imperialism, racism, and sexism. Yet she urges those who understand themselves to be either misrecognized, or writing on their behalf, to reject the intersubjective dynamic presupposed by the model of recognition. She makes what may be a startling suggestion that feminists and postcolonial thinkers forget about "the Other" and affirm the irrepressibly agonistic dynamics of nature and bodily forces. It is to her suggestive critique that I now turn.

Elizabeth Grosz's Critique of the Politics of Recognition

Grosz's call for a politics of imperceptibility first appears in a critical response to an essay by Cornell and Murphy, "Anti-racism, Multiculturalism, and an Ethics of Identification." Grosz applauds Cornell and Murphy for endeavoring to reformulate a politics of recognition that is not tied to the acknowledgment of an authentic, prepolitical, conscious cultural iden-

---

31. This is a very general gloss of Hegel's *Philosophy of Right*.
32. Poole, "On Being a Person," 48.
33. See chap. 5 of *The Struggle for Recognition*.
34. A critical assessment can be found in Markell, *Bound by Recognition*.

tity, a model they attribute to Charles Taylor. Cornell and Murphy aim to decouple the struggle for recognition from any notion of "authenticity," while advocating an "ethics of identification." The notion of authenticity derived from Johann Gottfried Herder and Lionel Trilling presupposes that we are all equally human, but each in our own unique way. Even as Taylor, with Hegel, insists that we become who we truly are only in time and in ongoing relationships with others, Cornell and Murphy contend that seeking "authenticity" entails an unacceptably static notion of personal and cultural identity.[35] Authenticity, for them, eclipses the recognition of individuals as the sources of the meanings of their identities, meanings that are continually being revised and reinterpreted.[36] Instead, they advocate an "ethics of identification," an ongoing transformative practice among diverse social actors, which allows for the emergence of incipient, novel identities. They emphasize the freedom to recreate oneself through the assertion and recognition of one another's humanity. The basis of their politics is the dignity and respect owed to all human beings *qua* human, which entails attention to each person's need to develop and transform her self-representation and cultural meaning. Theirs is a "personal politics" in the technical sense. It pertains to the struggles of diverse agents to *represent* themselves publicly as moral agents. Theirs is a neo-Hegelian (rather than neo-Kantian) personal politics, because it emphasizes democratizing the procedures through which representations are engendered and established. It highlights the concrete conditions and social processes by which particulars become universals. Specifically, Cornell and Murphy advocate the (state) provision of "the psychic and moral space" in which the oppressed are equally able to shape how they are seen through participation in public discourse, art, and literature.[37]

Although Grosz appreciates the move away from a politics of identity conceived in terms of authenticity, she remains highly critical of any language of recognition. She fears that any vision of justice predicated upon the validation of social subjects by other subjects belongs to "a politics that is fundamentally servile." Grosz acknowledges that minorities seek recog-

---

35. "Anti-racism, Multiculturalism, and an Ethics of Identification," 420, 444.
36. Ibid., 421.
37. The proposal by Cornell and Murphy demonstrates the difficulty Markell indicates. How is the state to confer recognition upon identities subject to constant revaluation and recreation? Although they suggest that the state guarantees "the psychic and moral space" necessary for such self-recreation, they still insist that the state recognize individuals and groups *as* bearers of identities, albeit shifting and provisional ones. "Recognition" comes to be an awkward term for whatever state policies might promote such fluid processes of identification.

nition from each other and not necessarily from the dominant culture, but she rejects any conception of the self that is "governed, in advance, by the image and value of the other," no matter who that other happens to be.[38] Elsewhere Grosz advocates a turn to a Nietzschean conception of the subject precisely because it is wholly "indifferent to the other."[39] She urges her readers to think instead about politics in terms of agonistic forces and impersonal "becomings."[40] She calls for the politics of recognition to be supplanted by a fight for "bodily activities and practices."[41]

Needless to say, Grosz's is an unusual feminist critique of Hegelian theories of intersubjectivity and recognition. Kelly Oliver, for example, endeavors to go "beyond recognition" because subjectivity need not be modeled on violence and antagonism, as it is in Hegel, Beauvoir, Sartre, and Butler.[42] Oliver objects to a flattening account of any and all social subjectivity on the model of trauma and a portrait of all otherness in the image of threat and hostility. She argues, persuasively in my view, that such a universal account elides the real differences between social subjectivity under conditions of radical oppression and social subjectivity in a context of privilege. Oliver elaborates an alternative account of dyadic intersubjectivity that neither presupposes violence nor covers over distinctively oppressive histories. Her theory aims to bear witness to the profound sufferings of particular others. Oliver's theory supports the feminist vision of a just world in which social subjects emerge in a context of responsiveness, attentive connection, and love.

Like Oliver, the vast majority of feminist theorists focus on ethical practices of attuning oneself better to others, especially the disadvantaged. They promote political strategies that modify and refine symbolic representation, social meaning, and communicative interaction. For example, Oliver advocates an alternative notion of vision in terms of sensual connectivity, counter to the speculative tradition in the history of philosophy. Without revising the very notion of visual apprehension, Cornell and Murphy insist upon the right to participate actively in one's social representations. In various ways, most feminist theorists advocate *seeing better*, conceiving others more appropriately, and becoming better able to perceive differences in subjective experiences.[43] At the same time, many

---

38. Grosz, "A Politics of Imperceptibility," 471.
39. Grosz, *Time Travels*, 86
40. Grosz, "A Politics of Imperceptibility," 469.
41. Grosz, *Time Travels*, 87.
42. Oliver, *Witnessing*.
43. Cf. Alcoff, *Visible Identities*.

acknowledge in a Levinasian vein that an ideal of mutual transparency is neither possible nor desirable.[44] Yet we are still called upon to become ever more sensitive to our failure to apprehend the needs, desires, and experiences of other subjects. Even as a traditional model of transparent, mutual recognition is typically rejected,[45] a nonperfectible effort to see, perceive, and imagine better remains a core aspiration in feminist and antiracist theory.

Vision, representation, and consciousness have concerned feminist and antiracist politics since their inception. Even as social movements have extended beyond juridical politics of abolitionism, suffrage, and women's rights, they are dominated by the problem of representation. How are gendered and racialized subjects portrayed? How do we mobilize counterimages and intervene in the production of stereotypes? How do we develop practices that avoid the mutilating distortion of people of color, lesbians, and sexual minorities?[46] In other words, as a politics of representation, feminist and antiracist ambitions remains centered on the problem of "personality" and moral agency.[47]

Grosz, in stark contrast, does not advocate a theory of social subjectivity that is more loving and responsive to particular others and their histories. Her Nietzsche-inspired paradigm of impersonal, nonsubjective forces renders violence and conflict both necessary and irresolvable. Grosz advocates a politics of imperceptibility because it privileges acts, forces, energies, and bodies. She rejects a dialectic of self and other, since "acts don't have an 'other.' Only Subjects have an 'other.'"[48] In advocating imperceptibility, she opposes a project of mutual clarification and disclosure, a meeting of minds, as a salve for pain caused by hatred and humiliation. She turns away from metaphors of vision, illumination, transparency, and representation. Instead, she urges her readers to join her in a political project that embraces opacity, dissolution, indiscernibility, and departicularization.

What motivates Grosz's strange exhortation to imperceptibility? To

---

44. See, e.g., Young, "Asymmetrical Reciprocity."

45. Both Taylor ("The Politics of Recognition," 26) and Honneth (*The Struggle for Recognition*, 121) insist on an ideal of recognition that eliminates distortion.

46. See Lugones, "Playfulness, 'World'-Travelling, and Loving Perception," and Frye, *The Politics of Reality*.

47. This is true despite the movement, originating in North America in the early 1990s (well before that in France), to take "the body" as a point of theoretical departure. It is no accident, however, that Grosz, a pioneer of what has been called "corporeal feminism," continues to resist the representationalist orientation of feminist and antiracist thought.

48. Found Objects Collective, "An Interview with Elizabeth Grosz," 4.

whom might it be attractive? When one examines her inspiration for a politics of imperceptibility, her counterprogram might appear even more perplexing. Grosz appropriates the notion of imperceptibility (without citation) from Gilles Deleuze and Félix Guattari's *A Thousand Plateaus*. The notion of becoming-imperceptible appears at the extreme end of a spectrum of "becoming-animal." Deleuze and Guattari propose becoming-animal as a notion of transformation that is not predicated on identification, imitation, resemblance, or analogy. Rather than the reflection of an unconscious urge to work out a psychic identification with a lost other (a parent, love object, or part of oneself), becomings-animal are impersonal communications between bodily forces that cannot be represented by concepts or explained through developmental narratives. If I represent myself as feeling "like a dog," it may be the way I imagine the destabilizing effect of a molecular exchange between the porous and dynamic assemblage I call "my body" and the myriad inhuman bodies by virtue of which I exist. Becomings-animal, according to Deleuze and Guattari, occur on a continuum that begins, on the one side, with what they call the "special introductory power" of becoming-woman and culminates, "at the far side," in becoming-imperceptible.[49]

In an early work, Grosz finds Deleuze and Guattari's affirmation of becoming-woman as a portal to becoming-imperceptible to be problematic.

> But there must remain a wariness, insofar as they too sever becoming-woman from being-woman, and make the specificities of becoming-woman crucial to men's quest for self-expansion. They render women's becomings, their subversions, their minoritarian and marginal struggles subordinate to a cosmic becoming-imperceptible which amounts, in effect, to a political obliteration or marginalization of women's struggles.[50]

Today, however, she urges feminists and postcolonial theorists to embrace what once appeared to her as a mystical "obliteration" of the demands, desires, and projects of women. Perhaps the link between becoming-imperceptible and becoming-woman as part of the project of becoming-animal is what prevents Grosz from noting that a politics of imperceptibility is conceptually inherited from Deleuze and Guattari. Yet insofar as the project of becoming-animal and becoming-imperceptible belongs to a

---

49. Deleuze and Guattari, *A Thousand Plateaus*, 248.
50. Grosz, "A Thousand Tiny Sexes," 179.

program of radical antihumanism in Deleuze and Guattari, its lineage is essential to her critiques of Cornell and Murphy as well as of Butler.

Cornell and Murphy preserve the language of recognition to affirm the necessity of contesting and opening up the symbolic content of the term "human." Butler claims in *Undoing Gender* that her project necessarily begins and ends with "the human."[51] Butler's recent work explicitly belongs to a "post-Hegelian politics of recognition," which comprises an effort to expand the designation of humanity in response to implicitly socially sanctioned violence against unrecognizable others.[52] Grosz consistently exhibits suspicion, however, of any discourse of the human. Although she often invokes Nietzsche to support her emphasis upon the "inhuman,"[53] she is at least equally inspired by Luce Irigaray's critique of the phallocentric logic of Western thought. When she defends her preference for a language of forces rather than subjects, she notes that feminists are likely to consider an idiom of force, power, and action to be masculine and patriarchal. "But this maneuver of identifying force with the masculine is already to humanize force (which in effect is to masculinize it, in a phallocentric logos), to anthropomorphize it and to refuse to see its role not as the effect but as the condition of subjectivity and subjective will."[54] In her parenthetical identification of humanization with masculinization, we can detect a distinctively feminist motivation for the language of force in the politics of imperceptibility. Because, for Grosz, any humanization and anthropomorphism falls into a phallocentric economy of the same, she rejects the possibility of stretching the category of the human to include its excluded others. Although many feminists argue that "the human" implies a masculine subject, most do not see any alternative to an appeal to this particular universal, especially if they are writing programmatic political theory. Yet Grosz does not shy away from promoting a turn to the inhuman: the multiplicity of natural, bodily forces and the nondiscursive terrain of actions, affects, and mutations. Although Grosz does not condemn all humanist political theories *tout court*, she claims that feminist and antiracist struggle is starved for new languages, concepts, and problems.[55] Perhaps only an uncompromising effort to exit the regime of recognition and eschew the desire for visibility and intersubjective affirmation can yield a new horizon for politics?

51. Butler, *Undoing Gender*, 17.
52. See Butler, *Giving an Account of Oneself*.
53. As well as the obvious allusion to Lyotard, *The Inhuman*.
54. Grosz, *Time Travels*, 187.
55. Grosz, "A Politics of Imperceptibility," 463.

Thinking beyond the (Hu)Man

One of the distinctive aspects of Grosz's counterproposal is her invocation of a more "primitive" and naturalistic language rather than a more sophisticated conceptualization of our increasingly diverse world. Although moral and political thought today operates almost exclusively in a "postcritical" idiom in which discussion of natural causality is all but verboten, Grosz writes of causes, forces, and conditions. She does not avoid characterizing nature itself. Nature, guided by her interpretation of Darwin, designates uncontainable dynamism, irrepressible mutation, and constant self-differentiation. She elaborates and calls for new models of nature that insist on our continuity with nonhuman agencies, while striving to avoid pitfalls identified by decades of denaturalizing critique.[56] Feminists, race theorists, and critical theorists, for good reason, evince strong suspicion of appeals to nature, which often function as discourses of domination that identify some social groups with animal functions and others with spiritual ones. In response, Grosz outlines a concept of nature that disrupts rather than promotes normalization. Nature, for her, is self-differentiation and thus cannot promote a stable model. This portrait of nature, she hopes, cannot be used as a norm against which to find anyone defective or inferior. Moreover, in contrast to the Cartesian and Hegelian traditions, nature is replete with various active powers, rather than a passive object that spiritual subjects might hope to master.

Most feminists and race theorists who appropriate the Hegelian intersubjective model do not accept it in its entirety.[57] Rather than modifying it to suit our purposes, Grosz argues that we ought "to begin with different working assumptions" that challenge our dependence upon a receptive audience. It is the fixation on the dyadic relation of master and slave that Grosz seeks to overturn. She thereby makes an urgent call for "new *intellectual* resources" to address domination.[58] Toward that end, she suggests that "[s]ubjects can be conceived as modes of action and passion, a surface of catalytic events, events which subjects do not control but participate in, which produce what history and thus what identity subjects may have."[59] Rather than a "psychical interiority inhabited by the specter of the other," she advocates a perspective in which "what marks the subject as such is

---

56. See, Grosz, *Time Travels*, part 1.
57. See, for example, Fanon's discussion, "The Negro and Recognition," *Black Skin, White Masks*.
58. Grosz, "A Politics of Imperceptibility," 463; emphasis in original.
59. Ibid., 468.

its capacity to act and be acted upon, to do rather than to be, to act rather than to identify."[60] Thus she endeavors to address the same phenomena (the social subjectivity of the oppressed) that preoccupy many feminists and antiracists today, but in an alternative idiom.

Grosz confronts us with "a theoretical choice" between a humanist "theory of the subject" and an inhuman "theory of impersonal," natural forces. We might also call this a theoretical choice between the "personal" (universal consciousness freed of natural determination) and the "impersonal" (the causal network of affects). Although Grosz develops this alternative theoretical lens through Nietzsche, it might just as easily be discovered in Spinoza.[61] Spinoza's challenge to anthropocentric thinking can supplement the impersonal approach she advocates. Moreover, compared with Nietzsche's philosophy, Spinoza's thought arguably exhibits less suspicion toward collective efforts and may, for that reason, have greater potential to support a feminist agenda. Indeed, a number of feminists recognize Spinoza's philosophy as a rich resource.[62] Nietzsche alerts modern subjects to our problematic assumptions, habits, and investments with more rhetorical force than perhaps any other philosopher. I would like to suggest, however, that Spinoza opens up still further avenues, especially for the practice of a politics of imperceptibility.

The fundamental premise of the politics of renaturalization—that humans are not different in kind from any other natural being—allies it with Grosz's program. Although Spinoza was writing well before Hegelian theories of recognition, his thinking was no less animated by a concern with the pervasiveness of hatred in human societies. He frequently laments that "men are naturally inclined to hate and envy" (*E* III p55s). Also as in Hegel (and many others in the history of philosophy), freedom depends upon coming to accept and affirm oneself as one truly is, in essence. Yet, rather than being essentially a free person by virtue of the infinity of the will, as Hegel maintains, each of us is essentially a part of nature, dependent upon both the infinite power of nature as a whole and the infinitely many finite forces to which we are ineluctably connected. Enmity and hatred are inevitable consequences of our finitude. Owing to the sin-

---

60. Ibid., 466.

61. Given that Grosz's Nietzsche is mediated by Deleuze, who finds very similar strains of thought in Spinoza, it is not a big leap from one to the other. Moreover, the precise language of acting and being acted upon is closer to Spinoza's, although he more often discusses the body as what "affects and is affected" by others.

62. Gatens, *Imaginary Bodies*; Gatens and Lloyd, *Collective Imagining*; Braidotti, *Metamorphoses*.

gularity of essences in nature, even if humans share many capacities and our bodies and minds are structurally similar, our distinct requirements and aspirations often do not coincide. Love, being prompted by joy from an external cause, is also possible only by virtue of finitude. Indeed, finitude and human psychology are such that we are constantly animated by love and hate, which determine us personally and anonymously, since "anything can be the accidental cause of joy, sadness, and desire" (III p15). Strife and enmity follow from hate and its derivatives: envy, mockery, disdain, anger, and vengeance (IV p45c1). Peace, or political unity, depends upon organizing our social relations to counter one of the most prevalent emotions among human beings: *odium*. Spinoza defines hate as "sadness with the accompanying idea of an external cause" and notes that each of us cannot but strive to "remove and destroy the thing he hates" (III p14s). Sadness, recall, is simply the feeling of a decrease in one's power to persevere in being (III p11s), and the mimetic character of our psychology virtually guarantees that we are most affected by the behavior and action of those whom we identify to be "like us" (III p27). The question for the politics of renaturalization becomes: how do we address hatred among us? In particular, how do we exorcise the self-hatred that follows from imitating the affects of the hateful other?

According to the politics of recognition, human conflict, whether it takes the form of direct confrontation, property crime, or self-mortification, is about the desire for the esteem of the other. The thief, in taking something, not only aims to satisfy his biological need for food but claims that his life is valuable, that he has a right to food, and seeks a response from the universal. This is how, for Hegel, "the criminal is intelligence. His inner justification is . . . to count as something, to be recognized."[63] Even if the ambition to be esteemed by others is potent in human psychology, Spinoza's ethics does not advocate overcoming enmity through mutual esteem. Although some, like Levinas, have found the lack of concern with the other in Spinoza's ethics to be its most objectionable aspect, Grosz suggests that preoccupation with the other has led to impasses in emancipatory politics. Spinoza advocates the cultivation of self-esteem (*acquiescentia*) in response to enmity, hatred, and self-hatred. Yet his understanding of self-esteem is not an egoistic affirmation of the unique value of the individual but a liberating appreciation of nature and the distinctive shape of one's power within it. It is liberating because it involves the experience of one's own agency, not as an illusory transcendence of natural

---

63. *Lectures on the Philosophy of Spirit 1827–1828*, 126.

determination but as a constitutive natural force (*E* IV p52, V p27). Thus, although Spinoza shares Hobbes's view that the ambitious desire for esteem must be presupposed in the successful organization of a state, good institutions redirect rather than satisfy the urge to find our worth in the eyes of fellow men. The politics of renaturalization seeks a new ethos and practical wisdom (by structural means) to revalue dependency and natural determination and produce a new understanding of action.[64] While the *Ethics* advocates an impersonal identification with God and nature, the political writings, in complementary ways, aim at a harmony of minds (peace) through a coordination of the powers of diverse agents (*TP* 6.4). Both of these trajectories depend upon overcoming an understanding of humanity as different in kind from nature.

In other words, the politics of renaturalization displaces the drive for that special kind of respect owed to one's humanity, so fundamental to contemporary liberal humanism. The desire to be esteemed imprisons us, as long as it depends upon being seen as an absolute special genre of being, elevated out of nature by virtue of one's rationality, consciousness, unconditioned will, or anything else. The hypothesis of the politics of renaturalization is that ceasing to imitate the hatred of others requires abandoning an economy of recognition, by which we determine who is human (fetuses? babies? women? slaves? the cognitively disabled?), and thereby demarcate our sphere of moral concern. Grosz and Spinoza contend, albeit in different ways, that self-love and the production of collective power and pleasure require a nonhumanist theory of agency and desire.

Spinoza's distance from humanism, as chapter 1 argues, is captured by his famous announcement that he will "consider human actions and appetites just as if it were a question of lines, planes, and bodies." In contrast to the humanist tradition, he refuses to treat "man" as though he is "outside Nature," as if the human realm is an "empire within an empire ... that disturbs, rather than follows, the order of Nature" (*E* III pref). What has been called Spinoza's "antihumanism" is not a denial of human freedom or worth, which is no less the preoccupation of his philosophy, but a rejection of the idea that there are special laws that belong to human existence alone, in any of its manifestations. As is surely familiar to readers by now, "the way of understanding the nature of anything, of whatever kind, must ... be the same, namely, through the universal rules of Nature." Spinoza contends that his denial of human freedom as it is traditionally understood "contributes to social life, insofar as it teaches us to hate no one,

---

64. I treat one of the structural means in detail in Sharp, "Feeling Justice."

to disesteem no one, to mock no one, to be angry with no one." Ceasing to regard humans as free, as different in kind, attenuates hate and its relatives. This claim may not seem especially political, since it concerns moral failures to respect others. Yet he proceeds to affirm that the renaturalization of human freedom likewise "contributes, to no small extent, to the common society insofar as it teaches how men are to be governed and led, not so they may be slaves, but that they may freely do those things that are best" (II p49s). Elsewhere, he directly connects the mitigation of hate to the effort of renaturalization: If we recall that "men, like other things, act from the necessity of nature," the hate we feel when suffering the common wrongs of men will "easily be overcome" (V p10). The view of humans as endowed with radically free wills that prompts hate, on Spinoza's account, is precisely what Hegel thinks requires recognition.[65]

Hegel's is a rich and demanding concept of human freedom and its social conditions. Yet it is unacceptable from the point of view of renaturalization, since recognition entails viewing humans as special kinds of beings. Although contemporary thinkers are not uncritical of Hegel's treatment of nature, the politics of recognition's valorization of "postconventional" societies confirms the insistence upon human transcendence.[66] Justice and freedom are more available insofar as a people progressively spiritualizes the natural world, including human bodies. To put my claim in the strongest possible terms, if Spinoza is right, the politics of recognition is a self-hating endeavor. To insist that we are other than we are, and to judge ourselves and others by a spiritual standard that can nowhere be met, invites mockery and contempt. It is no accident that Spinoza accuses most philosophers of writing "satire" and invective that offer little to understanding, rather than ethical and political theory (*E* III pref; *TP* 1.1). Especially when confronted with the pain we cause one another, philosophers divide humanity into those closer to God and those more bestial. Their own hatred of human wrong alienates them from an explanation of the causes of human frailty. The politics of recognition risks mocking humans as they really are by imagining them as one would prefer them to be.

Spinoza's challenges to humanism, in my view, aim precisely at misanthropy. Insofar as humanism grounds moral and political theory in special features of humanity that imply our transcendence of nature,

---

65. Cf. Pippin, "What Is the Question for Which Hegel's Theory of Recognition Is the Answer?"
66. "Postconventional society" is a term of art among Habermasians.

it fuels resentment every time we fail to rise above our circumstances. Philanthropic motivations animate what some have decried as Spinoza's dispassionate inhumanity.[67] Spinoza's polemic against a uniquely human perspective evinces his conviction that we can love ourselves only by getting over ourselves. Does this mean we can end oppression as soon as we acknowledge the iron laws of natural necessity? No, the politics of renaturalization understands "how foolish are attempts so often made to get rid of a tyrant while yet the causes that have made the prince a tyrant cannot be removed" (TP 5.7). Tyranny, for Spinoza, is not the independent action of a sovereign individual but rather an effect of a vast constellation of impersonal causes. We need an entire set of "new modes and orders" to transform current power relations.[68] As detestable as an oppressor is, "hate can never be good," for "we strive to destroy the man we hate," which will do little to reorder the causes of our hatred (E IV p45). We should act, as much as possible, with an informed understanding of the myriad impersonal causes hostile to our flourishing. Because we are finite, self-defense may require opposition and destruction, but that will likely be only a temporary abeyance of what ails us. Being part of causal networks means that political transformation is profoundly difficult. The tyrant's head cannot simply be cut off. Yet the extent to which "the common wrongs of men" torment us can be minimized by viewing one another and ourselves as parts of nature. The politics of renaturalization calls for a change in how we understand human existence. To see ourselves opposed to nature is to hate ourselves.

To return to the debate within feminist and antiracist politics, Grosz distinguishes herself from Judith Butler, who has radicalized social construction more than any other theorist by denaturalizing sex and gender. Grosz notes that "denaturalizing is important. But it is not my project. We have, by now, been denaturalized as much as we need to be. What I'm much more interested in [is a] sort of renaturalizing that has been taken away, redynamizing a certain kind of nature."[69] While we need denaturalization's suspicion toward discourses that eternalize social roles, attributing them to a transhistorical human nature, we also need to see our projects in terms of natural forces that exceed human powers. The politics of renaturalization, by way of Grosz and Spinoza together, decenters human reality by acknowledging its production within a force field of powers and

---

67. Alquié, *Le rationalisme de Spinoza*, and Nussbaum, *Upheavals of Thought*.
68. I allude to Machiavelli's *Discourses on Livy*, 5.
69. Found Objects Collective, "An Interview with Elizabeth Grosz," 5.

counterpowers indifferent to human flourishing. The project of renaturalization seeks an alternative response to the "crippling self-hatred" that is the object of a politics of recognition. Rather than yearning for the affirmation of our humanity, or insisting upon a satisfying self-representation within the social imaginary, we strive for a liberating knowledge of ourselves as natural beings.

What would it mean politically, however, to affirm our natural rather than human being? What kind of political practice is urged by the renaturalization of humanity? One of the virtues of the politics of recognition is its insistence that justice issues from a complex social dynamic that includes a robust affective dimension in excess of individual psychologies. The politics of recognition maintains that we cannot liberate ourselves. Although it does not seek the other's recognition, the politics of renaturalization is not solitary. We need (many) others, but it is important to consider those others to include more than human beings. Broadening our frame of reference, apprehending political power and individual agency as something that involves more than social relations, mitigates the sad passions that animate a culture of justice as retribution, recrimination, and reparation. Depriving humanity of its special status as part of a project of loving and knowing ourselves and the nonhuman beings on whom we depend is arguably of increasing importance in an epoch that threatens environmental catastrophe. I have yet to make any detailed suggestions about what kind of political practices and institutions Grosz's politics of imperceptibility, a contemporary articulation of what follows from renaturalization, might entail. I conclude with some thoughts toward that end.

A Politics of Imperceptibility

Grosz's terms are not precisely Spinoza's. While Spinoza rejects the view of man in nature as a dominion within a dominion, Grosz objects to the politics of recognition as a form of "identity politics." Identity politics is linked to recognition insofar as it seeks affirmation of group identity as a meaningful part of who one is. Black and feminist consciousness involve coming to see oneself in terms of a social identity and fighting to transform the meaning of that identity for oneself and others. Spinoza's effort is a rather generic effort to renaturalize "man." Among social movements today, it is not enough to see humans as a whole in a new light. We must attack particular abuses and local hatreds. Factionalism and radical prejudices were far from alien to Spinoza (cf. *E* IV p46), and he analyzes religious hatred in detail in his *Theological-Political Treatise*. Yet, in his day, he was not yet concerned with racist or sexist "biologization" of human differences. Denaturalization has been central to gender and race theory, because the oppression of women, non-orthosexuals, and racial minorities has often been justified, since at least the mid-eighteenth century, on biological grounds. Grosz's exhortation to renaturalization addresses an audience that is deeply skeptical of appeals to nature.

The politics of imperceptibility, as I understand Grosz, critiques orienting political action around human representations. Yet it is still concerned with "concepts." She proposes a project of emancipatory renaturalization through an appreciation of material forces that are indifferent to human conceptualizations even as they constitute them. While she takes inspiration from Deleuze and Guattari, note that they do not entirely reject identity politics. With respect to the feminist movement, they write: "It is, of course, indispensable for women to conduct a molar politics, with a view of winning back their own organism, their own history, their own subjectivity." At the same time, they warn that "to confine oneself to such a subject, which does not function without drying up a spring or stopping a flow," poses a constant threat to efforts at self-transformation.[70] Grosz advocates a "molecular" politics of impersonal flows. Rather than focusing on the visibility and social legitimation presupposed by molar politics of identity, impersonal and imperceptible politics likely takes inspiration from radical queer politics.[71]

The politics of queer nation and lesbian separatism have long argued, against the aspiration for inclusion in the dominant culture, that the failure of the dominant imaginary to represent us might have liberating potential.[72] The obscurity and illegibility of "abnormal" subjects may not only be a source of pain and exclusion, even if it is wretched to be hated and scorned. There have always been some radicals who contend that relative invisibility can be exploited toward new ends. Darkness might be enjoyed rather than illuminated. Consider Sartre's assessment of Aimé Césaire's poetry: "night is no longer absence, it is refusal. Black is not color, it is the destruction of this borrowed clarity which falls from the white sun."[73] Perhaps, in addition to the Irigarayan rejection of the masculine symbolic economy where humans can only ever be men, Grosz's exhortation to

---

70. *A Thousand Plateaus*, 304.
71. See, for example, Warner, *The Trouble with Normal*. Thank you, again, to Cristian Lo Iocano for suggesting the link between molecular and queer politics.
72. A point frequently made by lesbian politics, such as Wittig, *A Straight Mind and Other Essays*.
73. Sartre, "Black Orpheus," 124.

imperceptibility emerges from the queer affirmation of the autonomy of counterculture, of the pleasure, solidarity, and possibility of being outside the mainstream. While it is important not to romanticize oppression, it is also important not to overestimate the constitutive impact of the hegemonic gaze.[74] Emphasizing the spaces of creativity and possibility afforded by an underground movement that avoids the sun arguably contains some promise in an epoch when media are centralized and overwhelmingly controlled. Seizing the means of production of representation may be a futile project. At the same time, new media allow local groups to go viral and make unforeseen contacts. A politics of imperceptibility pursues contact and communication, but without striving for admission to universality.

Spinoza offers the politics of imperceptibility a rigorous and uncompromising critique of human transcendence. Moreover, Spinoza's philanthropic challenge to humanism is genetically linked to Grosz, in that it serves as an ontological foundation for her Deleuzian framework. When Deleuze and Guattari invite us to consider becoming-imperceptible, they do not advocate a retreat from perception absolutely, as if that were possible. Perception in itself is not necessarily problematic, and, for Spinoza, our minds and bodies perceive in excess of our consciousness. Spinoza contends that "nothing can happen in that body which is not perceived by the mind" that is an idea of that body (*E* II p12), and yet "the human mind does not know the human body" (II p19s) and usually only marvels at what it can do (III p2s). For Spinoza, perception happens in nature but is not a uniquely human phenomenon. Deleuze and Guattari target not the perceptive power of nature itself but the dominant regime of perception, the social imaginary that filters, contours, and categorizes beings into intelligible entities. Their imagery of becoming-imperceptible challenges, sometimes through evasion rather than self-assertion, the hegemonic sociosymbolic order.

Children and the insane figure as Deleuze and Guattari's examples of becoming-animal on the way to becoming-imperceptible. Children are exemplary because they do not perceive the world as divided into atoms. Children apprehend "assemblages" of proximate beings producing effects in unison, as when little Hans notices the horse-omnibus-street.[75] Children of a certain age do not yet operate in terms of the hegemonic sociosymbolic order, fail to use names appropriately, and often imitate the affects of beasts or trains and thereby affirm nature as replete with

---

74. Cf. Butler, *Frames of War*, 1.
75. Deleuze and Guattari, *A Thousand Plateaus*, 284.

possibilities for relationships and transformative involvements. Children and madmen, for Deleuze and Guattari, do not become imperceptible absolutely, in the sense of being inaccessible to other bodies and minds. Rather, they fail to conform to the dominant order and thereby travel a less manifest path, among the infinitely many that compose nature. If the examples in *A Thousand Plateaus*, however, are largely children, werewolves, and (socially defined) madmen, how does this translate into a politics of imperceptibility? And what is especially feminist or antiracist about such a politics?

Grosz's schema offers inspiration and redirection without much positive guidance. A politics of imperceptibility entails a reconsideration of "the subject," be it an individual or group, in terms of vital forces. In her words, "Rethinking the concept of the subject in terms of force means profound transformations in all related concepts—of objects, of the social, of actions and agency."[76] Grosz promotes an increasingly "abstract" feminist theory as a means to overhaul fundamental ontological categories. Her work is increasingly autonomous from specific problems that traditionally preoccupy feminist and antiracist thought. She does not often discuss particular institutions of oppression and instead elaborates new ways to consider time, space, and force. Her early work on gender and embodiment has given rise to a style of thinking that is not confined to responding to the most manifest exigencies in the lives of women or racialized groups. It risks appearing detached from lived experiences of oppression. Yet the circumscription of feminist theory to women's issues domesticates and restrains feminist thought. It treats feminism as an application of philosophy rather than as a comprehensive philosophical effort. In Grosz's intervention into the debate surrounding the politics of recognition, we can see that her style of thinking is not devoid of political prescription.

Grosz's thought shares with Spinoza's a kind of irony. Grosz explicitly advocates greater abstraction in feminist theory, and, similarly, Spinoza's philosophy strikes critics (as well as admirers) as hyperrational and distant from sensual experience. The truth to these characterizations lies in the fact that Spinoza and Grosz advocate, first and foremost, a radical transformation of thought. While each presents a picture of nature as a realm of agonistic forces indifferent to human well-being, their projects promote and exemplify intellectual efforts that appear distinct in character from an arena of bodies struggling to survive and thrive. Yet, as I argue in chapter 2, Spinoza's "parallelism" of mind and body supports a

---

76. Grosz, "A Politics of Imperceptibility," 469.

portrait of ideas themselves as forces, desiring powers in nature, striving to prolong and enhance their existence. Bodily servitude entails mental servitude, and vice versa. Spinoza's and Grosz's intellectual interventions into the discourses of their day are energetic, forceful activities that combat and suppress certain ideas and enjoin others to form countermodes of thinking and being. Although agonism inevitably belongs to the effort to change one's causal milieu, thinking in terms of force is not the same as thinking only in terms of opposition. Forces thrive and suffer by virtue of their relationships to ambient others. The arguments contained in Grosz's and Spinoza's philosophies represent not only inspiration for alternative ways of thinking and living, endeavoring to affect and displace other modes of thinking. They are lived enactments of those very alternatives. Their challenging ideas are evidence that they have enjoyed fortuitous encounters with other minds and bodies and marshaled the power to know themselves and live in their worlds according to different norms. Spinoza's *Ethics*, a treatise on the pleasure and power of understanding, is a product and project of assembling forces to think, feel, live, and love oneself, like any other thing, as a part of nature. Similarly, Grosz's ideas are both nourished and constrained by a history of suffering and acting among feminist and antiracist ideas, since these traditions comprise ecosystems of ideal forces in which her ideas exist and act.

While only time will reveal what differences their theories might make for any of us, Grosz promotes the effort "to become more mobile, more fluid and transformable." Instead of an effort to be valued as persons, feminism becomes a "struggle to mobilize and transform the position of women, the alignment of forces that constitute that 'identity' and 'position,' that stratification that stabilizes itself as a place and an identity."[77] She advocates the politics of imperceptibility as an intellectual effort, which is not the effect of willing subjects. An optimism of the intellect and a pessimism of the will,[78] it leaves its "traces and effects" everywhere but is acknowledged only retrospectively as increased mobility, surprising encounters, and enabling energies that transform gendered and raced subjectivity. How might we engage in a politics of imperceptibility? How do we galvanize imperceptible destabilizations of identity?

Like the plateau from which Grosz takes her inspiration, one might wonder whether becoming-imperceptible just happens, independent of any subjective effort, or whether one may undertake such "becomings" as

77. Ibid., 471.
78. Negri reformulates Gramsci's phrase in *Subversive Spinoza*, 41, among other places.

a project. Imperceptible politics makes no sense as a teleological plan to be drawn up and executed according to the transparent intentions of human actors. Yet Grosz advocates a politics and not just a mystical attunement to subterranean transformations. Since she does not develop her politics in detail, however, I offer Spinoza's political thought as a notion of practice that acknowledges the imperceptible forces operative in our affective engagements with human and nonhuman beings. The politics of renaturalization, like imperceptibility, engenders different indices of effectivity from a humanist politics oriented around seeing one another as fellow men. In contrast to a recognitive measure of justice, which depends upon satisfying "self-consciousness," the politics of renaturalization aims at the collective production of joy in ourselves as natural powers. The project of renaturalization maintains that mutual understanding remains elusive as long as we seek to find ourselves reflected in one another as equally human, equally transcendent of nature. For Grosz, striving to be equally human necessarily implies seeking to be equally masculine, to which others would surely add, yearning to be equally white. If seeking to be equally masculine, white, and superior to nature is the basis of humanism, we clearly need a new aspirational horizon.

Let us consider again Spinoza's frequent counsel for the organization of large deliberative assemblies. The insistence upon collective deliberation productive of rationality links Spinoza to today's neo-Hegelians. It is no accident that thinkers of freedom as a relational phenomenon emphasize communication and public interaction among political practices. Collective reasoning, however, need not be seen as a stage for the conscious expression of reason and identities seeking recognition. For the politics of imperceptibility, as I interpret it in a Spinozan vein, the index of a successful "meeting of the minds" will be the ability of collectivities to produce potent and enabling ideas, ideas that allow us to think and act more capably given that we cannot but be parts of nature. The "goal," then, will be not the satisfaction of self-consciousness or the achievement of humanity but the affirmation of radical mutual dependency and natural determination as conditions of our agency.

In the *Theological-Political Treatise*, Spinoza advocates democracy on the basis that a large number of thinking powers assembled together generate better ideas: "there is less reason in a democratic state to fear ridiculous proceedings. For it is almost impossible that the majority of a large assembly would agree on the same absurdity" (*TTP* 16.9). He develops this claim in the *Political Treatise*:

When all decisions are made by a few men who have only themselves to please, freedom and the common good are lost. The fact is that men's wits are too obtuse to get straight to the heart of every question, but by discussing, listening to others, and debating, their wits are sharpened, and by exploring every avenue they eventually discover what they are seeking, something that meets with general approval and that no one had previously thought of. (TP 9.14)

Discussion, discord, and listening produce what the deliberative body is seeking, something no one previously considered. Rather than the identical character of each person's fundamental yearning, deliberation exposes what the general approval determines to be useful. If we recall, Spinoza defines utility as what enables one to be affected and to affect others in a great variety of ways (E IV p38). Large assemblies are valuable, as I argued in chapter 2, because being moved and moving others require corporeal proximity.[79] Forces and energies need to combine and act in excess of the particular imaginings, desires, and volitions of the individuals involved.

A space of conflictual speaking is liberating not only because we may come to respect the powers of other reasoners and find our moral agency confirmed. It might liberate because other bodies and minds are the only possible source of our own power. We think only because others think (*homo cogitat* not *ego cogito*); we act only because others act. As parts of nature, our powers are synergetic combinations with other natural forces. The collective basis of any activity confirms the enabling aspects of our unavoidable dependency. Even if we are diminished and disabled by hatred and oppression, we manage to think and feel otherwise only by forming and fortifying alternative constellations of affect. Black does not become beautiful because those in power agree that it is beautiful. Rather, Black is beautiful because a group articulates and proliferates the words, feelings, institutions, and practices that erode the destructive forces institutionalizing the antithetical proposition. An oppressed person cannot simply see

---

79. Spinoza's advocacy of large deliberative assemblies does not exhaust his political philosophy, which I treat only selectively throughout this book. His political philosophy is a complex treatment of the uneasy relationship between passions and actions, irrationality and rationality, in the collective body. Although most interpretations exaggerate the difference between the ethical and the political projects, especially with respect to the putative pessimism Spinoza evinces about the potential for mass empowerment and collective activity, I select the example of deliberation by virtue of its proximity to the politics of recognition.

the truth in the claim that Black is beautiful but must join herself to those other counterpowers to engender new ways of being. At an exhilarating march, regardless of whether any new adjustments to the universal are achieved, protestors will feel beautiful. They will feel that their presence engenders joy and power in others and be strengthened by the recursive effect of the passionate exchanges. A successful march, then, is one that feels good, connects agents to one another, and thereby produces a circuit of empowerment. For the politics of imperceptibility, the agency constituted at such an occasion is limited as long as we measure success by either the index of humanization or the representations of the oppressed in the Other.

Imperceptible politics, as Grosz articulates it, does not have a particular end in view, other than seeking vitality, connection, and sharing of power in terms other than those prescribed by the dominant order. The politics of imperceptibility, as a particular expression of the project of renaturalization, may not, in my view, entail a wholesale revision of what counts as political practice. Even public deliberation, the realm of politics that is most often viewed in terms of intersubjectivity, recognition, and communicative action as the dialogical generation of rationality, can fruitfully be considered an open-ended project of vitality and discovery .

Just as public deliberation has been central to neo-Hegelian politics, consciousness-raising has been a core practice of feminist and Black liberation movements. Consciousness-raising might seem anathema to a theory that decenters self-consciousness and intersubjectively derived truth. As it is conventionally understood, consciousness-raising coincides neatly with the commitments of the politics of recognition to mitigate self-loathing. Catharine MacKinnon describes consciousness-raising as an intersubjective practice aimed at engendering a positive identity. She cites Sheila Rowbotham approvingly: "In order to discover its own identity as distinct from that of the oppressor, [an oppressed group] has to become visible to itself."[80] MacKinnon associates feminist liberation with becoming visible to oneself and others through a process of mutual self-clarification and group identification. Group identification engenders solidarity and new sources of self-esteem. Women find validation in other women who can recognize their contributions to society as meaningful, necessary, and world-sustaining. The method of discussing women's quotidian lived experience reveals patriarchy (a systematic form of "identity

---

80. Rowbotham, *Woman's Consciousness, Man's World*, 27; cited in MacKinnon *Toward a Feminist Theory of the State*, 84.

invalidation" for women) to be the source of their feelings of inadequacy.[81] The moral regeneration this feminist technique promoted resembles the aims of the politics of recognition. Consciousness-raising aims to attenuate self-loathing, produce solidarity and self-esteem, and generate a more accurate apprehension of oneself and other oppressed women. It aspires to see through patriarchal social conventions and undo the psychic mutilation they have wrought. The ultimate goal is to restore to women their moral agency as persons, eroding the conditions that maintain women as objects. It is unsurprising that "[t]he analysis that the personal is political came out of consciousness raising."[82]

Grosz's plea for an impersonal politics of bodies and natural forces may seem utterly alien to consciousness-raising. And it is contrary to such a practice as it is traditionally understood. Grosz would likely share the suspicions that Wendy Brown articulates with respect to feminist efforts to unveil the "'hidden truth' of women's experience."[83] An impersonal politics inspired by Nietzsche might have little more than contempt for a project that institutes a unitary female experience armed with Truth against patriarchy, a regime of distorting lies. Nonetheless, we might approach the practices around consciousness-raising from an impersonal perspective. Consciousness-raising among liberation groups involves gathering to speak, listen, and argue, as well as to plan public actions like marches, boycotts, campaigns, institutional reform, and sometimes more radical acts of sabotage, etc. An assembly of the oppressed might be reimagined as a collective production of powers, linkages, and transformations. Assembling to think and act with others who desire to live, feel, and experience themselves otherwise might find a place as an experimental process grounded in little more than the yearning to generate a counterpower, a new arrangement of corporeal forces, and alternative sources of pleasure and agency. Such consciousness-raising will not endeavor to recognize one another's experiences as analogous, or our relationships to the social structure as interchangeable. It will not be an effort to recognize "who we are." Rather, a politics of impersonality might focus on what we desire.[84] Following Grosz and Spinoza, impersonal politics takes its point of departure from the desire to enhance our pleasure and power the only way it can be done: together. It is an affective politics that seeks enabling relationships, wherever they may be found.

81. MacKinnon, *Toward a Feminist Theory of the State*, 91, 93.
82. Ibid., 95.
83. Wendy Brown, *States of Injury*, 42.
84. Ibid., 75.

An impersonal politics that endeavors to renaturalize rather than humanize the oppressed does not necessarily invalidate traditional feminist or antiracist practices of resistance, even as it reimagines and approaches them with new criteria of success. As renaturalists, we do not aim primarily to be understood and valued by our fellows. We pursue strength, affinities with other vital forces, and alternative futures. A politics of imperceptibility, like the politics of renaturalization, begins from the insistence that human existence is within and not above nature. We depend upon and affect innumerable forces, human and nonhuman. The measure of our agency that is determined by other's perceptions may be significant, but it is hardly the totality of our power and freedom. Preoccupation with our need to be seen as who we really are may be self-defeating. If our identities are constantly being revised, reinterpreted, and experienced differently in response to new encounters and relationships, we will often find what we never knew we were seeking. Although Spinoza himself exhibited little concern for women, a feminist politics of imperceptibility does not need him to recognize its validity. The politics of imperceptibility siphons enabling energy and power wherever it happens to find it. It infects and enjoins whichever beings and forces might aid in the construction of a joyful insurgency against patriarchy, misanthropy, imperialism, and, yes, "crippling self-hatred."

6

Nature, Norms, and Beasts

> People who study animals often say more about themselves than they do about animals.
> —CATHARINE MACKINNON

> All the notions by which ordinary people are accustomed to explain Nature are only modes of imagining, and do not indicate the nature of anything, only the constitution of the imagination.
> —BENEDICT DE SPINOZA

> We are the veal.
> —Bumper sticker

Spinoza insists that humans are not different from other natural beings, relentlessly criticizes the tendency to imagine God in anthropomorphic terms, and denies the existence of any special moral laws inscribed in nature or the heavens that might guide human endeavor. Yet he does not advocate humility with respect to nature, God, or other species.[1] Deep ecologists celebrate Spinoza for undermining the bases for human

---

1. At least, he does not advocate humility for the rational (*E* IV p53). More on this below.

exceptionalism. Similarly, poststructural Marxists find in Spinoza an ally against liberal notions of humanity that imply a given dignity as the ground of universal equality. These critics interpret Spinoza as an "antihumanist," meaning that his principles deny philosophical humanism's treatment of man as a special kind of being who chooses his fate, independent of structural forces and unconscious influences.[2] Ecological philosophers embrace and develop Spinoza's profound critique of anthropocentrism and the instrumentalization of nature.[3] Yet readers are troubled by the fact that despite his denial that man "through rank and dignity is a being entirely different from *things*, such as irrational animals," he asserts that we can do whatever we like with nonhuman things.[4] Although Spinoza does not place any special metaphysical value on humanity, he urges us to prefer ourselves and one another to other natural things. He appears to authorize the exploitation of nonhuman nature, even as he excoriates those who fantasize a God who might "direct the whole of Nature according to the needs of their blind desire and insatiable greed" (*E* I app).

I will argue that even if Spinoza's remarks on animals do not limit human exploitation, their principal point is not to determine anything about the relationship between human practices and flesh and blood beasts. Although Spinoza will not bolster a case for vegetarianism, his remarks on beasts are not even about animals per se. Rather, he admonishes us not to treat nonhuman nature and animals in particular as paradigms for human virtue. This admonishment has important implications for ecological as well as democratic appropriations of Spinoza. Deep ecologists have been most forcefully taken to task for disregarding that, for Spinoza, nature sets no standards for human behavior.[5] Yet commentators regularly imply that nature functions in Spinoza's thought as a standard against which to judge certain political forms and ways of life as defective.[6] Admittedly, it is tricky to navigate Spinoza's critique of anthropocentrism and his remarks on animals, because he rejects the elevation of humanity with such force that his objection to the humiliation of human-

---

2. See Althusser, "On Spinoza," and Tosel, *Du matérialisme de Spinoza*. Their chief targets were Kant and the German idealists for whom rationality and free will produce an "infinite" chasm between humans and the rest of nature, including animals.

3. For example, Mathews, *The Ecological Self*; Naess, "Spinoza and Ecology"; Sessions, "Spinoza and Jeffers on Man in Nature."

4. Kant, *Anthropology from a Pragmatic Point of View*, 15.

5. Lloyd, "Spinoza's Environmental Ethics"; Houle, "Spinoza and Ecology Revisited"; and de Jonge, *Spinoza and Deep Ecology*.

6. Israel, *Radical Enlightenment*, 274.

ity can easily be overlooked.[7] His remarks on animals demonstrate that he was not only concerned to deflate human pretension with respect to natural determination. He likewise opposed the direct inversion of a human-centered perspective, in which nonhuman nature becomes the model for existence, and human culture comes to appear as corrupt and subnatural. Thus, green and radical democratic Spinozists must beware of finding in the account of nature implicit norms to which humans ought to subordinate themselves.

The desire to find in the beast an alternative moral vision, a more natural idea of man, stripped of social distortion arguably lurks in democratic theory in the Rousseauvian vein as well as some ecological theory and animal ethics. If Spinoza is to be linked to these causes, each of us must be wary of the affects driving our critique of anthropocentrism. The politics of renaturalization must avoid enshrining nature as a new idol. To go beyond man, I argue in this chapter, we should not humiliate him. A rejection of humanism does not entail an ennoblement of the cosmos or animal instinct. A posthumanist politics sensitizes us to our permeability and involvement with nonhuman powers, without requiring us to subordinate ourselves to them. A liberating framework for thinking about who and what we are cannot emerge from self-hatred and a desire to repent, by virtue of which we are only "twice wretched" (*E* IV p54).

Although several commentators note Spinoza's lamentable attitude toward animals,[8] no one has discussed the keen psychological insight animating his remarks. His claims about animals militate against the misanthropic despair that can erupt as a reaction to impossible ideals and superhuman norms. Political norms derived from the presumption of perfect rationality and sovereign free will, or other putatively human traits that make us unlike any other "thing," can generate what I call "an antinomian dialectic." Spinoza's declaration that we can kill animals by virtue of their different "natures" takes aim at those who prefer animals to human company. He criticizes the retreat from the demands of civilization as a response to the harshness of the moral law. Thus, while the self-humiliation of man before nature appears to be the opposite of the celebration of philosophical humanism's deification of man, Spinoza finds that they are not really opposites at all. The admirer of beasts shares the

---

7. His earliest critics, however, were most struck by his removal of humility from the column of the virtues, and saw his philosophy as, first of all, a dethronement of God and an abominable inflation of man. Cooper, "Spinoza on Humility."

8. The sharpest condemnations are in Berman, "Spinoza's Spiders, Schopenhauer's Dogs," and Wolloch, *Subjugated Animals*.

humanist's desire for moral law but becomes corrupted by humility, the "sadness that arises from the fact that man considers his lack of power" (*E* III p55s). His feeling of impotence before the law makes antinomianism, the life of brutes, attractive.

In order to substantiate my interpretation, I systematically examine Spinoza's remarks on beasts (*bruta*). After elaborating his concern about what I call "the antinomian dialectic"—the human attraction to uncultivated savagery precisely because it is nonhuman, or more precisely *antihuman*—I proceed to discuss his conviction that we require a human exemplar in order to guide our actions. Spinoza's meditations on beasts must be understood in light of what he identifies as a necessary but problematic human need for exemplars, what we would today call "norms," to guide and measure our projects, aspirations, and institutions. As an alternative to the models of man or beast for a politics of renaturalization, I examine the posthumanist suggestion that the paradigm of "man" has become an obstacle to our collective vitality. If in the seventeenth century Spinoza identified a powerful "desire to form an idea of man, as a model of human nature which we may look to" (*E* IV pref), more recently Deleuze and Guattari strive to displace man with new and various figures of becoming. Man as the paradigm for human activity is first unseated by becoming-woman, a portal to the more profound transformations dubbed "becoming-animal" and "becoming-imperceptible." Deleuze reads Spinoza's ethics as an ethology to forge an understanding of Spinozism compatible with becoming-animal. I conclude with a discussion of ethology as a possible alternative to the humanist morality that opposes humanity to "things," including animals. This chapter is thus a critical effort to explore the limits and promises of an ethics and politics beyond the image of man.

The Beast Within

To date, Spinoza's scattered remarks on nonhuman animals have been discussed in relationship to an agenda of animal rights or a deep ecological stance toward nature.[9] By virtue of his remarks on animals, scholars object to the ecological appropriation of Spinoza. They claim that his antianthropocentric metaphysics does not translate into an argument for self-

---

9. Environmental ethics does not necessarily entail animal rights, but these are the terms that have been used in the debate around Spinoza's place in the environmental movement. For a treatment of the antagonism between the two, see Hargrove, *The Animal Rights/Environmental Ethics Debate*.

imposed human restraint when it comes to the exploitation of animals or other aspects of nonhuman nature. Indeed, they find that it is precisely Spinoza's anti-anthropocentrism that leads him to disregard nonhuman animals, since, by virtue of being unexceptional, humans have no obligation of stewardship toward nonhuman nature.[10] The argument concerns whether his rather lamentable attitude toward nonhuman animals is compatible with an ecological agenda. What this argument misses is that Spinoza's concern with beasts is almost entirely unrelated to the codification, legal or moral, of human behavior toward nonhuman animals. When Spinoza mentions animals, he is concerned, above all, with the desire to retreat from human community and to emulate nonhuman animals. In my view, Spinoza is not interested in nonhuman animals in their own right, but rather in the eruption of an anticivilization ethos that treats beasts as exemplars for humans to imitate and to admire.

Spinoza's ethics and politics remain necessarily inscribed within his naturalism, such that "reason demands nothing contrary to Nature" (*E* IV p18s). Living the best life in accordance with reason in no way entails belief in a uniquely human code that contravenes the brute forces of nature. By "nature," Spinoza, of course, does not mean primal wilderness, uncontaminated by civilization. Spinoza is not a protoromantic philosopher who encourages humans to discover the call of the wild. Indeed, he rejects back-to-nature cults as childish (*E* IV appXIII). Just as he is critical of humans' imagining themselves to be quasi-gods, able to transcend the laws that determine the rest of natural existence, he rejects the elevation of nature into something higher than humanity.[11] Spinoza's opposition to supernaturalism is based on the notion that it is precisely the norm of a godlike human who obeys a "higher law" that prompts so many philosophers, theologians, and moralists to look upon humanity with disgust. Indeed, he hopes that viewing humans to be like any other thing in nature contributes to social harmony (II p49s), for when we view each person, including ourselves, as the unique cause of his actions, we are overcome with hate, an urge to destroy the cause of harm (V p10s). But the best response to the deification of humanity, implicit in today's humanism, is not

---

10. See Berman, "Spinoza's Spiders, Schopenhauer's Dogs," 207; Curley, "Man and Nature in Spinoza"; and, Lloyd, "Spinoza's Environmental Ethics," 294.

11. For this reason, within my own text, I do not preserve Spinoza's capitalization of the word "nature" unless I am referring to the ideological tendency to revere Nature. This can be awkward, since lower-case nature refers to finite natures, or essences, and upper-case Nature designates infinite nature. Nevertheless, context can distinguish these natures sufficiently and avoid the misleading ideological implications of an overarching Nature that transcends finite natures.

the humiliation of man, understood as the association of ourselves only with our weakness (III p55s). A common psychological response to the idea that we *ought* to be like God (infinite forces of thought and will) too easily mutates into contempt for those, including ourselves, who fail to determine themselves, who "see the better but do the worse" and proceed to repentantly associate themselves and our kind with sadness (III p51s). In some cases, contempt for humanity prompts a celebration of bestial existence as more natural, more harmonious, and, paradoxically, less brutal. These cases are the subject of Spinoza's remarks on beasts.

Those who decry Spinoza's notorious "antitheriophilic" remarks neglect the primary object of his critique.[12] Spinoza, we will see, is not making pronouncements on human-animal relations in general but addressing those who romanticize "brutish" existence, seek a bond with beasts, and evince a preference for animal over human community. Spinoza takes aim at the (human) representation of animals *as exemplars* to be emulated and admired. Rather than a doctrine concerning the lives of flesh-and-blood animals, Spinoza's remarks issue warnings about tendencies of human imagination and identification. Although what he says about animals appears to many to reinstate anthropocentrism, I will argue that the imaginative tendencies he diagnoses and challenges are precisely those of the anthropocentric and narcissistic imagination.

A number of thinkers in the deep ecology movement find, with Arne Naess, that "[n]o great philosopher has so much to offer in the way of clarification and articulation of basic ecological attitudes as Baruch Spinoza."[13] In addition to Spinoza's staunch rejection of human exceptionalism, deep ecologists appreciate his view of reality as an "inter-connected whole" in which each and every being, be it a river or an antelope, is endowed with a *conatus* and strives toward "self-actualization."[14] While ecological interpreters tend to obscure the fact that, from a Spinozist perspective, computers, landfills, and consumer culture are equally parts of nature, they have also been taken to task for sidestepping Spinoza's "speciesism," evinced in his commitment to human well-being over and against that of nonhuman animals.[15] Naess defends his interpretation by alluding to what others have called Spinoza's "antihumanism."[16] Whereas Lloyd claims that

12. Wolloch, *Subjugated Animals*.
13. Naess, "Spinoza and Ecology," 54.
14. See, for example, Mathews, *The Ecological Self*.
15. Lloyd, "Spinoza's Environmental Ethics."
16. Cf. Melamed, "Spinoza's Antihumanism."

Spinoza's morality can never be anything but anthropocentric, Naess insists that Spinoza's affirmation of all right as natural is anathema to the moralism involved in a calculus of human versus animal rights.[17] While Naess's point is certainly valid, and I will build upon it in the final section of this chapter, he evades the problem of understanding Spinozist hostility toward a movement like deep ecology, which demands that humans radically limit their impact upon other life forms through, for example, aiming to decrease our population.[18] Naess does not directly confront Spinoza's claim that "whatever there is in Nature apart from men, the principle of seeking our own advantage [utilitatis] does not demand that we preserve it. Instead it teaches us to preserve or destroy it according to its use, or to adapt it to our use in any way whatever" (E IV appXXXVI).

The claim that anything other than fellow humans may be "used" to "our advantage" appears to exemplify "speciesism": "a prejudice or attitude of bias in favor of the interests of members of one's own species and against those members of another species."[19] As I argue in chapter 3, however, Spinoza does not understand "use" or "advantage" (utile) in instrumental terms. Spinoza affirms that "to man . . . there is nothing more useful than man" (E IV p18s) and that "when each man most seeks his own advantage [utile] for himself, then men are most useful to one another" (IV p35c2). "Use" has no derogatory connotations for Spinoza. A relationship of "use" implies neither exploitation nor instrumental utility. Humans are most useful to one another because we enable one another to affect and be affected in increasingly diverse ways, which enhances the receptive and active powers of our minds and bodies (IV p38). Moreover, the principle of *utile* implies not an exclusive good but rather a self-enhancing impulsion to community with others, where "community" ought to be understood as a (not exclusively human) multiplicity, able to communicate and join forces effectively. Nonetheless, Spinoza insists that our "advantage" consists in the cultivation of bonds and associations with other "similar things," above all, other "men." "Similar things" are those with the most corporeal commonalities. These commonalities are essential to our thriving, since those properties our bodies share include the common notions, the foundations of reason.

Given the privilege that Spinoza accords to similar things with which

17. Naess, "Environmental Ethics and Spinoza's Ethics."
18. For a good philosophical introduction to the deep ecology movement, see Zimmerman, *Contesting Earth's Future*.
19. Singer, *Animal Liberation*, 6.

we might best be able to "join forces," he holds that we are only prudentially obligated to preserve other natural beings that are useful to us. We can note an element of his antihumanism here, in that we are likewise, for better or for worse, only prudentially obligated, driven by our interest (*utile*), to preserve and enable other humans. There is no special duty to preserve human life as such, but the prudential mandate to augment the powers of our fellow humans is stronger in the case of those whose minds and bodies we can most enjoy (*E* IV appIX). The dictates of reason teach us to dedicate our energies to the preservation of any being that enhances our agency, understood as our active and passive powers to affect and to be affected by other bodies. Certainly, we are justified in interpreting the category of useful beings broadly to include much of nonhuman nature, as our survival clearly depends upon clean air, pacemakers, sewage treatment, and the myriad microorganisms in mutual symbiosis with our bodies.

Nevertheless, Spinoza puts humans capable of reason in a special, maximally beneficial category and explicitly allows for killing animals. He denies the desirability of alliance or identification with nonhuman animals. It is not with Spinoza that one will "run with the wolves." He rejects even sympathy toward the plight of slaughtered animals. He contends that "the law against killing animals is based more on empty [*vana*] superstition and womanish [*muliebri*] compassion than sound reason" (*E* IV p37s1). This assertion, along with Spinoza's repeated insistence that our bodies require "continuous and varied food so that the whole body may be capable of doing everything which can follow from its nature, and consequently, so that the mind may be equally capable of conceiving many things" (IV appXXVII), suggests that a Spinozan case for vegetarianism is not forthcoming. While we might argue that, in many cultural contexts, meat eating results in a less varied and imaginative diet, there appears to be no "manly" moral argument for curtailing human interests in order to promote the "self-actualization" of animals. There is no room in Spinoza's philosophy for a justice movement on behalf of animal flourishing for its own sake.[20]

Still, we must understand why Spinoza is so concerned with the "womanish" tendency to sympathize and identify with brutes that he introduces it no fewer than four times in the part of the *Ethics* dedicated to a study of human servitude. We can observe that Spinoza's remarks on "brutes" arise in similar contexts. The topic of animals usually appears

---

20. Cf. Rodman, "The Liberation of Nature?"

in the context of an acknowledgment of the preponderance of human irrationality and the near inevitability of violent conflict among us. In what remains of this section, let us consider his remarks systematically. Spinoza's "antitheriophilic" mentions of *bruta* can all be found in part IV of the *Ethics*, on human servitude. Spinoza refers to beasts in the discussion of three separate propositions and in one of the essential points listed in the long appendix. Three cases concern those who seek out animal community, or even prefer it to human association (*E* IV p35s1, IV p37s1, IV appXIII). The fourth case, which I will treat separately in greater detail, is an account of someone communing with beasts rather than with another human. The person who identifies with brutes over humans is no other than "the first man," Adam. Spinoza offers a peculiar account of the Genesis story in which the Fall is explained by Adam's mistaken belief (or perhaps "womanish" feeling) that the beasts in his vicinity resemble him more than his human mate, Eve (IV p68s). This rather odd interpretation of the human creation story—a text Spinoza surely studied with great care—suggests that he is eager to make a didactic point about the dangers of idealizing relationships with nonhuman animals. In fact, a zoophilic and misanthropic figure appears so many times in the *Ethics* that it may even signal a recurrent anxiety of Spinoza's. The misanthropic zoophile represents a perversion, a turning away from one's fellows ("similars"), by virtue of compassion for or mutual affection with beasts. I argue that the zoophile marks Spinoza's concern with a deification of nature as the inversion of human arrogance. The zoophile, rather than displacing it, succeeds only in inverting the image of an anthropocentric cosmic order in which the natural world reflects and serves human caprice. Nevertheless, we might glimpse in the recurrence of the zoophile a repressed challenge to his assertion that the affects of beasts are simply "different in nature from human affects" (IV p37s1). The zoophile might trouble Spinoza because it destabilizes the species frontier and the ethical community it promises to circumscribe, a permeable frontier according to Spinoza's relational ontology.

The zoophile first appears when Spinoza is in the course of demonstrating that reason's dictates urge each to "love himself, seek his own advantage, what is really useful to him, want what will really lead a man to greater perfection, and absolutely, that everyone should strive to preserve his own being as far as he can" (*E* IV p18s). At this point in the *Ethics*, he seeks to demonstrate that our basic drive toward self-enhancement leads not to a war of all against all but to the most robust expression of human community. Although passions can render people opposed to one another

(IV p34), insofar as we "agree in nature" we are necessarily good for one another (IV p31c). "Things which are understood to agree [*convenire*] in nature are understood to agree in power" (IV p32s). Thus, insofar as we act, or use our reason, we *convenire*, come together, fit, or form an enabling composition. The passions that prompt humans to "disagree in nature" are not fixed features of the human essence but rather expressions of our finitude, our inability to surpass those infinitely many forces in nature that do not accord with our striving (IV p3). We are not bound to enmity but easily become opposed to one another as well as ourselves by virtue of the passive affects that contradict our vital efforts. Although we can never bring it about that we are not subject to passions (IV p4), if we acted only from the laws of our singular natures, we would live in accordance with the adage "man is a God to man" (IV p35s).[21]

Yet, as Spinoza frequently laments, very few live in accord with reason's dictates, and as a result, humans are so often "burdensome to one another." The dangers and inconveniences of social life, however, are exaggerated by some to the extent that they elevate the life of brutes over that of humans.

> So let the satirists laugh as much as they like at human affairs, let the theologians curse them, let melancholics praise as much as they can a life that is uncultivated and wild, let them disdain men and admire brutes. Men still find from experience that they can provide themselves much more easily with the things they require, and only by joining forces can they avoid the dangers that threaten on all sides—not to mention that it is preferable and more worthy of our knowledge to consider the deeds of men, rather than those of brutes. (*E* IV p35s)

Who are these melancholic admirers of brutes? Who disdains humanity and endeavors instead to enjoy a savage and brutish existence?

Montaigne could conceivably have been the "womanish" melancholic Spinoza had in mind.[22] In his essay "On Cruelty," Montaigne confesses that he is easily perturbed by the death of an animal.

---

21. The "we" here is problematic from the point of view of contemporary political theory. Spinoza privileges rational or potentially rational actors. While one must be careful to understand by "reason" naturalized reason and to include many in the potentially rational category, his focus on power and capacity might neglect certain portions of "the least well off." I plan to discuss this elsewhere.

22. Nadler suggests that Spinoza read Montaigne, and the moralism inspired by him was alive and well in seventeenth-century Europe. See Nadler, *Spinoza: A Life*, 111.

> For myself, I have not even been able without distress to see pursued and killed an innocent animal which is defenseless and does us no harm. And as it commonly happens that the stag, feeling himself out of breath and strength, having no other remedy left throws himself back and surrenders to ourselves who are pursuing him, asking for our mercy by his tears . . .[23]

With the mention of the stag's tears, Montaigne evokes the mention of his own tears a few pages earlier: "There is nothing that tempts my own tears but tears."[24] Montaigne describes a communication of affect between himself and nonhuman animals. He does not acknowledge a firm distinction between humans and animals and avows a human obligation toward not only animals but all beings with "life and feeling," including trees and plants. The community of feeling, the involuntary imitation of affects that circulates between human and animal, prompts his declaration: "We owe justice to men, and mercy and kindness to other creatures that may be capable of receiving it."[25] Certainly, the stag whose tears and moans implore human mercy ought to be admitted into a community of moral consideration, for Montaigne.

What is melancholy in Montaigne's appeal? Is openness to animal affect necessarily a recipe for sadness and impotence? Not only is Montaigne a defender of "womanish" compassion for animals, he stands for a whole movement of moralists who viewed animals not only as rational and moral but as *more* rational and upright than human beings. Animal figures were seen to play a didactic role, serving as exemplars of distinctive virtues that humans should strive to imitate. The study of nature and nonhuman animals up until the seventeenth century was seen as a way of learning the moral order of the universe. As Peter Harrison puts it, "the behaviors of animals are so many representations of human passions, virtues, and vices, presented in a living pageant, accessible to the meanest minds, to the end that we might all learn moral rectitude."[26] Such a view is anathema to Spinoza's ontology for multiple reasons. Nature as a teleological moral diorama points only to man. On this model of Renaissance humanism, we ought to study animals and natural phenomena because they point to God's design for *us* and not to anything outside of us. "Animals are ciphers, insignificant in themselves, yet useful for humans

---

23. Montaigne, "Of Cruelty," *The Complete Works*, 383.
24. Ibid., 381.
25. Ibid., 385.
26. Harrison, "The Virtues of Animals in Seventeenth Century Thought," 468.

at every level."[27] Thus, Spinoza's rejection of anthropocentrism, even if it does not disapprove of cruelty toward animals, rejects this particular use of them. Animals are not for us. They are not role models that God placed on earth to teach us specific virtues. He condemns using beasts as indications of who we are and how we should behave. Spinoza's objective in his remarks on animals is to reject the notion that nonhuman animals are moral exemplars whose virtue and sagacity ought to be emulated by humanity, who, by virtue of our estrangement from nature, our "infinite difference" from things, tend toward corruption.

Montaigne's theriophilic celebration of natural virtue sits comfortably alongside an extraordinarily demanding moral paradigm for humanity. The very same essay that condemns cruelty against nonhuman animals could be viewed as a remarkable act of self-laceration. The opening pages hold up Socrates and Cato as models of human virtue. Montaigne expresses profound admiration of the pleasure and beauty Cato and Socrates found in their deaths.

> Witness the younger Cato. When I see him dying and tearing out his entrails, I cannot be content to believe simply that he then had his soul totally free from disturbance and fright; I cannot believe that he merely maintained himself in the attitude that the rules of the Stoic sect ordained for him, sedate, without emotion, and impassible; there was, it seems to me, in that man's virtue too much lustiness and verdancy to stop there. I believe without any doubt that he felt pleasure and bliss in so noble an action, and that he enjoyed himself more in it than in any other action in his life. *He so departed from life, as if he rejoiced in having found a reason for dying.*[28]

We ought to cultivate souls that would be "grateful to fortune" for such extraordinarily painful deaths to test us. For the virtuous, the pain of losing their entrails is an occasion for self-admiration, prompting secret joy like that of someone watching a tragic play.[29]

Montaigne's is a classical vision of a life that is measured by its death, which ought to be experienced with Stoic equanimity. Montaigne's particular representation of these ideals consists in both holding them out as exemplary and punishing himself (and, implicitly others) for any natural

---

27. Ibid.
28. Montaigne, "Of Cruelty," *The Complete Works*, 374,
29. Cf. Descartes's letter to Elisabeth, May or June 1645.

inclination toward virtuous action. Montaigne thus anticipates a Kantian suspicion toward morality prompted by inclination.[30] When we are naturally drawn to appropriate behavior, ours are "counterfeit virtuous actions" that merit blame rather than praise.[31] Only when a higher nature is acquired with great effort is the pleasure in virtue deserved. We must admire Cato and Socrates and even imitate them, but there is little hope that any of us will approximate the virtue they represent. They serve in Montaigne's own reflections as an occasion for self-castigation, since even though he has appropriate moral attractions and aversions, he owes them to a good father, his noble "race," and the ministrations of his tender nursemaid. His path to virtue was not arduous, not guided by reason or engendered by a "deliberate stiffening of the soul." Even when he is good, or rather even *because* he is good, he feels bad. Compare this to Spinoza's equation of virtue and power (*E* IV def8), his frequent claim that virtue is an expression of self-love, whose only reward is the joy and power that accompany it (IV p18s). Montaigne and his theriophilic followers in the seventeenth century are good candidates for that self-abnegating, melancholic admiration of beasts that concerns Spinoza.

Spinoza defines melancholy as a sadness in which "the body's power of acting is absolutely diminished or restrained" (*E* IV p42d). The "absolutely" suggests that melancholy is the ultimate expression of powerlessness. Elsewhere, he affirms the exigency of combating such total pain, which might be considered trivial by virtue of being emotional. "For why is it more important to relieve our hunger and thirst than to rid ourselves of melancholy?" (IV p45c). The transformation of our passionate disposition is as fundamental to our well-being as the basic factors of hydration and nutrition. Melancholy, applying as much to the soul as to the body, indicates a generalized impotence. Melancholics feel devoid of any capacity to improve their lot or that of others.

The importance of curing melancholy arises in the treatment of the proposition "Hate is never good" (*E* IV p45). Envy, mockery, disdain, and vengeance are all among affects that flow from hate: "sadness with the accompanying idea of an external cause" (III p13s). Hate and its derivatives are often a consequence of measuring humanity against a supernatural, unattainable norm, as I have argued throughout this book. The more we affirm humanity as a part of nature, subject to the same necessary determinations as any other being, the less we are prone to antipathy (II p49s,

---

30. Kant, *Grounding for the Metaphysics of Morals*.
31. Montaigne, "Of Cruelty," *The Complete Works*, 376.

V p10s). If we come to terms with our irreducible subjection to passions, we can better avoid being anti-pathetic, fleeing our inevitable condition. To invert Sartre, for Spinoza, we have a tendency to flee our servitude. The more we can renaturalize the idea of man that governs the social imagination, the less intense conflicts that issue from hateful affects will be. Hate, however, often has its way with love. When this happens to individuals, they can become melancholic such that their disgust with humanity mutates into a blanket valorization of the nonhuman. The failure to be a Cato or a Socrates can prompt one to seek the beast within (the inner beast rather than the inner child) as a site of freedom from the threatening ideal of man without.

The admiration of brutes is one reaction to human ideals predicated upon the transcendence of nature. The cult of the noble beast expresses hopelessness, a despairing urge to give up on one's own cultivation and to insulate oneself from suffering at the hands of other humans. Freud called this recoiling from any and all suffering, the withdrawal from relationality in general, "the death drive." When the demands of a rational life appear to be too great, one can come to desire a-rationality, the paradoxical desire for nothingness, the desire not to desire any longer.[32] For Spinoza, melancholy names the radical attenuation of drive, the overwhelming experience of being diminished, reduced to near total passivity.[33]

Further remarks concerning the melancholic appear in the appendix to part IV, which details key points to retain from Spinoza's examination of servitude. The note concerning animals appears on the heels of his reminder that "it is especially useful to men to form associations, to bind themselves by those bonds most apt to make one people out of them, and absolutely, to do those things which strengthen friendships." As usual, he qualifies his affirmation of the ethical and political desirability of becoming a single community built on friendship and mutual empowerment with a lament that too few live according to reason. When made to suffer the evils of men, humans are generally "more inclined to vengeance than to compassion." Great "art" and "vigilance" are required, he counsels, to deal well with our fellows, to understand them in terms of their peculiar

---

32. Freud, *Beyond the Pleasure Principle*.

33. Since there are only positive drives in Spinoza, this cannot be understood in precisely the same terms as Freud's death drive. Nevertheless, Butler may have a point when she claims that Spinoza's ethics has a place for the consideration of the death drive, in "The Desire to Live," 127. In my discussion of this article, I give her insufficient credit for this insight, although she does not consider the appropriate textual evidence. See Sharp, "Melancholy, Anxious, and *Ek-static* Selves."

dispositions, and to respond to them in constructive ways when they are hateful. Notably, the attraction to brutes appears, again, in close connection to misanthropy.

> But those who know how to find fault with men, to castigate vices rather than teach virtues, and to break men's minds rather than strengthen them—they are burdensome both to themselves and to others. That is why many, from too great an impatience of mind, and a false zeal for religion, have preferred to live among the brutes rather than men. They are like boys or young men who cannot bear calmly the scolding of their parents, and take refuge in the army. They choose the inconveniences of war and the discipline of an absolute commander in preference to the conveniences of home and the admonitions of a father. (*E* IV appXIII)

The comparison between those seeking to escape human society to live among savage brutes and impertinent adolescents who flee home to join the army may seem rather peculiar. This juxtaposition characterizes the youthful, zealous soldier and the misanthropic zoophile as similarly perverse. The admirer of brutes may fancy himself an iconoclast who enjoys unconstrained and natural freedom, but Spinoza suggests that he is rather like the impassioned soldier who desires an ineffable law, a law with no explicit rationale, that offers an alternative to the delicate art of constituting a life in common with others.

Both the young soldier angry with his critical father and the misanthrope disgusted with human frailty present melancholic figures. The desire to emulate wild brutes or yield to an anonymous commander instead of the all-too-knowing and familiar father indicate felt powerlessness. Like the boy who flees the authority of one father only to end up with another patriarch, a patriarch even less responsive to his idiosyncratic needs and desires, those whom Spinoza calls the "melancholic admirers of brutes" are bound in a spiral of misanthropy: they escape the demands of the moral law only to institute a new one, the law of brute Nature. Those who prefer community with beasts have much in common with the melancholic who is diminished to the point of giving up on enhancing his own agency through the most effective means, the cultivation of human association and friendship.

The *animi impatientia* resent the suffering of passions, a painful reminder of the human condition as one consisting of greater patience than agency. Spinoza admonishes nameless philosophers and theologians for surrendering the arduous task of educating and improving others, taking refuge in misanthropic criticism, and endeavoring to disable mental power through extolling the virtues of beasts as signs pointing to God's wishes for man. He accuses the moral zealot, of whatever cast, of relishing the defects of his fellows. Spinoza detects a sadistic pleasure of tearing out one's entrails among moralists. Even if one is vulnerable to violent death at war, the adolescent moralist finds consolation in the high and patriotic principles animating a soldier's life. In contrast, a virtuous education, on Spinoza's model, entails coming to understand oneself and others as vulnerable in perhaps a more radical way. All of one's relationships and contacts come to matter as constitutive determinations of one's being and power. Rather than being vulnerable to violent death—which is, of course, Hobbes's greatest concern—one is vulnerable to the transformations that genuine education provokes and the burden of continuing to transform oneself and others.

Throughout these propositions, *bruta*, while they are admired by those who feel impotent in the face of human evils, represent to Spinoza bellicose and violent tendencies. Those who prefer an uncultivated existence are analogous, according to Spinoza, to those who pursue war rather than a social human life. Spinoza's association of animals with warlike behavior, of course, has a long history. Grotius, for example, warns humans against the imitation of beasts: "Violence is characteristic of wild beasts, and violence is most manifest in war; wherefore the more diligently effort should be put forth that it be tempered with humanity, lest by imitating wild beasts too much, we forget to be human."[34] Spinoza is not unique in associating humanity with peace and violence with brutes. Yet he does not claim that there is a "human way" of interacting inscribed in each human heart that only needs to be heeded. No, men are inclined by nature to enmity (TP 2.14). Thus the misanthropic zoophile erupts regularly to qualify Spinoza's exhortations to human unity.

The connections Spinoza draws between religious zealotry, animal admiration, and war, moreover, imply that it is precisely the spiritual norm against which man is measured that produces solace to be had in war. Linking animal emulation to religious zealotry points to what I am calling the "antinomian dialectic," since war is the state of exception that suspends law. When the goodness at which spiritual education aims excludes most flesh-and-blood human beings, it easily yields repulsion at human frailty. Such disgust mutates from an excessive enthusiasm for the spiritual law into a rejection of human order altogether. Spinoza suggests that

---

34. Grotius, *De Jure Belli ac Pacis* 30.25.2, quoted in Rodman, "Animal Justice," 13.

the desire for the uncultivated life represented by the brute is akin to the desire for the absolute, indifferent, and unsympathetic regulation of the commander. The soldier receives no detailed rationale but only the principle that what he does is for God and Country. Similarly, the zoophile bows to the law of nature as something uncontaminated by human design and thereby unknowable. The Commander and Nature are brute, beyond and higher than the natural light of reason.

For the zealot who turns to nonhuman animal exemplars, man is fallen and beasts offer a path to salvation. Beasts appear to be untethered by the unforgiving human ideals that lead to self-castigation, misery, and misanthropy, but they remain mere expressions of those ideals insofar as they imply human failing. Spinoza's words on beasts diagnose the desires and affects engendering the figure of the animal as a model for human virtue. The image of the animal is not an animal in its own right but a wild, uncultivated anti-man and therefore an image *of* man (in both senses of the genitive). In turning away from the demands implied in the reigning model of man, they erect a new law, the law of nonhuman nature, the law *avant la lettre*, or, rather, *contre la lettre*.

If Spinoza rejects the standards of what became the hallmarks of liberal humanism—unconstrained will, disembodied mind, and incorruptible rationality—he also objects to a protoromantic naturalism that embraces animal instinct and disdains human order. What alternative does he provide? The resources for another kind of ethical norm—a philanthropic norm that avoids implying that we are either supernatural or subnatural—is implicit in his account of "the first man." Let us turn to the story of the garden of Eden to see how a politics of renaturalization might avoid both the deification involved in human exceptionalism and the turn to wild nature as ideal.

Animal Affects (and) the First Man

A parable for the human condition, the story of the expulsion from the garden of Eden is, of course, one of the most discussed stories in the Jewish and Christian traditions. It gives voice to a notion of human self-consciousness as that paradoxical grasp of ourselves as perfect and close to God but also weak and alienated from the natural world. What dualism attributes to the difference between our spiritual and our corporeal natures, the Fall portrays in temporal terms. Our sense of immortality, infinite intelligence, and uniqueness is a primordial memory, which was lost by virtue of an original sin, through which we were condemned to be, in the words of Augustine, "mortal, ignorant, and enslaved to the flesh."[35] To scan the history of philosophy and theology for interpretations of the story is to find innumerable accounts of what human perfection consists in and what precipitates its loss. For Maimonides, an example surely well-known to Spinoza, Adam's original perfection was his flawless intellectual grasp of truth and falsity, which, by virtue of appetite, devolved into the lesser, practical knowledge of good and evil.[36] In contrast, as Nancy Levene points out, for Augustine prelapsarian perfection consists in a perfect will, which is imperfectly exercised by the first man.[37] Original sin is the paradoxical necessity of the entirely uncoerced will, which, in its total indetermination, can choose evil as easily as good.

Spinoza invokes the story a number of times to illustrate aspects of the human condition (*E* IV p68s; *TTP* 2.14, 4.9–11; *TP* 2.14). Spinoza thereby participates in the tradition of treating Adam as an exemplar of humanity, an archetype of typical human existence, and, as we might expect, he puts his characteristic naturalist spin on the well-known tale. Adam serves, especially, as an example of our limitations, with which we must come to terms if we are to optimize our natural powers rather than fantasizing about a lost resemblance to divinity. Spinoza retells a rather peculiar version of the story in the *Ethics*, in which Adam's identification with beasts precipitates the Fall. In contrast to other philosophical glosses on the story, Spinoza's Adam is not originally perfect in either intellect or will. He is, in mind and body, "like us . . . subject to affects" (*TP* 2.6). The only perfection in the garden that Adam lost was the perfect accord between himself and Eve. Although she barely appears in his retelling, the only intimation of prelapsarian perfection in Spinoza's account of the Fall is the "mate, who agreed completely with his nature," or rather the perfect suitability of the pair, the fact that "there could be nothing in Nature more useful to him than she." Yet Adam forsook the perfect communion (*convenientia*) he might have enjoyed with Eve "after he believed the beasts to be like himself" and "began to imitate their affects" (*E* IV p68s).

The didactic story of paradise lost, on Spinoza's naturalized rendition, instructs us, just like his other remarks on beasts, that as detestable as human behavior can be, the perfection of our power can be had only in the human bond. Thus, Spinoza's account of "the Fall" reveals that even if he is sharply critical of the philosophical pillars maintaining human*ism*,

---

35. Augustine, *On Free Choice of the Will*, 105.
36. Maimonides, *Guide of the Perplexed*, bk. I, chap. 2.
37. Levene, "The Fall of Eden," 9.

he in no way advocates a turn away from humans. Insofar as it is true to Spinoza, then, the politics of renaturalization must, at the same time, negate human exceptionalism and seek human unity more than anything else.

Let us consider more closely his account of "the first man."

> And so we are told that God prohibited a free man from eating of the tree of knowledge of good and evil, and that as soon as he should eat of it, he would immediately fear death, rather than desiring to live. Then, man having found a mate who completely agreed with his nature, he knew that there could be nothing in Nature more useful to him than she; but that, believing that the beasts were similar to him (*bruta sibi similia esse credidit*), he soon began to imitate their affects (see III p27) and allowed his freedom to escape.

In an unusual version of the story in which neither Eve nor a deceitful animal seems to do anything, Adam loses his freedom by virtue of a belief in his similarity to nonhuman animals, which prompts him to incorporate brutish affects. The "social psychology" of the *Ethics* describes an involuntary circulation of affect among those beings we imagine to be similar to us (III p27), which, as we see in this case, is not restricted to fellow humans. As we noted above, Spinoza is opposed to "the law against killing animals" on the basis that animal affects are "different in nature from human affects" and do not agree with ours (IV p37s1). The lack of accord between human and bestial bodies, however, does not prevent them from communicating with one another. If our affects are different in nature, they are not so different that we are not highly susceptible to genuine transformations provoked by animal affect. If the affects of beasts disagree with our natures, it is because they decompose our power.[38] We can observe Spinoza erecting a boundary between man and beast precisely because nothing actually prevents profound community between us. The frontier between human and beast is sufficiently permeable to prompt Spinoza's repeated concern that animal attractions will divert us irrevocably away from "the rational principle of seeking our own advantage[, which] teaches us to establish a bond with men, but not with the beasts" (IV p37s1). However (un)justified we may find Spinoza's concern with grizzly men and cat women, his worry is that humans may come to prefer beasts to one another.

Adam, in particular, had before him in the garden another human

---

38. See Montag, "Imitating the Affects of Beasts."

whose nature (essence) agreed perfectly with his own. Recall that to agree in nature is to agree in power (*E* IV p32d), and thus Adam and Eve might have joined minds and bodies to engender great joy and lively ideas. Had he turned toward Eve rather than undergoing the affects of beasts, Adam might have enjoyed the freedom that emerges when "two individuals of entirely the same nature are joined to one another," composing "an individual twice as powerful as each one" (IV p18s). There was no other being in the garden with which he could have combined powers more joyously or to better effect. Yet despite the fact that he "knew that there could be nothing in nature more useful to him than she," his feeling of kinship with the beasts disrupted the human bond that might have allowed him to live, like philosophers, beyond good and evil (*Ep* 19).

Spinoza's odd recapitulation of the Fall follows the proposition that reads, "If men were born free, they would form no concept of good and evil so long as they remain free." The counterfactual in the proposition suggests that Spinoza does not, like other interpreters of the story, maintain that Adam was originally free and thereby equipped with perfect knowledge. Indeed, he begins his account of the Fall elsewhere with what I have deemed the fundamental thesis of renaturalization.

> Yet most people believe that the ignorant violate the order of Nature rather than conform to it; they think of men in Nature as a dominion within a dominion. They hold that the human mind is not produced by natural causes but is directly created by God and is so independent of other things that it has an absolute power [*potestatem*] to determine itself and use reason in a correct way.

Spinoza proceeds to meditate again on the Fall and concludes that "it must be admitted that it was not in the power of the first man to use reason aright, and that, like us, he was subject to affects" (*TP* 2.6). Thus, in contrast to Maimonides' account, Spinoza's Adam does not begin with a perfect intellect that is corrupted by appetite. The story of the Fall, through his eyes, is not a story of the infinite mind limited by its earthly body. Rather, Adam shows us that, originally and irreducibly, the human condition is one of "intellectual vulnerability."[39] Our minds are vulnerable, moreover, not because they are entwined with our bodies, but because they are "produced by natural causes." Minds, no less than bodies, are

---

39. Ravven, "The Garden of Eden," 29.

bound in a community of cause and effect, necessarily affecting and affected by ambient forces, including nonhuman ones, like beasts.

Neither Adam nor any of us is born free and omniscient. Spinoza takes "as a foundation what everyone must acknowledge: that all men are born ignorant of causes" (E I app). As a result, we are compelled to look to a "model [*exemplar*] of human nature" and to form concepts of good and evil relative to this model. "I shall understand by good what we know certainly is a means by which we may approach nearer and nearer to the model of human nature we set before ourselves," and by evil "what we certainly know prevents us from becoming like that model" (E IV pref). Thus, as for Maimonides and in contrast to many in the Christian tradition, knowledge of good and evil is not an index of our perfection. Maimonides invokes what is "well-known to every Hebrew scholar" to resolve the apparent contradiction whereby Adam and Eve seem to become wiser by virtue of eating the fruit. Namely, he claims that "and ye shall be as *Elohim* knowing good and evil" (Genesis 3:5) likens humans not to God (one possible meaning of *Elohim*) but rather to "princes" (a justifiable and more plausible meaning, on his account). Knowing good and evil, then, does not elevate human knowledge but demotes it to the imaginative, practical wisdom of rulers.

Heidi Ravven argues that for Maimonides and Spinoza, moral knowledge, the adjudication of good and evil, is necessarily imperfect, imposed by the limitations of the intellect. Thus, for Maimonides, "Adam's fall signals a regretful turn to a life focused on a lower ideal, a negative ideal, that of self-control, social justice and harmony."[40] Likewise, Shlomo Pines remarks that for Spinoza and Maimonides it appears not that Adam illicitly tasted knowledge of good and evil and was thus punished, lest he become too powerful, but that knowledge of good and evil, being an inferior mode of knowing, is itself the punishment![41] Put more naturalistically, moral knowledge is a consequence of our finitude. The human condition forces us to act like princes, such that we are constrained to calculate the relative virtues of good and evil in a given situation to remain viable. To have a moral sensibility means that we must, like Adam, affect and be affected with highly imperfect knowledge of what our decisions will yield. We reach out for the means of becoming more powerful, but there is never

---

40. Ibid., 13.
41. Pines, "On Spinoza's Conception of Human Freedom and Good and Evil," 149, quoted in Ravven, "The Garden of Eden," 28.

any guarantee that we will discern the best means, or that we will become more powerful in the ways anticipated. Like a prince, as Machiavelli tells us, we must remain ever vigilant and responsive to the vicissitudes of fortune.

As compelling and instructive as the comparison with Maimonides is, we can also note differences precisely in relationship to the question of the animal. For Maimonides, prelapsarian Adam enjoyed a perfect intellect, but appetite derailed his powers and constrained him to a lower ideal of self-regulation. To those who see knowledge of good and evil as an increase in human perfection, it may imply that, prior to the Fall, "God originally intended for humanity to be 'like the beasts, devoid of intellect.'"[42] Maimonides is keen to reject this notion on the basis that Adam must have been rational in order to receive God's command. Yet perfect knowledge of God's directive is precisely what Spinoza denies. For Spinoza, we find Adam originally embedded in nature, subject to affects, and unable to discern what is conveyed by the natural light. "The command given to Adam consisted solely in this, that God revealed to Adam that eating of that tree brought about death, in the same way that he reveals to us through our natural intellect that poison is deadly" (*Ep* 19). Adam's idea of the noxious fruit was confused and inadequate, and he thereby believed he was prohibited from eating the fruit rather than warned about potential ill effects of doing so. For Spinoza, then, it is not that humanity came to think prudentially like a prince but that God, or nature itself, appeared "as a kind of legislator exclusively with respect to Adam" (*TTP* 4.9). What, adequately conceived, is nothing other than the natural fact of disagreeability between Adam's body and the fruit was perceived imperfectly as a rule that he could obey or disobey.[43]

Whether Spinoza tells the story as one of decomposition provoked by toxic fruit or of the affects of beasts, it is a story of a finite, imperfect being, undermined by a disabling relationship. Adam loses freedom (power) because he does not know what kind of being he is. He does not adequately understand that he is a part of nature and therefore profoundly affected by his involvements with others, human and nonhuman. The abstraction of the garden of Eden allows one to see a man in relationship to some of the greatest influences on his freedom and power: God/nature, woman, and beast. We observe the human tendency to imagine God as a legislator, his

---

42. Ravven, "The Garden of Eden," 6.
43. Deleuze forcefully brings out Spinoza's naturalistic account of good and evil on the model of poisoning in *Spinoza: Practical Philosophy*, chap. 3.

human mate as a helper, and beasts as worthy of emulation. We see several mistakes of religious consciousness, according to Spinoza. Humans go astray when we dream that we are God or beast and thereby estrange ourselves from those to whom we are most similar. The tragedy of the Fall is a tragedy Spinoza observes every day: it is the failure to regard the human bond as the most essential source of power and freedom. At least one moral of the story, on my interpretation, is that despite his denial of a self-same human essence, Spinoza avows a need to consider ourselves to be human. When he refers to our "desire to form an idea of man, as a model of human nature to which we may look," he warns us against striving to be other than we are. He notes that "a horse is destroyed as much if it is changed into a man as if it is changed into an insect" (*E* IV pref) to remind us that no being is liberated by transcending its nature.[44] To engage in liberatory practices, "it is necessary to come to know both our nature's power and its lack of power" (IV p17s). Adam, our archetype, reminds us that we will never enjoy a mind "so independent of other things that it has absolute power to determine itself and use reason in a correct way" (*TP* 2.6). Yet Adam's story is not such a tragic story, since the portal to freedom has not been closed, even if it can be difficult to produce the conditions under which we might enter it. He, and perhaps we, need only to overcome our estrangement from Eve. If only we did not feel the allure of gods or beasts. Yet we will not cease feeling torn in different directions, because we are still part of nature, still mutating in response to the human as much as the inhuman.

The temporal aspect of the Fall points to our inevitable reliance on norms. Because we are in time, we cannot apprehend all that happens to us *sub specie æternitatis*. We must act, which means we must respond to and enter into relations with others. These others are not under our control or fully known to us, just as we remain largely unknown to ourselves. Thus, we conjure and act in light of ideas of human nature to help us to identify those with whom we might relate in the most enabling ways. Finitude thereby imposes morality on us, but we can think about this morality in different ways. For philosophical humanism, moral norms follow from the idea that to be human is to be capable of reason and responsible for subordinating our actions to universal principles. Morality gestures toward our infinite natures, our putative ability to transcend inclination and affect, in favor of reason. But for Spinoza, Adam tells us no less than

---

44. Spinoza is thus not a friend to "transhumanism," a peculiar philosophical vision of technologically produced immortality. See Wolfe, *What Is Posthumanism?* xv.

our own experience that "it is no more in our power to have a sound mind than a sound body" (*TP* 2.6). Perhaps following Maimonides, Spinoza tells us that the need for moral law, and the corresponding image of man to guide our actions and identifications, is an expression of our finitude, our inability to be determined only by what we perceive to be true and false.

Spinoza believed, for better or for worse, that the figure to guide us in our practical effort to persevere in being and enhance our power must be human. Spinoza acknowledges that we often resist thinking of ourselves in relation to "the universal idea of man or animal" (*E* III p55s), but he hopes that we can form an idea of humanity that will be a source of strength, even if it will never be purely rational. Much of the *Ethics* concerns itself with the disabling effects of a superhuman ideal, a godlike being who does not suffer the natural determinations of cause and effect. To dismantle this ideal, Spinoza undoes the whole theological architecture upon which supernaturalism depends. Yet he also warns us not to err in the other direction by subordinating ourselves to a figure of unadulterated nature. Even if philosophers are more prone to illusions of grandeur than to self-debasing melancholy, it is important to take heed of his lesson for several reasons: First, it underlies the constitutive impact of fantasy. Adam imitates the beast, and insofar as the Fall marks a genuine transformation in his existence, we can see that affects and emotions are not transient experiences. Who we think we are and those with whom we identify matter. Affects materialize the contours of our bodies and selves. Second, to entertain a false idea of ourselves is to overlook one another and thus the real sources of our power. To dream we are either God or beast is to forget that it is all about Eve.

Spinoza's naturalism aims to regard singular beings, especially "men," as he says many times, as they are, and not as we would like them to be. If we were free, we would not require these exempla that abstract from the singularity of each individual. But, no less than Adam, we are born ignorant of the causes shaping our desire and our fantasies about ourselves. Our bondage is such that we desire in relationship to an exemplar, a norm that embodies what we hope to become, but we must be wary of any disabling features of this ideal. Spinoza's suspicion of universals notwithstanding, he maintains the need for provisional boundaries to our exempla in order to avoid allowing our fantasies of other kinds of beings to govern our guiding fiction, the human ideal. Spinoza's story of the Fall suggests that Adam suffered because his self-ideal excluded Eve. Despite Spinoza's insistence elsewhere that women are naturally inferior to men (*TP* 11.4), sexual difference does not diminish the perfect agreement between Adam and Eve. We might even see in Adam's mistaken identification with beasts an acknowledgment, probably unconscious, on Spinoza's part of the barrier posed to human community by (male perception of) sexual difference. If Adam had been perfectly free, he would have acted on his clear and distinct perception of the perfect agreement between his body and Eve's. Moreover, he would have done so not because he viewed himself and her to be equally human but because he perceived their distinctive natures to be perfectly compatible with one another. Without perfect awareness of which bodies best agree with ours, Spinoza thinks we can lay down a general maxim that agency is most fortified by human community and friendship. Adam's exemplarity reveals that, first and foremost, humans need compatible partners to enhance their minds and bodies. An enabling exemplar of humanity shows that paradise is regained when we "so agree in all things that the minds and bodies of all would compose, as it were, one mind and one body" and men "want nothing for themselves which they do not desire for other men" (*E* IV p18s; cf. IV p68s, conclusion of the parable of the Fall).

Much of the *Ethics* makes the point well recognized by current social criticism that when our models are supermodels we can come to feel hateful toward ourselves and others. The less recognized lesson is that humanity appears equally defective if it is measured against the model of the beast, where "beast" stands for unmodified natural instinct or unmediated harmony with the natural order. Spinoza's remarks on beasts, including the tale of the Fall, concern animals as images *of* man. The story of Adam warns us about how not to think of ourselves as parts of nature. While it is absolutely necessary to affirm that we are part of nature, this does not imply a natural ideal for human existence, especially where "natural" connotes nonhuman or antihuman. Spinoza diagnoses a turn away from humanity toward the emulation of beasts as a corrosive despair in relation to one's own kind Thus, even when our models are hairy and shameless, they may be expressions of self-hatred.

Deleuze reads the parable of Adam as a great challenge to moralism. With Spinoza's naturalistic model of good and bad, he takes ethics beyond the bounds of Spinoza's philanthropic antihumanism to a more radical posthumanism. As part of an effort to think without the crutch of a human exemplar, an avowed fiction in Spinoza's philosophy, Deleuze reads the ethics as an ethology, a horizontal plane of beings affecting one another and striving to form fruitful compositions of agency. In the final section, I will explore Deleuze's alternative to Spinoza's insistence on an exemplar of man to avoid the temptation of imagining ourselves as divinities or noble savages.

Ethics as Ethology?

The flight to nonhuman nature is not a practice of renaturalization but a flight from (our) nature. To strive to act from joyful affects, Spinoza commands that we love ourselves and our fellows, warts and all, for better and for worse. He insists that we be guided by an image of *man*, rather than of God or animal, superman or anti-man, because his project is philanthropic. Spinoza identified a desire for a self-loving and self-emancipating exemplar of man, against the background of quasi-divinity and pseudo-brutality, but today there is a desire for something stranger, something other than either man or even humanity.

If in the seventeenth century Spinoza identified a powerful "desire to form an idea of man, as a model of human nature which we may look to" (*E* IV pref), in the second half of the twentieth century, Deleuze and Guattari suggest displacing man with various alternative figures of desirous becoming. Man as the paradigm for human activity is first unseated by becoming-woman, which comprises a portal to even more transformative becomings in the form of becoming-animal and, ultimately, becoming-imperceptible. Deleuze's suggestion that Spinoza's ethics should be read as an ethology is proper to an understanding of Spinozism compatible with becoming-animal. Deleuze displaces anthropocentric moralities with ethics as ethology.

Deleuze claims that because an "individual is first of all a singular essence" or "a degree of power" rather than a class of being, Spinoza's ethics should be considered to be an "ethology." Ethology is the study of animal, including human, behavior. It thus treats human and nonhuman animals on the same horizontal plane. From the perspective of ethology, "animals are defined less by the abstract notions of genus and species than by a capacity for being affected, by the affections of which they are 'capable,' by the excitations to which they react within the limits of their capability."[45] Deleuze proposes ethology as a matrix of intelligibility for Spinoza's ethics for several reasons. First, he aims to mark the distance between Spinoza's ethics and moral theories, which are generally predicated upon the uniqueness of humans as a class of being opposed to animal or natural

---

45. Deleuze, *Spinoza: Practical Philosophy*, 27.

being.[46] To undermine a system of generic laws grounded in human exceptionalism, Deleuze's somewhat peculiar appropriation of ethology highlights the irrelevance of species boundaries. He accents how Spinoza's philosophy destabilizes ontological differences between beings, as much as between Being (God or Nature) and beings.[47] Likewise, because ethology concerns effective singularities rather than generic types, it is better able to treat transindividual powers, or what are called "assemblages" in Deleuze's vocabulary. The notion of ethological ethics strives to renaturalize human existence and underscore the genuine alternative that Spinoza's philosophy offers. In this section, I will proceed to explore what ethics as ethology entails and conclude with a consideration of whether it escapes the concerns that Spinoza raises with respect to animal emulation as an expression of misanthropy.

For Deleuze, Spinoza's ethics must be understood in opposition to morality. Whereas morality implies a doctrine of what rational beings *ought* to do, ethics concerns the question of liberating what it is "a body *can* do." Ethological ethics is an affective alternative to a spiritual rationality, which circumscribes the moral community within a zone of prescriptive principles or universal laws. Rather than aiming to define the moral community based on shared spiritual or moral powers, as humanism and politics of "personality" inevitably do, ethology ascertains singular units of agency, where agency refers to the power to affect and to be affected. "Singularities" name provisional effective assemblages rather than stable, selfsame spiritual identities or indivisible souls. Deleuze's understanding of singular being recalls Spinoza's definition: "if a number of individuals so concur in one action that together they are the cause of one effect, I consider them all, to that extent, as one singular thing" (*E* II def7). Ethology, for Deleuze, concerns the capacities of individuals as singular degrees of power, while "consideration of genera and species still implies a 'morality.'"[48]

---

46. Lloyd and Gatens also discuss this aspect of ethology in *Collective Imaginings*.

47. On Spinoza's thought as a rejection of ontological difference, see also Negri, *The Savage Anomaly*.

48. Deleuze, *Spinoza: Practical Philosophy*, 27. Deleuze clearly adopts a somewhat peculiar notion of ethology, however faithfully, from Jacob von Uexküll. For others, ethology belongs precisely to a mode of thinking in terms of species norms and regularities. A very different argument for the relevance of ethology for ethics makes the following claim: "To the degree that human nature is homogenous, the very general principles according to which men may flourish, or fail to flourish, as individuals or groups, will also be homogenous. And it is such principles on which both morality ultimately depends, and ethology may be expected to shed some light." Meynell, "Ethology and Ethics," 291.

A taxonomy of genera and species "implies a morality," because morality subordinates individual cases to general laws. As Hegel's unhappy consciousness illustrates, morality is most basically the subjection of the changeable to the unchangeable, the submission of the natural and evolving self to the unyielding eternal law.[49] A moral perspective encounters a singular being, event, or circumstance and refers it to the principles appropriate to its type, class, or natural kind. Moral reasoning affirms that to be human, for example, is to conform one's actions to a stable, universalizable principle valid for all rational beings (divine, human, and/or alien), rather than to inclination, impulse, or biological "nature." Thus universal, spiritual principles unify apparently diverse individuals by guiding and judging their multifarious actions and life choices.

Morality often functions by using one notion of nature (human nature) against another notion of nature (mere or animal nature). As the moral perspective evolves from Descartes to Kant and Hegel, "human nature" becomes "personhood," which isolates the spiritual and rational from sensuous determination, aligning moral agency only with the rational aspect of ourselves.[50] In other words, human existence is increasingly defined against nature, as antinature.[51] What distinguishes and unites humans is their being thinking things, entities who operate according to a purely spiritual logic, freed from natural determination, unencumbered by the forces governing corporeal life. In Spinoza's time, Descartes is clear that morality involves the mastery of nature, in the form of both the body and external nonhuman beings. Arguably, the perspective of morality reaches its most nuanced expression in Hegel, who finds that ethical life composes its necessary ground and supplement. Even as the body and nature are not reduced to pure instrumentality in Hegel, they are progressively internalized by Spirit, which aims to know itself as the whole of reality. Moreover, this realization of Spirit must take the form of "forgiveness," since nonconforming nature will stubbornly erupt and disrupt Spirit's self-concept. Nature always remains a problematic factor for Hegel, which must be either domesticated or forgiven for ethical life to reach its highest expression. The perspective of morality in the humanist tradition elevates

---

49. Hegel, *Phenomenology of Spirit*, chap. 4, sec. B.
50. Poole argues that the opposition of person to human has disastrous consequences for moral thought ("On Being a Person"). Posthumanists go even further by suggesting the cleavage between human and nonhuman is likewise disastrous and, as I have suggested, has become inextricable from the notion of humanity.
51. Humanism is, in truth, to use a Hegelianism, transhumanism.

the human species out of the natural order of cause and effect precisely through a process of dominating, mastering, or "educating" brute nature within and without. Morality is an expression of the anthropocentric cosmos that bifurcates spirit and nature, self and world, mind and body. By virtue of the ostensibly unique ability to act in accordance with a self-authorized law that is valid for one's species as a whole, morality endows humanity with a "second nature" that subordinates its given nature. Humanist politics absorbs a notion of morality as the force by which brute nature, the nature of brutes, becomes properly human nature, a nature that is increasingly antinature.

Morality entails an attractive universalism whereby all those who fall into the category of human are due, in contemporary terminology, "equal consideration" or "respect." Moral arguments have been and will likely continue to be important political tools by which women, racialized groups, and more recently (humans on behalf of) nonhuman animals can insist on the injustice of being treated as means to the ends of others. The ongoing struggle among humans and nonhumans to be included within the class of humankind, however, reveals how particular universal categories remain. The duties and obligations that follow from a moral law vary depending upon whether one is recognized as belonging to the human species, or whether one is "sufficiently" and "relevantly" similar to humans.[52] One hardly needs to point out that those from another nation, culture, religion, or ethnic group, as well as those who are not recognizably gendered, often receive a different sort of moral consideration than those who belong to the type with which one identifies. The category of humanity is always subject to interpretation by the dominant institutions, as Foucault demonstrates so clearly in his career-long examination of the "human sciences." Yet given the appeal and effectivity of moral strategies, however imperfect they may be, it is not surprising that efforts to improve the lot of nonhuman nature generally aim to extend rather than problematize the category of humanity.[53] Deleuze and others suggest that perhaps a greater challenge to human imagination and narcissism is in order. Rather than extending human principles, posthumanists suggest that we embrace an ethical perspective that interrupts them altogether. Given the mixed success of humanist arguments, a nonjuridical activism inspired by ethology rather than morality is a promising alternative. A perspective that advo-

---

52. I am alluding here to Regan's language in *The Case for Animal Rights*.
53. Rodman presents a trenchant critique of this strategy in "The Liberation of Nature?"

cates equal respect based upon a shared ability to subordinate our natural to our spiritual selves involves significant losses along with any gains, from the perspective of renaturalization. Even so, given that we stand to lose the moral grounds for demanding equal respect, what do we stand to gain by pursuing a nonmoral, ethological ethics?

Deleuze finds that, rather than "laws," ethology involves a complicated and "lasting prudence."

> Such studies as [von Uexküll's tick], which define bodies, animals or humans by the affects they are capable of, founded what today is called *ethology*. The approach is no less valid for human beings, than for animals, because no one knows ahead of time the affects one is capable of; it is a long affair of experimentation, requiring a lasting prudence, a Spinozan wisdom that implies the construction of a plane of immanence or consistency. Spinoza's ethics has nothing to do with a morality; he conceives it as an ethology, that is, a composition of fast and slow speeds, of capacities for affecting and being affected on this plane of immanence.[54]

Ethology demands a patient and tentative prudence that entails experimentation and "the construction of a plane of immanence or consistency." Rather than internalizing a set of principles that will be valid for any occasion and situation, ethology constructs and organizes a plane, a flat horizon of action and passion. As obscure as this may sound, with the notion of the "plane of immanence," Deleuze suggests that there is only one order of being. Thus, there is no superior aspect of the self, or realm of being, that might order the other part. There is no rational principle that ought to command the "natural," corporeal, affective, or sensuous aspect of oneself or the world. The plane of immanence expresses an ontology with a "flat geography." The plane of immanence, what he sometimes calls "the univocity of being," names a horizontal field of powers and counterpowers that can be arranged from within in more or less enabling ways from the perspective of distinct agents, or "degrees of power," but that cannot be directed from without to reflect an external or higher principle.

Deleuze and Guattari call Spinoza "the prince of immanence" by virtue of his comprehensive effort to eliminate any distance between God and nature, Creator and creation.[55] Spinoza affirms that God is an "immanent

---

54. Deleuze, *Spinoza: Practical Philosophy*, 125.
55. Deleuze and Guattari, *What Is Philosophy?* 60.

cause" of all that exists (*E* I p18), which dissolves any gulf between the spiritual and the natural. All that exists is in God, and God is in all that exists (I p15). As Spinoza's *Ethics* progresses, God "disappears" into nature and we are left with an infinitely complex but flat horizon of being.[56] If everything is nature, for Spinoza, there is no extracausal realm of freedom, truth, or reason to which bodies, impulses, and feelings ought to be made to conform. Likewise, there is no corrupt or defective nature that needs to be realigned with a given natural harmony. Neither Nature nor Spirit functions as a normative horizon against which to judge actually existing beings. The plane of immanence eliminates any external standards.

Ethological ethics, therefore, must be enacted within a terrain of horizontal relationality rather than upon a vertical axis of subordination. Since the relationships that constitute one's power and vitality vary for each and every being, we must become practiced at arranging and rearranging our affective communities. Rather than internalize universal laws of self-governance, the ethological agent slowly acquires prudential rules of composition and becomes alert to forces of decomposition.

Deleuze proceeds to make the rather abstract claim that ethology entails "a composition of fast and slow speeds." This remark refers to Spinoza's physics, upon which his ethics is based (*Ep* 27). Bodies retain their singular integrity only by virtue of preserving a certain "ratio of motion and rest" (*E* II p13L6). To persevere in being, bodies must be able to undergo many changes, interact with myriad ambient beings, and avoid entering into composition with those beings that can destroy their "natures" or "essences." A human body that enters into composition with a sufficient quantity of arsenic, for example, will no longer be able to retain its essence. It will undergo an alteration beyond what its nature allows and mutate into a new form (i.e., die). One who frequently has occasion to note Oscar Wilde's observation that "alcohol, taken in sufficient quantities, produces all of the effects of intoxication" may transform her body to the extent that its nature (essence) is extinguished. One may appear to maintain a continuous identity, but, Spinoza notes, death does not require a corpse (*E* IV p39s). How often we transgress our characteristic threshold of motion and rest is an open question in Spinoza's text, but it is clear that fatal decomposition takes many forms.

In the other direction, Spinoza highlights the enabling composition

---

56. The imagery of "disappearance" comes from Montag, "Spinoza: Politics in a World without Transcendence."

into greater and greater communities of affect, such that singulars of the same nature might join and become twice as powerful (*E* IV p18s). Deleuze underscores how virtue names the enhancement of one's vital power, such that ethological ethics becomes a sometimes unconscious, sometimes knowledgeable, praxis of entering into relations with other beings in enabling ways. Such compositions will not necessarily be recognizable, and the threshold of transformation, as Spinoza implies in multiple places, does not remain confined to individual or specific identity.

Ethology, with its focus on affects rather than individuals or species, is especially well equipped to renaturalize a conception of agency. A qualitative examination of affects foregrounds concrete and particular compositions of power. Ethology takes the "body as model," never presuming in advance that anyone knows what a body can do.[57] If the body is a model, it is not a blueprint, since Spinoza emphasizes the opacity of the body. Like a body, agency is a provisional effective unity of myriad diverse parts. The prudential cultivation of agency, then, is not the transparent light of the moral law. Spinoza clearly rejects the dualist model of agency as self-rule implied by morality. Action within a plane of immanence opposes any notion of activity that depends upon the transcendence of one's situation, impulse, or causal environment. Action becomes an endeavor to cultivate a sensuous receptivity, in order better to determine the relations of composition that most enable one to think and thrive. Since one can exist and act only by virtue of the affects that circulate in one's environment, ethological ethics entails the development of mutually beneficial affective compositions.

The musical metaphor that "composition" suggests is apt, since it points to the passivity involved in listening as well as the need to hear not only discrete notes but the involvement and play between them. While agents as composers certainly act, we are constrained by the tones available and guided by the relationships *between* them, what they do in concert with one another. Spinozan ethics involves contact, receptivity, and openness to the effects that various encounters and combinations yield. Spinoza's ethics does not involve a blanket embrace of all others, since there are certainly many bodies that will decompose our own, including, of course, fellow human bodies (*E* III p34). Yet, he emphasizes throughout that one exists only among a multiplicity of others. We must strive to join forces with those others with whom one can compose ever more vital assemblages, ever more potent arrangements. Ethics imagined as ethology

---

57. Deleuze, *Spinoza: Practical Philosophy*, 17.

may galvanize more surprising and enabling encounters than Spinoza allows with his emphasis on humans with a corporeal basis for reason.

Nevertheless, if we take our cue from Deleuze and embrace an ethological language that emphasizes the zoological aspect of life as political animals, we ought to bear in mind Spinoza's concerns. A turn to the animal, to be liberating, must not be an expression of melancholy or felt powerlessness. Antipathy and misanthropy will, according to Spinoza, infect any political program with sad passions that will ultimately hamstring any efforts at liberation. Spinoza's invocation of the adage "man is a God to man" serves as a rebuttal to Hobbes's suggestion that humans have an irreducible lupine tendency that political organization must suppress, precariously and constantly. For Hobbes, one must not forget that "man is a wolf to man," even if the sword can maintain godly relations among citizens.[58] Although humans can be political animals, this possibility, for Hobbes, must be vigilantly maintained by the pact and the sword. If the natural condition of humankind that is never overcome for Hobbes is one of perpetual fear and restless desire for more in order to maintain a precarious security against our rapacious fellows, we see the necessity by which he deduces a need for absolutist government. It is a sad politics, motivated and preserved by anxious passions. This is but one example of how an image of man can motivate self-negation rather than the discovery of those who might be standing beside us, already in perfect agreement with our natures. In Hobbes's state of nature, one sees the threat of the wolf, responds in kind, imitating his affects, and overlooks Eve.

Spinoza asserts that the difference between himself and Hobbes is that he maintains "natural right in its entirety," as much in the state of nature as in the civil order (*Ep* 50). Indeed, Spinoza is arguably more concerned with the possibility that civil order will turn us into brutes than with the inability of sovereigns to suppress our viciousness (*TP* 20.6). Nevertheless, Spinoza's renaturalization of humanity such that neither language nor reason distinguishes man finally from beasts[59] may render Spinoza even more vulnerable to the accusation, so often hurled at Hobbes by his contemporaries, of animalizing man.[60] Indeed, there is no clear moment of anthropogenesis for Spinoza. The lack of opposition between humanity and nature, however, is precisely what I find so promising for a politics of renaturalization. At the same time, I want to keep in mind the reasons

---

58. See the epistle dedicatory to Hobbes, *On the Citizen*.
59. Melamed notes that even rocks may be said to possess common notions, in "Spinoza's Antihumanism."
60. See Ashcraft, "Hobbes' Natural Man."

Spinoza asks us to hold onto a distinctive sense of ourselves as particular kinds of beings. Holding certain characteristics in common, having bodies and minds that can potentially agree and form powerful unions, is important for Spinoza to counter the melancholy to which we are prone in the face of violence, social strife, and enmity. Without some sense that we genuinely need and benefit from one another, community with Eve remains a lost possibility for freedom and power.

Today, in taking up a politics of renaturalization inspired by Spinoza, the term human appears in a markedly different landscape. Human was, for Spinoza, a rallying call to oppose sectarian conflict and deny that some peoples are favored above all others by God (*TTP* 3.5). In our own epoch, we may need a new universal, a new image to assist our efforts to assemble our powers effectively to promote our continued vitality and flourishing. I suspect human-animal alienation is a greater danger to us than human-animal identification. Remaining faithful to Spinoza's imperative that we find ways to love ourselves as parts of nature with distinctive capacities, the politics of renaturalization can learn from the posthumanist claims, found in figures like Deleuze and Haraway, that an exclusionary paradigm of humanity that exiles dogs, plants, and robots from our sphere of primary concern may be precisely a self-negation, a separation of ourselves from our own power. In disavowing that we are who we are only by virtue of bacteria, nematodes, pacemakers, affections and labors of companion animals, and so many other involvements with nonhumans, we mutilate ourselves and the sources of power in our midst. Just as Adam was weakened by forgetting his need for Eve, we are diminished if we disregard our need, to take only the example of beasts, for animal affection. There is clear evidence that our minds no less than our bodies are enabled by relationships with nonhuman animals. We are enabled not only by instrumentalizing them as food or test subjects for pharmaceuticals but by simple attentive co-presence or companionship. Alzheimer's patients, for example, show improved memory upon friendly interaction with cats or dogs.[61] Research reveals a "cardiovascular benefit" for males with dogs (perhaps Adam had a heart defect?). Children who have difficulty reading can be helped significantly by a canine audience, and mere pet presence improves arithmetic calculations, something Spinoza would surely appreciate.[62]

---

61. Hines and Frederickson, "Perspectives on Animal Assisted Activities and Therapy."
62. Garrity and Stallones, "Effects of Pet Contact on Human Well-Being."

The "animal holocaust" that is our food industry notwithstanding,[63] it would be difficult to deny that many nonhuman animals deeply enjoy their relationships with humans. Moreover, not all human-animal relationships are products of conquest. It is suspected, for example, that wolves deliberately entered into cooperative relationships with humans for food, shelter, and companionship.[64] I hope that the politics of renaturalization can promote and nourish the enabling relations we enjoy with nonhuman animals and call into question the many destructive relations that ultimately threaten our existence as much as theirs.

Yet in our struggle to find new and better ways to honor the nonhuman in and outside of us, Spinoza's words on beasts suggest that we ought to be wary of any reactionary antihumanism that may animate our turn away from the human. Misanthropy is easily observed in the ecological movement, for example. In lamenting that humanity has ceased to be a part of nature, research biologist David Graber declares that "we have become a plague upon ourselves and upon the Earth. . . . Until such time as Homo sapiens should decide to rejoin nature, some of us can only hope for the right virus to come along."[65] Less drastically, some animal rights activists argue that humans should voluntarily withdraw contact from any nonhuman animals. The fantasy that humans could voluntarily circumscribe the effects they have on nonhuman nature, however, is a perfectly humanist ambition predicated on an empirically false human exceptionalism. It is a moral vision that erects an illusory wall between the human world and the natural world.[66] It imagines that humans might undo having been constituted by their nonhuman animal relations, such that our encounters with animals are contingent and optional. In other words, it preserves the antinaturalist notion that humans are a "dominion within a dominion."

Spinoza warns that a turn to nonhuman nature, if motivated by sad affects, represents only a perverse effect of an anthropocentric worldview and hence a reactionary politics that can only promote the moral fantasies of beautiful souls. Thus, even as I endorse a politics of renaturalization that is not governed by the image of man, or even the human, ours must be a philanthropic posthumanism, lest we remain captive to our melancholy. Spinoza's words on beasts remind us that affirming ourselves as

---

63. This is an allusion to Coetzee's provocative novel, *Elizabeth Costello*.
64. See Haraway, *The Companion Species Manifesto*.
65. Graber, "Mother Nature Is a Hothouse Flower."
66. As much as I admire the uncompromising character of the argument in this book (as well as his legal work for animal rights), I am thinking of Francione, *Animals as Persons*.

parts of nature is not tantamount to subordinating ourselves to Nature. Although we have no special value as preferred parts of nature and we are not the reason for nature's existence, neither are we a perversion of nature's order. In order to avoid destroying the very powers by virtue of which we exist, we have to learn to love ourselves, to feel the peculiar and distinctive joys that make us who we are. Otherwise, we will remain alone in paradise.

WORKS CITED

Ahmed, Sara. *The Cultural Politics of Emotions*. London: Routledge, 2004.
Alaimo, Stacey, and Susan Hekman. *Material Feminisms*. Bloomington: Indiana University Press, 2007.
Alcoff, Linda. *Visible Identities: Race, Gender, and the Self*. New York: Oxford University Press, 2005.
Allen, Amy. "Dependency, Subordination, and Recognition: On Judith Butler's Theory of Subjection." *Continental Philosophy Review* 38, no. 3 (2005): 199–222.
Alquié, Ferdinand. *Le rationalisme de Spinoza*. Paris: Presses Universitaires de France, 1981.
Althusser, Louis. "Ideology and Ideological State Apparatuses: Notes toward an Investigation." In *Lenin and Philosophy and Other Essays*, trans. B. Brewster. New York: Monthly Review Press, 1971.
———. "Marxism and Humanism." In *For Marx*, trans. B. Brewster. London: Verso, 2005.
———. "On Spinoza." In *Essays in Self-Criticism*, trans. Graham Locke. London: New Left Books, 1976.
———. "The Only Materialist Tradition, Part 1: Spinoza." Trans. T. Stolze. In *The New Spinoza*, ed. Warren Montag and Ted Stolze. Minneapolis: University of Minnesota Press, 1997.
———. "Underground Current of the Materialism of the Encounter." In *Philosophy of the Encounter: Later Writings, 1978–1987*, ed. François Matheron and Olivier Corpet, trans. G. M. Goshgarian. London: Verso, 2006.

Althusser, Louis, and Etienne Balibar. *Reading Capital*. Trans. B. Brewster. London: Verso, 1970.

Anzaldúa, Gloria. *Borderlands/La Frontera: The New Mestiza*. San Francisco: Aunt Lute Books, 1987.

Armstrong, Aurelia. "Autonomy and the Relational Individual: Spinoza and Feminism." In *Feminist Interpretations of Benedict Spinoza*, ed. M. Gatens. University Park: Pennsylvania State University Press, 2009.

Ashcraft, Richard. "Hobbes' Natural Man: A Study in Ideology." *Journal of Politics* 33 (1971): 1076–1117.

Augustine. *On Free Choice of the Will*. Trans. T. Williams. Indianapolis: Hackett, 1993.

Balibar, Etienne. *The Philosophy of Marx*. Trans. Chris Turner. London: Verso, 1995.

——. *Spinoza and Politics*. Trans. Peter Snowdon. London: Verso, 1998.

——. *Spinoza: From Individuality to Transindividuality*. Delft: Eburon, 1997.

——. "Spinoza, the Anti-Orwell: The Fear of the Masses." In *Masses, Classes, Ideas*, trans. J. Swenson. London: Routledge, 1994.

Barbone, Steven. "What Counts as an Individual for Spinoza?" In *Spinoza: Metaphysical Themes*, ed. Olli Koistinen and John Ivan Biro. Oxford: Oxford University Press, 2002.

Bartky, Sandra Lee. "On Psychological Oppression." In *Femininity and Domination: Studies in the Phenomenology of Oppression*. London: Routledge, 1990.

Beauvoir, Simone de. *The Second Sex*. Trans. H. M. Parshley. New York: Vintage Books, 1989.

Benjamin, Jessica. *Bonds of Love: Psychoanalysis, Feminism, and the Problem of Domination*. New York: Pantheon Books, 1988.

Bennett, Jane "The Force of Things: Steps toward an Ecology of Matter." *Political Theory* 32, no. 3 (2004): 347–72.

——. *Vibrant Matter: A Political Ecology of Things*. Durham: Duke University Press, 2010.

Berman, David. "Spinoza's Spiders, Schopenhauer's Dogs." *Philosophical Studies* 29 (1982): 202–9.

Bernstein, J. M. "From Self-Consciousness to Community: Act and Recognition in the Master-Slave Relationship." In *The State and Civil Society: Studies in Hegel's Political Philosophy*, ed. Z. A. Pelczynski. Cambridge: Cambridge University Press, 1984.

Beyssade, Jean-Marie. "*Nostri Corpori Affectus:* Can an Affect in Spinoza Be 'of the body'?" In *Desire and Affect: Spinoza as Psychologist*, ed. Y. Yovel. New York: Little Room Press, 2000.

Biko, Steve. "We Blacks." In *I Write What I Like: A Selection of His Writings*, ed. Aelred Stubbs. Oxford: Heinemann, 1978.

Bordo, Susan. "Are Mothers Persons?" In *Unbearable Weight: Feminism, Western Culture, and the Body*. Berkeley: University of California Press, 1993.

——, ed. *Feminist Interpretations of René Descartes*. University Park: Pennsylvania State University Press, 1999.

———. *Flight to Objectivity: Essays on Cartesianism and Culture*. Albany: State University of New York Press, 1987.
Bove, Laurent. *La stratégie du conatus: affirmation et résistance chez Spinoza*. Paris : J. Vrin, 1996.
Brace, Laura. "The Tragedy of the Freelance Hustler: Hegel, Gender, and Civil Society." *Contemporary Political Theory* 1, no. 3 (2002): 329–47.
Braidotti, Rosi. *Metamorphoses: Toward a Materialist Theory of Becoming*. Cambridge, UK: Polity Press, 2002.
Brennan, Teresa. *The Transmission of Affect*. Ithaca: Cornell University Press, 2004.
Brown, Deborah J. *Descartes and the Passionate Mind*. Cambridge: Cambridge University Press, 2006.
Brown, Wendy. *States of Injury: Power and Freedom in Late Modernity*. Princeton: Princeton University Press, 1995.
Butler, Judith. "The Desire to Live: Spinoza's *Ethics* under Pressure." In *Politics and the Passions, 1500–1850*, ed. V. Kahn, N. Saccamano, and D. Coli. Princeton: Princeton University Press, 2006.
———. *Frames of War: When Is Life Grievable?* London: Verso, 2009.
———. *Gender Trouble: Feminism and the Subversion of Identity*. London: Routledge, 1990.
———. *Giving an Account of Oneself*. New York: Fordham University Press, 2005.
———. "Performative Acts and Gender Constitution: An Essay in Phenomenology and Feminist Theory." *Theatre Journal* 40.4 (1988): 519–31.
———. *The Psychic Life of Power*. Stanford: Stanford University Press, 1997.
———. "Sexual Ideology and Phenomenological Description: A Feminist Critique of Merleau-Ponty's *Phenomenology of Perception*." In *The Thinking Muse: Feminism and Modern French Philosophy*, ed. J. Allen and I. M. Young. Bloomington: Indiana University Press, 1989.
———. *Subjects of Desire: Hegelian Reflections in Twentieth Century France*. New York: Columbia University Press, 1987.
———. *Undoing Gender*. London: Routledge, 2004.
Casarino, Cesare, and Antonio Negri. *In Praise of the Common: A Conversation on Philosophy and Politics*. Minneapolis: University of Minnesota Press, 2008.
Clough, Patricia Ticineto, ed. *The Affective Turn: Theorizing the Social*. Durham: Duke University Press, 2007.
Code, Lorraine. *Rhetorical Spaces: Essays on Gendered Locations*. London: Routledge, 1995.
Coetzee, J. M. *Elizabeth Costello*. New York : Penguin, 2004.
Combes, Muriel. *Simondon: Individu et collectivité*. Paris: Presses Universitaires de France, 1999.
Connolly, William. *Neuropolitics: Thinking, Culture, Speed*. Minneapolis: University of Minnesota Press, 2002.
Cooper, Julie. "Freedom of Speech and Philosophical Citizenship in Spinoza's *Theological-Political Treatise*." *Law, Culture and the Humanities* 2, no. 1 (2006): 91–114.

———. "Spinoza on Humility." Unpublished paper.
Cornell, Drucilla. *The Imaginary Domain: Abortion, Pornography, and Sexual Harassment.* London: Routledge, 1995.
Cornell, Drucilla, and Sara Murphy. "Anti-racism, Multiculturalism, and an Ethics of Identification." *Philosophy and Social Criticism* 28, no. 4 (2002): 419–49.
Cotten, Jean-Pierre. "Althusser et Spinoza." In *Spinoza au XXième Siècle,* ed. Paul-Laurent Assoun. Paris: Presses Universitaires de France, 1993.
Crenshaw, Kimberlé. "Mapping the Margins: Intersectionality, Identity Politics, and Violence against Women of Color." In *The Public Nature of Private Violence: Women and the Discovery of Abuse,* ed. Martha Fineman and Roxanne Mykitiuk. New York: Routledge, 1994.
Curley, Edwin. "Experience in Spinoza's Theory of Knowledge." In *Spinoza: A Collection of Critical Essays,* ed. Marjorie Grene. Garden City: Anchor Books, 1973.
———. "Man and Nature in Spinoza." In *Spinoza's Philosophy of Man,* ed. J. Wetlesen. Oslo: Universitetsforl., 1978.
Dalla Costa, Mariarosa, and Selma James. *The Power of Women and the Subversion of the Community.* Bristol, UK: Falling Wall Press, 1975.
Damasio, Antonio. *Descartes' Error: Emotion, Reason, and the Human Brain.* New York: Penguin, 2005.
———. *Looking for Spinoza: Joy, Sorrow and the Feeling Brain.* New York: Mariner Books, 2003.
Davies, Tony. *Humanism.* London: Routledge, 1997.
de Jonge, Eccy. *Spinoza and Deep Ecology: Challenging Traditional Approaches to Environmentalism.* Aldershot, UK: Ashgate, 2004.
Deleuze, Gilles. *Expressionism in Philosophy: Spinoza.* Trans. Martin Joughin. New York: Zone Books, 1992.
———. *Spinoza: Practical Philosophy.* Trans. R. Hurley. San Francisco: City Lights Books, 1988.
Deleuze, Gilles, and Félix Guattari. *A Thousand Plateaus.* Trans. B. Massumi. Minneapolis: University of Minnesota Press, 1987.
———. *What Is Philosophy?* Trans. J. Tomlinson and G. Burchell III. New York: Columbia University Press, 1996.
Della Rocca, Michael. *Spinoza.* London: Routledge, 2008.
Del Lucchese, Filippo. *Conflict, Power, and Multitude in Machiavelli and Spinoza.* London: Continuum, 2009.
———. "Democracy, Multitudo and the Third Kind of Knowledge in the Works of Spinoza." *European Journal of Political Theory* 8, no. 3 (2009): 339–63.
———. "Monstrous Individuations: Deleuze, Simondon, and Relational Ontology." *differences* 20, no. 2 (2009): 179–93.
Descartes, René. *The Correspondence.* Vol. 3. of *The Philosophical Writings of Descartes,* ed. J. Cottingham, A. Kenny, R. Stoothoff, and D. Murdoch. Cambridge: Cambridge University Press, 1991.

———. *The Philosophical Writings of Descartes.* Vols. 1–2. Ed. J. Cottingham, R. Stoothoff, and D. Murdoch. Cambridge: Cambridge University Press, 1985–86.

de Sousa, Ronald. "Emotion." In *Stanford Encyclopedia of Philosophy* (June 2007 edition), ed. Edward N. Zalta. http://plato.stanford.edu/entries/emotion/.

Du Bois, W. E. B. "Of Our Spiritual Strivings." In *The Souls of Black Folk*. New York: Penguin, 1995.

Eagleton, Terry. *Ideology: An Introduction.* London: Verso, 1991.

Eisenberg, P. D. "Is Spinoza an Ethical Naturalist?" *Philosophia* 7, no. 1 (1977): 107–33.

Fanon, Frantz. *Black Skin, White Masks.* New York: Grove Press, 1967.

Feuer, Lewis. *Spinoza and the Rise of Liberalism.* Edison, NJ: Transaction Publishers, 1987.

Feuerbach, Ludwig. *The Essence of Christianity.* Trans. George Eliot. Buffalo, NY: Prometheus Books, 1989.

Foucault, Michel. *Power/Knowledge: Selected Interviews and Other Writings 1972–1977.* Ed. Colin Gordon. New York: Pantheon Books, 1980.

———. *The Use of Pleasure.* Vol. 2 of *The History of Sexuality.* Trans. R. Hurley. New York: Vintage, 1990.

———. "What Is Critique?" *The Politics of Truth*, ed. S. Lotringer. Los Angeles: Semiotexte, 2007.

Found Objects Collective. "An Interview with Elizabeth Grosz." http://web.gc.cuny.edu/csctw/found_object/text/grosz.htm (accessed 14 December 2007).

Francione, Gary. *Animals as Persons: Essays on the Abolition of Animal Exploitation.* New York: Columbia University Press, 2008.

Fraser, Nancy. "From Redistribution to Recognition? Dilemmas of Justice in a 'Post-socialist' Age." *New Left Review* 212 (1995): 68–93.

Frazer, Elizabeth, and Nicola Lacey. *The Politics of Community: A Feminist Critique of the Liberal-Communitarian Debate.* London: Routledge, 1993.

Freud, Sigmund. *Beyond the Pleasure Principle.* In *The Standard Edition of the Complete Psychological Works of Sigmund Freud*, vol. 18. Trans. James Strachey. London: Hogarth, 1920–22.

Frye, Marilyn. *The Politics of Reality: Essays in Feminist Theory.* Berkeley: Crossing Press, 1983.

Garrity, Thomas F., and Lorann Stallones. "Effects of Pet Contact on Human Well-Being." In *Companion Animals in Human Health*, ed. C. Wilson and D. Turner. London: Sage Publications, 1997.

Gatens, Moira. *Imaginary Bodies: Ethics, Power, and Corporeality.* London: Routledge, 1996.

———. "The Politics of the Imagination" In *Feminist Interpretations of Benedict Spinoza*, ed. M. Gatens. University Park: Pennsylvania State University Press, 2009.

Gatens, Moira, and Genevieve Lloyd. *Collective Imaginings: Spinoza, Past and Present.* London: Routledge, 1999.

Gilligan, Carol. *In a Different Voice: Psychological Theory and Women's Development*. Cambridge: Harvard University Press, 1993.

Gombay, André. *Descartes*. Oxford: Blackwell, 2007.

Graber, David. "Mother Nature Is a Hothouse Flower." *Los Angeles Times*, 22 October 1989.

Gramsci, Antonio. *Selections from the Prison Notebooks*. New York: International Publishers, 1971.

Grassi, Paula. "Adam and the Serpent: *Everyman* and the Imagination." In *Feminist Interpretations of Benedict Spinoza*, ed. M. Gatens. University Park: Pennsylvania State University Press, 2009.

Grosz, Elizabeth. "A Politics of Imperceptibility: A Response to 'Anti-racism, Multiculturalism and the Ethics of Identification." *Philosophy and Social Criticism* 28, no. 4 (2002): 463–72.

———. "A Thousand Tiny Sexes: Feminism and Rhizomatics." *Topoi: An International Review of Philosophy* 12, no. 2 (1993): 167–79.

———. *Time Travels: Feminism, Nature, Power*. Durham: Duke University Press, 2005.

Grotius, Hugo. *Rights of War and Peace*. Ed. R. Tuck. Indianapolis: Liberty Fund, 2005.

Guenther, Lisa. "How Does the Light Get In? Phenomenology and Solitary Confinement." Unpublished paper.

Gullan-Whur, Margaret. "Spinoza and the Equality of Women." *Theoria* 68, no. 2 (August 2002): 91–111.

Gunnel, John G. "Are We Losing Our Minds? Cognitive Science and the Study of Politics." *Political Theory* 35, no. 6 (December 2007): 704–31.

Gutmann, Amy, ed. *Multiculturalism: Exploring the Politics of Recognition*. Princeton: Princeton University Press, 1994.

Haraway, Donna. *The Companion Species Manifesto: Dogs, People, and Significant Otherness*. Chicago: Prickly Paradigm Press, 2003.

———. "A Cyborg Manifesto." *Simians, Cyborgs, and Women: The Reinvention of Nature*. New York: Routledge, 1991.

———. *When Species Meet*, Minnesota: University of Minnesota Press, 2008.

Hardt, Michael. "Foreword: What Affects Are Good for." In *The Affective Turn: Theorizing the Social*, ed. P. T. Clough. Durham: Duke University Press, 2007.

Hardt, Michael, and Antonio Negri. *Empire*. Cambridge: Harvard University Press, 2000.

———. *Multitude: War and Democracy in the Age of Empire*. Cambridge: Harvard University Press, 2009.

Hargrove, Eugene. *The Animal Rights/Environmental Ethics Debate: The Environmental Perspective*. Albany: State University of New York Press, 1992.

Harris, Errol. *Spinoza's Philosophy: An Outline*. Atlantic Highlands, NJ: Humanities Press International, 1992.

Harrison, Peter. "The Virtues of Animals in Seventeenth Century Thought." *Journal of the History of Ideas* 59, no. 3 (1998): 463–84.

Haslanger, Sally. "Social Construction: The Debunking Project." In *Socializing*

Metaphysics: The Nature of Social Reality, ed. F. Schmitt. New York: Rowman and Littlefield, 2003.
Hegel, G. W. F. *Elements of the Philosophy of Right*. Ed. A. Wood. Cambridge: Cambridge University Press, 1991.
———. *Lectures on the History of Philosophy*. Trans. E. S. Haldane. New York: Humanities Press, 1996.
———. *Lectures on the Philosophy of Spirit 1827–1828*. Trans. Robert Williams. Oxford: Oxford University Press 2007.
———. *Phenomenology of Spirit*. Trans. A. V. Miller. Oxford: Oxford University Press, 1977.
Held, Virginia. *Feminist Morality: Transforming Culture, Society, and Politics*. Chicago: University of Chicago Press, 1993.
Hines, Linda, and Maureen Frederickson. "Perspectives on Animal Assisted Activities and Therapy." In *Companion Animals in Human Health*, ed. C. Wilson and D. Turner. London: Sage Publications, 1997.
Hirschman, Albert O. *The Passions and the Interests: Political Arguments for Capitalism before Its Triumph*. Princeton: Princeton University Press, 1997.
Hobbes, Thomas. *Leviathan*. Ed. C. B. Macpherson. Indianapolis: Hackett, 1994.
———. *On the Citizen*. Ed. R. Tuck and M. Silverthorne. Cambridge: Cambridge University Press, 1998.
Honneth, Axel. *The Struggle for Recognition: The Moral Grammar of Social Conflicts*. Cambridge: MIT Press, 1996.
Honneth, Axel, and Nancy Fraser. *Redistribution or Recognition? A Political-Philosophical Exchange*. London: Verso, 2003.
Houle, Karen, "Spinoza and Ecology Revisited." *Environmental Ethics* 19, no. 4 (1997): 417–31.
Hull, Gordon. "Spinoza in a Fabulous Red Scarf: Judith Butler on the Fragility of the *Conatus*." Paper presented at the Society for Phenomenology and Existential Philosophy, 2007.
Israel, Jonathan I. *Enlightenment Contested: Philosophy, Modernity, and the Emancipation of Man, 1670–1752*. New York: Oxford University Press, 2006.
———. *Radical Enlightenment: Philosophy and the Making of Modernity, 1650–1750*. New York: Oxford University Press, 2001.
James, Susan. *Passion and Action: The Emotions in Seventeenth Century Philosophy*. New York: Oxford University Press, 2000.
Kant, Immanuel. *Anthropology from a Pragmatic Point of View*. Ed. R. Louden. Cambridge: Cambridge University Press, 2006.
———. *Critique of Pure Reason*. Trans. W. Pluhar. Indianapolis: Hackett, 1999.
———. *Grounding for the Metaphysics of Morals*. Trans. J. W. Ellington. Indianapolis: Hackett, 1981.
King, Martin Luther, Jr. "The Sword That Heals." In *Why We Can't Wait*. New York: Penguin, 1964.
Kittay, Eva. *Love's Labor: Essays on Women, Equality, and Dependency*. London: Routledge, 1998.

Kojève, Alexandre. *Introduction to the Reading of Hegel*. Ithaca: Cornell University Press, 1980.
Lachterman, David. "The Physics of Spinoza's Ethics." In *Spinoza: New Perspectives*, ed. R. Shahan and J. Biro. Norman: University of Oklahoma Press, 1978.
Laclau, Ernesto. "The Death and Resurrection of the Theory of Ideology." *Journal of Political Ideologies* 1, no. 3 (1996): 201–20.
Levene, Nancy. "The Fall of Eden." *Philosophy Today* 50 (2006): 6–23.
———. *Spinoza's Revelation: Religion, Democracy, and Reason*. Cambridge: Cambridge University Press, 2004.
Lin, Martin. "Spinoza's Account of Akrasia." *Journal of the History of Philosophy* 44, no. 3 (July 2006): 395–414.
Lloyd, Genevieve. *Man of Reason: "Male" and "Female" in Western Philosophy*. Minneapolis: University of Minnesota Press, 1993.
———. *Part of Nature: Self-Knowledge in Spinoza's Ethics*. Ithaca: Cornell University Press, 1994.
———. "Spinoza's Environmental Ethics." *Inquiry* 23 (1980): 293–311.
Lloyd, Genevieve, and Moira Gatens. *Collective Imaginings: Spinoza, Past and Present*. New York: Routledge, 1999.
Lugones, María. "Playfulness, 'World'-Traveling, and Loving Perception." *Hypatia* 2, no. 2 (1987): 3–19.
Lyotard, Jean-François. *The Inhuman: Reflections on Time*. Stanford: Stanford University Press, 1991.
Macherey, Pierre. *Hegel ou Spinoza*. Paris: Maspero, 1979.
———. *Introduction à l'Ethique de Spinoza*. Vols. 1–5. Paris : Presses Universitaires de France, 1995–98.
———. "Towards a Natural History of Norms." In *Michel Foucault: Philosopher*, ed. T. Armstrong. London: Harvester Wheatsheaf, 1992.
Machiavelli, Niccolo. *Discourses on Livy*. Trans. Harvey C. Mansfield and Nathan Tarcov. Chicago: University of Chicago Press, 1996.
MacKinnon, Catharine A. "Of Mice and Men: A Feminist Fragment on Animal Rights." In *Animal Rights: Current Debates and New Directions*, ed. Cass Sunstein and Martha Nussbaum. Oxford: Oxford University Press, 2004.
———. *Toward a Feminist Theory of the State*. Cambridge: Harvard University Press, 1989.
Macpherson, Crawford B. *The Political Theory of Possessive Individualism: Hobbes to Locke*. Oxford: Oxford University Press, 1964.
Maimonides, Moses. *The Guide of the Perplexed*. Trans. C. Rabin. Indianapolis: Hackett, 1995.
Mara, Gerald. "Liberal Politics and Moral Excellence in Spinoza's Political Philosophy." *Journal of the History of Philosophy* 20 (1982): 129–50.
Marcus, George. *The Sentimental Citizen: Emotion in Democratic Politics*. University Park: Pennsylvania State University Press, 2002.
Markell, Patchen. *Bound by Recognition*. Princeton: Princeton University Press, 2003.

———. "The Recognition of Politics: A Comment on Emcke and Tully." *Constellations* 7, no. 4 (2000): 496–506.
Marx, Karl. *Capital: A Critique of Political Economy*. Vol. 1. Trans. B. Fowkes. New York: Penguin Books, 1976.
Massumi, Brian. *Parables of the Virtual: Movement, Affect, Sensation*. Durham: Duke University Press, 2002.
Matheron, Alexandre. "L'anthropologie spinoziste?" *Revue de Synthèse* 99, no. 89 (1978): 175–88
———. "Femmes et serviteurs dans la démocratie spinoziste." *Revue philosophique de la France et de l'étranger* 167 (1977): 181–200
———. *Individu et communauté chez Spinoza*. Paris: Presses Universitaires de France, 1968.
———. "Spinoza and Sexuality." In *Feminist Interpretations of Benedict Spinoza*, ed. M. Gatens. University Park: Pennsylvania State University Press, 2009.
Mathews, Freya. *The Ecological Self*. New York: Rowman and Littlefield, 1991.
Melamed, Yitzhak Y. "Acosmism or Weak Individuals? Hegel, Spinoza, and the Reality of the Finite." *Journal of the History of Philosophy* 48, no. 1 (2010): 77–92.
———. "Spinoza's Antihumanism: An Outline." In *Montreal Studies in the History of Philosophy*, vol. 1: *The Rationalists: Between Tradition and Revolution*, ed. C. Fraenkel, D. Perinetti, and J. E. H. Smith. Dordrecht: Springer Press, 2010.
Meynell, Hugo. "Ethology and Ethics." *Philosophy* 45, no. 174 (1970): 290–306.
Montag, Warren. *Bodies, Masses, Power: Spinoza and His Contemporaries*. London: Verso, 1999.
———. "Imitating the Affects of Beasts: Interest and Inhumanity in Spinoza." *differences* 20, no. 2 (2009): 54–72.
———. *Louis Althusser*. London: Palgrave Macmillan, 2003.
———. "Spinoza: Politics in a World without Transcendence." *Rethinking Marxism* 2, no. 3 (1989): 89–103.
Montaigne, Michel de. *The Complete Works*. Trans. D. Frame. New York: Everyman's Library, 2003.
Moore, Donald, Jake Kosek, and Anand Pandian, eds. *Race, Nature, and the Politics of Difference*. Durham: Duke University Press, 2003.
Moreau, Josef. "Spinoza: est-il moniste?" *Revue de Théologie et de Philosophie Lausanne* 115, no. 1 (1983): 23–35.
Moreau, Pierre-François. *Spinoza, l'expérience et l'éternité*. Paris: Presses Universitaires de France, 1994.
Morfino, Vittorio. "An Althusserian Lexicon." Trans. Jason Smith. *Borderlands e-journal* 4, no. 2 (2005).
———. "Spinoza: An Ontology of Relation?" *Graduate Faculty Philosophy Journal* 27, no. 1 (2006): 103–27.
Nadler, Steven. *Spinoza: A Life*. Cambridge: Cambridge University Press, 1999.
Naess, Arne. "Environmental Ethics and Spinoza's Ethics. Comments on Genevieve Lloyd's Article." *Inquiry* 23 (1980): 313–25.
———. "Spinoza and Ecology." *Philosophia* 7, no. 1 (1977): 45–54.

Negri, Antonio. *The Savage Anomaly: The Power of Spinoza's Metaphysics and Politics.* Trans. Michael Hardt. Minneapolis: University of Minnesota Press, 1991.

———. *Subversive Spinoza: (Un)Contemporary Variations.* Trans. Timothy Murphy. Manchester: Manchester University Press, 2004.

———. "Value and Affect." Trans. Michael Hardt. *Boundary 2* 26, no. 2 (1999): 77–88.

Neuhouser, Frederick. *Foundations of Hegel's Social Theory: Actualizing Freedom.* Cambridge: Harvard University Press, 2000.

Norris, Christopher. *Spinoza and the Origins of Modern Critical Theory.* London: Blackwell, 1991.

Nussbaum, Martha. *Upheavals of Thought.* Cambridge: Cambridge University Press, 2001.

Oliver, Kelly. *Family Values: Subjects between Nature and Culture.* London: Routledge, 1997.

———. *Witnessing: Beyond Recognition.* Minneapolis: University of Minnesota Press, 2001.

Pateman, Carol. *The Sexual Contract.* Stanford: Stanford University Press, 1988.

Pines, Shlomo. "On Spinoza's Conception of Human Freedom and Good and Evil." In *Spinoza: His Thought and Work,* ed. N. Rotenstreich and N. Schneider. Jerusalem: Israel Academy of Sciences and Humanities, 1983.

Pippin, Robert B. "What Is the Question for Which Hegel's Theory of Recognition Is the Answer?" In *European Journal of Philosophy* 8, no. 2 (2000): 155–72.

Pitts, Edward I. "Spinoza on Freedom of Expression." *Journal of the History of Ideas* 47, no. 1 (January–March 1986): 21–35.

Plumwood, Val. *Feminism and the Mastery of Nature.* London: Routledge, 1993.

Poole, Ross. "On Being a Person." *Australasian Journal of Philosophy* 74, no. 1 (1996): 38–56.

Power, Nina. *One-Dimensional Woman.* Ropley, UK: O Books, 2009.

Ravven, Heidi. "The Garden of Eden: Spinoza's Maimonidean Account of the Genealogy of Morals and the Origin of Society." *Philosophy and Theology* 13, no. 1 (2001): 3–51.

———. "What Spinoza Can Teach Us about Embodying and Naturalizing Ethics." In *Feminist Interpretations of Benedict Spinoza,* ed. M. Gatens. University Park: Pennsylvania State University Press, 2009.

Regan, Tom. *The Case for Animal Rights.* Berkeley: University of California Press, 1983.

Rice, Lee. "Action in Spinoza's Account of Affectivity." In *Spinoza on Reason and the "Free Man,"* ed. Yirmiyahu Yovel and Gideon Segal. New York: Little Room Press, 1999.

———. "*Tanquam Naturae Humanae Exemplar*: Spinoza on Human Nature." *Modern Schoolman* 58 (1991): 291–304.

Rodman, John. "Animal Justice: The Counter-revolution in Natural Right and Law." *Inquiry* 22, no.1 (1979): 3–22.

———. "The Liberation of Nature?" *Inquiry* 20, no. 1 (1977): 83–131.

Rorty, Amélie. "The Politics of Spinoza's Vanishing Dichotomies." *Political Theory* 38, no. 1 (2010): 131–41.
Rosenthal, Michael. "Spinoza on Why the Sovereign Can Command Men's Tongues but Not Their Minds." *Nomos* 48 (2008): 54–77.
———. "Why Spinoza Chose the Hebrews: The Exemplary Function of Prophecy in the *Theological-Political Treatise*." *History of Political Thought* 18, no.1 (Summer 1997): 207–41.
Rowbotham, Sheila. *Woman's Consciousness, Man's World*. Harmondsworth, UK: Penguin, 1973.
Sartre, Jean-Paul. "Black Orpheus." In *Race*, ed. Robert Bernasconi. Oxford: Blackwell, 2001.
Sekyi-Otu, Ato. *Fanon's Dialectic of Experience*. Cambridge: Harvard University Press, 1996.
Sessions, George. "Spinoza and Jeffers on Man in Nature." *Inquiry* 20, no. 1 (1977): 481–528.
Sharp, Hasana. "Feeling Justice: The Reorientation of Possessive Desire in Spinoza." *International Studies in Philosophy* 37, no. 2 (2005): 113–30.
———. "The Force of Ideas in Spinoza." *Political Theory* 35 (2007): 732–55.
———. "Melancholy, Anxious, and *Ek-static* Selves: Feminism between *Eros* and *Thanatos*." *Symposium: Canadian Journal of Continental Philosophy* 11, no. 2 (Fall 2007): 313–31.
———. "'*Nemo non videt*': Intuitive Knowledge and the Question of Spinoza's Elitism." In *Montreal Studies in the History of Philosophy*, vol. 1: *The Rationalists: Between Tradition and Revolution*, ed. C. Fraenkel, D. Perinetti, and J. E. H. Smith. Dordrecht: Springer Press, 2010.
———. "Why Spinoza Today? Or, 'A Strategy of Anti-Fear.'" *Rethinking Marxism* 17, no. 4 (2005): 591–608.
Sharpe, Matthew. "The Aesthetics of Ideology, or 'The Critique of Ideological Judgment' in Eagleton and Žižek." *Political Theory* 34, no. 1 (2006): 95–120.
Simondon. Gilbert. *L'individuation à la lumière des notions de forme et d'information*. Grenoble: Editions Jérôme Millon, 2005.
———. "The Position of the Problem of Ontogenesis." Trans. G. Flanders. *Parrhesia* 7 (2009): 4–16.
Singer, Peter. *Animal Liberation*. New York: Harper Collins, 1975.
Smith, Steven B. *Spinoza, Liberalism, and the Question of Jewish Identity*. New Haven: Yale University Press, 1998.
———. "What Kind of Democrat was Spinoza?" *Political Theory* 33, no. 1 (2005): 6–27.
Spinoza, Benedictus de. *The Collected Works*. Vol. 1. Ed. Edwin M. Curley. Princeton: Princeton University Press, 1985.
———. *The Letters*. Trans. S. Shirley. Indianapolis: Hackett, 1995.
———. *Political Treatise*. Trans. S. Shirley. Indianapolis: Hackett, 2000.
———. *Theological-Political Treatise*. Trans. J. Israel and M. Silverthorne. Cambridge: Cambridge University Press, 2007.

Steinberg, Diane. "Belief, Affirmation, and the Doctrine of *Conatus* in Spinoza." *Southern Journal of Philosophy* 43, no. 1 (2005): 147–58.
Strauss, Leo. *Liberalism Ancient and Modern*. Chicago: University of Chicago Press, 1995.
Sturgeon, Noël. *Ecofeminist Natures: Race, Gender, Feminist Theory and Political Action*. New York: Routledge, 1997.
Taylor, Charles. "The Politics of Recognition." In *Philosophical Arguments*. Cambridge: Harvard University Press, 1995.
Thiel, Udo. "Individuation." In *The Cambridge History of Seventeenth-Century Philosophy*, ed. Daniel Garber and Michael Ayers. Cambridge: Cambridge University Press, 1998.
Thomas, Keith. *Man and the Natural World: Changing Attitudes in England 1500–1800*. New York: Oxford University Press, 1996.
Thomas, Peter. "Philosophical Strategies: Spinoza and Althusser." *Historical Materialism* 10, no. 3 (2002): 71–113.
Timmermans, Benoît. "Descartes et Spinoza: De l'admiration au désir." *Revue Internationale de le Philosophie* 48 (1994) : 327–39.
Tosel, André. *Du matérialisme de Spinoza*. Paris: Editions Kimé, 1994.
Uyl, Douglas den. *Power, State, and Freedom: An Interpretation of Spinoza's Political Philosophy*. Assen: Van Gorcum, 1983.
Warner, Michael. *The Trouble with Normal: Sex. Politics, and the Ethics of Queer Life*. Cambridge: Harvard University Press, 1999.
Wartofsky, Marx. "Action and Passion: Spinoza's Construction of a Scientific Psychology." In *Spinoza: A Collection of Critical Essays*, ed. Marjorie Grene. Notre Dame: University of Notre Dame Press, 1973.
West, David. "Spinoza on Positive Freedom." *Political Studies* 49, no. 2 (1993): 284–296.
Wetlesen, John. *The Sage and the Way*. Assen: Van Gorcum, 1979.
Wilkin, Rebecca. "Descartes, Individualism, and the Fetal Subject." *Differences* 19, no. 1 (2008): 96–127.
Williams, Caroline. *Contemporary French Philosophy: Modernity and the Persistence of the Subject*. London: Athlone Press, 2001.
———. "Thinking the Political in the Wake of Spinoza: Power, Affect, and Imagination in the *Ethics*." *Contemporary Political Theory* 6 (2007): 349–69.
Williams, Robert. *Hegel's Ethics of Recognition*. Berkeley: University of California Press, 1997.
Wilson, Cindy, and Dennis Turner, eds. *Companion Animals in Human Health*. London: Sage, 1997.
Wilson, Margaret. "Objects, Ideas, and 'Minds': Comments on Spinoza's Theory." In *Ideas and Mechanism: Essays on Early Modern Philosophy*. Princeton: Princeton University Press, 1999.
Wittig, Monique. *The Straight Mind and Other Essays*. Boston: Beacon Press, 1992.
Wolfe, Cary. *What Is Posthumanism?* Minneapolis: University of Minnesota Press, 2009.

Wolloch, Nathaniel. *Subjugated Animals: Animals and Anthropocentrism in Early Modern European Culture*. New York: Humanity Books, 2006.
X, Malcolm. "The Ballot or the Bullet." In *Malcolm X Speaks: Selected Speeches and Statements*, ed. George Breitman. New York: Grove Press, 1965.
———. Speech given in Los Angeles, 22 May 1962. Viewed at http://www.youtube.com/watch?v=gRSgUTWffMQ (accessed August 30, 2010).
Young, I. M. "Asymmetrical Reciprocity: On Moral Respect, Wonder, and Enlarged Thought." In *Judgment, Imagination, and Politics: Themes from Kant and Arendt*, ed. R. Beiner and J. Nedelsky. Lanham, MD: Rowman & Littlefield, 2001.
Yovel, Yirmiyahu. *Spinoza and Other Heretics*. Princeton: Princeton University Press, 1989.
Zimmerman, Michael. *Contesting Earth's Future: Radical Ecology and Postmodernity*. Berkeley: University of California Press, 1997.
Žižek, Slavoj, ed. *Mapping Ideology*. London: Verso, 1994.

INDEX

acquiescentia (self-esteem/self-satisfaction), 31, 144, 146, 171
action/adequate cause, 22–37, 41–47, 51, 53–54, 66, 72, 78, 80, 83, 85, 106, 111, 144–45, 152, 168–69, 172, 174, 178, 181n79, 189, 211, 214, 216
Adam and/or Eve, 96n12, 103n22, 193, 202–9, 218. *See also* Fall, myth of the
adequate ideas, 31n19, 67, 72–80, 82–84, 92, 95–97, 102, 104–5, 135, 141, 146, 206
Althusser, Louis, 57–60, 62, 64–67, 70–72, 75–77, 85, 107n25, 118n4, 186n2
ambition, 139–45, 149, 153, 171–72
anger, 22, 31, 46, 171, 173, 199
animals: becoming-, 167–68, 177, 188, 210; companion, 98, 101, 218; -human relations, 11n17, 153, 190, 218–19; humans as more than mere, 13, 22–23, 42, 56, 91–92, 123–25, 130, 136–37, 163, 169, 192–93, 210, 212; humans as political, 217; lack of boundary between humans and, 27, 94, 106–7, 111–13, 134, 203, 217; as merely serving human interests, 109, 136, 186–87, 192; as models for humans, 5, 18, 187–90, 192–93, 195–96, 200–201, 203, 209–11; as parts of nature, 2; possible rationality in higher, 12, 27, 97; rights of, 10, 25, 110–12, 188, 191, 213–14, 219; and war, 200
anthropomorphism, 1, 52, 58, 168, 185
antihumanism, 120n18, 168, 172–74, 177, 186, 188, 190, 192, 201, 209, 219
antiracism, 17, 80, 142, 155, 158, 163, 166, 168, 170, 174, 178–79, 184
appetite, 5, 21, 31, 47–48, 51, 58, 123, 134–36, 172, 202, 204, 206
Aquinas, Thomas, 124
aristocracy, 53, 81
Aristotle, 24
attribute, 3, 26–28, 49, 57, 68–70, 72–73, 95n10, 98, 132
Augustine of Hippo, 202

Balibar, Etienne, 16, 31, 35, 39, 41, 54, 57n5, 62n22, 77n52, 148n78, 152
beatitude, 56, 139, 147. *See also* glory (*gloria*)
becoming-animal. *See under* animals
becoming-imperceptible, 167, 177, 179, 188, 210

235

Biko, Steve, 155, 158n12
Butler, Judith, 177n74; and denaturalization, 6–7, 107, 174; and performativity, 43; and recognition, 13, 149–53, 163, 165, 168; on Spinoza's *conatus* doctrine, 17, 117–21, 124–25, 128–29, 132, 149–53, 198n33

care, feminist ethics of, 34n24, 55, 78n54, 108
Cato, 196–97
Christian/Christianity, 23, 124, 135, 137, 201, 205
common notions, 67, 86, 92, 95n10, 96–98, 102, 105, 191, 217n59
compassion, 109, 192–93, 195, 198
compatibilism, 2, 24
conatus (striving/endeavor), 17, 28–32, 38–39, 41, 54, 56, 61n18, 65–66, 69, 71, 73–74, 76, 80–83, 86, 90–91, 94–96, 99, 101, 103–6, 109, 112, 119–25, 131–35, 139–51, 158, 171, 174–75, 179, 190, 193–94, 209–10, 216
consciousness: and the aims of renaturalization, 9; of appetite, 134, 136; black, 155, 175; false, 60, 83; and feminism, 155–56, 175, 166; as essentially human trait, 25; of God, 29n15; and ideology, 75; and the illusion of freedom/finality/providence, 64–65, 135, 145; as part of nature, 40, 152; -raising, 182–83; religious, 207; self-, 3, 11, 118, 126–27, 130–31, 137–38, 150–52, 180, 201; as subordinate to thought, 69–70, 177; as transcending nature, 17, 128, 170, 172; unhappy, 212
convenire/convenientia (to agree/agreement), 93, 96–99, 101–3, 105, 142, 194, 202–4, 208–9, 217–18
Cornell, Drucilla, 44n42; and Sara Murphy, 143n70, 163–65, 168
courtesy (*modestia*), 145n71, 146
creation/creator, 135, 137, 193, 214
critical theory, 6–7, 11, 108, 169

Damasio, Antonio, 23n4, 26n10, 94
death: and the aims of the *conatus*, 101; Butler on, 119, 121, 150; as external to each being, 123–24, 134; fear of, 203; Freud on, 198; Hegel on, 118–19, 123–24, 128; Hobbes on, 131; and the interdependence of finite modes, 40, 76; as lowest degree of power to affect and be affected, 103; Montaigne on, 150–51; and the myth of the Fall, 203, 206; of political regimes, 42; as preoccupation of contemporary philosophy and politics, 151; and ratio of motion and rest, 215; Simondon on, 36
Deleuze, Gilles: on the difficulty of ideology critique, 77n52; on ethology (conceiving Spinoza's ethics as), 188, 209–11, 214–18; and Félix Guattari, 26n11, 167–68, 176–78, 188; on immanence, 214; as influence on Grosz's interpretation of Nietzsche, 170n61; on the nature of good and evil in Spinoza, 206n43; on the nature of reason in Spinoza, 95n11; on Spinoza as philosopher of pure affirmation (in contrast to Hegel), 117–19, 123–24, 151; on Spinoza's doctrine of the attributes, 68; on the subordination of consciousness to thought in Spinoza, 69–70; on the triple illusion of consciousness in Spinoza, 135
Del Lucchese, Filippo, 76n47, 87–88, 148n77
democrat/democracy: anti-essentialism and the theory of, 107; nature as norm in the theory of, 3, 186–87; Spinoza on the need for large deliberative assemblies in a, 53, 81, 91, 180; Spinoza's challenge to traditional oppositions in the theory of, 15; Spinoza's championing of, 81, 91, 132, 180; Spinoza's exclusion of women from citizenship in a, 112; and the struggle for recognition/representation as persons, 159, 164
Den Uyl, Douglas, 11n18, 132n57
depersonalization, 139, 149
Descartes, René: and the *cogito*, 126–27; and doubt, 45; and the dualism of mind and body, 23–25, 29, 32, 127; on freedom, 50n50; on free will (and its role in judgment), 2, 23–25, 32, 44–45, 65n28; on heroic self-sacrifice, 196n29; the humanist tradition and, 5–6, 212;

on humans as both finite and infinite, 92n7; on love and desire, 125n32; and the mastery of nature, 108; on the passions, 23, 25, 29, 31–32; and women, 48
determinism/determinist, 24, 30
disdain, 144, 171, 194, 197, 201
duration/endurance: of external/objective representations of one's freedom, 127–28; of joy, 78; as mere survival in Butler, 125; of the mind independently of the body, 29n15; and resistance, 90; of the state, 143; as the striving for more than mere (biological) survival, 139; as the striving to persevere in being of finite beings in time, 106

ecology: of ideas, 56; and Spinoza, 4, 9, 108–11, 185–91; theories of, 3–4, 9, 108–11, 185–91, 219
empire within an empire (conception of humans as an), 10, 21–22, 87, 172
envy, 22, 31, 46, 89, 170–71, 197
equality/equal: humans as inherently, 213–14; and the imitation of the affects in Spinoza, 140; of individuals as impossible ideal for Spinoza, 53; not a function of inherent human dignity for Spinoza, 186; and renaturalization, 180; and the stability/endurance of the state in Spinoza, 143; striving for recognition as more than striving for formal, 161; the theory and politics of recognition and, 11–12, 129, 138, 156, 158, 163–64, 213–14
essence(s): agreement and/or disagreement in, 103, 204, 215; of the attributes, 68; denaturalization and the critique of, 6, 107; as desire or an individual's striving to persevere in being, 31, 39, 101, 125, 132–35; of humans as thought/reason/spirit, 25, 92–107, 131; knowledge of God's, 98; of man and the common good, 92; of nature as cause of all things, 74; never self-destructive, 122, 134; no universal human, 86–88, 92, 100–107, 207; properties of or following from an, 45; as relational/affective, 8, 39, 105, 133; as singular (expressions of God's power),

40, 80, 86–87, 101, 133, 141–45, 171, 210; of a thing as cause of its (adequate) ideas, 71–72, 95; of a thing as identical with its power, 54, 133
esteem (including self-), 14, 17, 46, 139, 143–44, 171–73, 182–83
eternal/eternity, 7–8, 29n15, 31, 88, 94, 96, 98, 106–7, 132, 174, 207, 212
evil, 78, 123, 146, 198, 200, 202–6
exemplar: animal (nonhuman), 18, 187–90, 195–96, 201, 209; human, 2, 5, 103–7, 112–13, 147, 188–89, 201–2, 205, 207–10
extension, 3, 10, 26–28, 49, 62, 68–69, 75, 97–99

Fall, myth of the, 103n22, 193, 201–9
false/falsity, 16, 45–46, 56–57, 72–73, 79, 202, 208
Fanon, Frantz, 156n4, 156n7, 157, 158n12, 169n57
fear, 26, 50, 90, 129, 137, 203, 217
feminism/feminist: and the denaturalization of human beings, 6–7, 43–44, 55; ethics of care, 34n24, 78n54, 108; and gossip, 48; and imperceptibility (the politics of), 17; of joy and affirmation inspired by Spinoza, 118–19; on the power of images/models, 80, 106; and the power of true ideas/reason, 79–80, 108; and the relational character of existence/agency, 9, 39, 71; and the renaturalization of human beings, 6–7, 11, 18, 44, 153, 155–84; and the theory and politics of recognition, 12, 118–20, 142; and unorthodox/appropriative interpretations of the history of philosophy, 151
finite/finitude, 33, 38, 122, 141, 207
Foucault, Michel, 6–7, 14, 56, 61–63, 74, 81, 120n17, 213
freedom: of expression, 24, 43, 51–52; political aspects of, 10, 13, 24, 34, 43, 50–54, 77, 81; Spinoza's conception of, 4, 15–16, 26, 34, 41–42, 50–54, 57, 66, 69, 76–77, 123–24, 147; of the will (individual autonomy/self-determination), 2, 3, 5, 11–13, 15, 17, 22–24, 30, 32, 35–36, 44, 46, 48–52,

freedom (*continued*)
  58–60, 65–67, 70, 78, 90, 107, 117, 123
  135, 156, 157–58, 162, 172–73, 186n2,
  187, 201
friend/friendship, vii, 17, 81, 86, 140,
  198–99, 209

glory (*gloria*), 31, 139, 143–49, 153
good: Aquinas on our apprehension of
  the, 124; the common and/or highest
  (human), 81, 89, 92–93, 99–100,
  104, 181, 191; Deleuze on Spinoza's
  conception of the, 123, 219; Descartes
  on the, 31–32; desire as principle of
  the, 124–25; difficulty of developing
  a common conception of the, 105;
  government, 53; hate is never, 32, 174,
  197; and human exemplars, 147, 200,
  205; for humans, is what agrees with
  our nature, 194; humility as, 33n23;
  lack of content to Spinoza's conception
  of the, 105; nonobjectivity of the, 124;
  and reason/adequate ideas, 93, 95,
  100, 104, 158; relativity of the, 104;
  Spinoza permits the use of whatever we
  deem to be, 111; Spinoza's counsel to
  focus only the, 14; Spinoza's discussion
  of the affects and the, 30, 51; the (true)
  knowledge of evil and the, 78, 107,
  202–6
Grosz, Elizabeth, 6, 17, 153, 157–59, 163–
  72, 174–80, 182–83

Haraway, Donna, 11n17, 113, 218, 219n64
hate/hatred, 22, 31–33, 46, 89, 139, 155,
  170–76, 189, 197–99, 209
Hegel, Georg Wilhelm Friedrich:
  collectivism/organicism and, 34; on
  desire, 17; and feminism, 162, 169; on
  freedom as self-acceptance/affirmation,
  170; and the humanist tradition, 6; on
  humans as both finite and infinite, 92;
  on the person and/or the politics of the
  person/recognition, 10–12, 117–53,
  156–57, 160–65, 170–71, 173; reason
  as working on and improving nature
  in, 108n29; on self-actualization in
  time/history, 164; on Spinoza, 37; and
  the unhappy consciousness, 212
Herder, Johann Gottfried von, 164

Hobbes, Thomas: on desire (especially
  as the primary/most fundamental
  affect), 124, 131; on the fear of death,
  121, 200; Hegel on, 125–26, 131,
  136, 138; as influence on Spinoza,
  131; and the justification of political
  domination/sovereign power, 129, 217;
  and liberalism, 117, 121; on man as a
  wolf to man, 217; and negative freedom,
  138; on the non-existence of anything
  incorporeal, 48; and possessive
  individualism, 121; on the power
  of deliberation as characteristically
  human, 24; and the reduction of
  deliberation to appetite, 48; on the
  relation between desire and the *conatus*,
  125, 131; and Spinoza on the role of
  ambition in a well-ordered state, 172;
  and Spinoza's view that God can only
  improperly be called one or single, 37
Honneth, Axel, 125, 143n69, 163, 166n45;
  and Nancy Fraser, 160n21
humanism/humanist: as characterizing
  our epoch, 107; impossible ideals in
  the politics of, 18; and misanthropy,
  173, 177; and the politics of the
  person/recognition, 121, 151, 158–59,
  170, 172, 180, 211; as radically opposing
  humans to (the rest of) nature, 5–6,
  110, 158, 172–74, 187–89, 201, 207,
  211–13, 219; Renaissance, 195
humanitas, 142, 145n71
humility, 31, 33n23, 185, 187n7, 188

ideas. *See* adequate ideas; image;
  imagination/imaginary; intellectual love of God; intuition;
  knowing/knowledge; thought
ideology, 6–8, 15–16, 55–84
image, 14, 32n21, 52, 58, 61, 77, 80, 141,
  143–44, 147, 166; of man (*see under*
  exemplar)
imagination/imaginary: and
  ambition/glory, 144–45, 149; compared
  to rational and intuitive knowledge,
  148; and exemplars, 106, 190, 198; and
  freedom, 52, 59–60, 66; idea of human
  nature as product of the, 107, 112;
  and ideology/prejudice/superstition
  (generally), 57, 59, 63, 66, 156, 185; as

ineradicable, 76; and the knowledge of good and evil (practical reason), 106, 205; and love/desire, 103, 135; and the multitude, 132; and representations of unity/simplicity/wholeness, 37–38; social, 145–46, 149, 175–77, 198; as subject to external causal forces, 44, 57, 60, 67, 95; and teleology/providence, 22, 58–59, 143; and true/adequate ideas, 72n41, 76–77
immanence/immanent, 27n12, 37, 57, 123, 131–32, 137, 214–16
impersonal: causal force(s) of nature, 13–14, 63, 111, 146–47, 165–67, 170, 174, 176; glory / intellectual love of god as, 139, 149, 172; politics, 10–11, 13–14, 157–59, 176, 183–84
inadequate idea, 31n19, 67, 71, 84, 92, 135, 206
intellectual love of God, 89, 91, 94, 99, 147–48
intuition, 40, 95, 146–48
Irigaray, Luce, 168, 176
Israel, Jonathan, 4n6, 51n52, 186n6

jealousy, 31, 88
joy, 8, 14, 30–33, 41, 50, 52, 76, 78–82, 99–101, 104–5, 117, 119, 139–47, 159, 171, 180, 182, 184, 196–97, 204, 210, 220
Judaism, 201
judgment, 44–46, 110, 150

Kant, Immanuel, 2, 6, 24, 117, 186n2, 186n4, 197, 212; neo-Kantian, 164
knowing/knowledge: Althusser on Spinoza's first kind of, 77; of appetite, 135; of the attributes, 68; the better but doing the worse, 91; of the body, 69, 102; causes that determine us often beyond our, 13; and doubt, 45; of God/nature, 86, 89, 91, 93–94, 98–100, 105, 139; of good and/or evil, 78, 93, 104, 202–6; gossip as social, 48; humans as preferred objects of, 194; individual unavailable to, 36; intuition as highest form of, 40, 148; local, 108; of oneself as free, 130–31; power-, 61; as relations between relations for Simondon, 39; self-, 71, 96, 99–100,

113, 130–31, 147–48, 175; of singular things in intuition, 147; third form of, 146–47; as transindividual, 68

law(s): against killing animals, 109, 192, 203; civil/positive, 13, 51, 88, 91, 110, 131, 160, 163; ethology and, 214–15; moral, 88, 108, 163, 185, 187–88, 199, 208, 212–13, 216; of the motion and rest of bodies, 49, 65; of nature (including human nature), 2, 21, 23, 28, 39, 85, 87–90, 92, 97, 105, 121, 172, 174, 189, 199, 201; no uniquely human, 22, 121, 134, 172, 211; of singular natures, 194; suspension of, 200
Leibniz, Gottfried Wilhelm, 28, 148n78
Levinas, Emmanuel, 166, 171
liberal/liberalism: antiessentialism and, 107; conception of the self according to, 35–36, 38, 117, 158, 160; as concerned with the justification of authority, 117; as focusing on rights owed to individuals and the just distribution of goods, 159; Hegel and Spinoza as (differing) alternatives to mainstream, 17, 117, 121, 124, 160–61; reduction of man to *homo œconomicus* in neo-, 107; and respect for the inherent dignity of human beings, 172, 186, 201; Spinoza as (proto-), 15, 34, 38, 51; *vis-à-vis* the politics of recognition, 158, 160–63
Lloyd, Genevieve, 85n1, 108n28, 109–12, 186n5, 189n10, 190–91; and Moira Gatens, 170n62, 211n46
Locke, John, 108n29, 117
love: affect of (generally), 31–32, 80, 89, 99, 103–4, 124–25, 139–43, 163, 165, 171, 198; of freedom, 15; of God or nature (subjective and objective genitive), 22, 59, 89, 91–94, 99, 105, 109, 135, 137, 139, 144, 147–49; self-, 4–5, 17, 80, 101, 141–44, 147–48, 155–56, 172, 174, 179, 193, 197, 210, 218, 220

Macherey, Pierre, 28nn13–14, 57n5, 68n34, 117, 118n4, 120n17, 122, 134n62
Machiavelli, Niccolo, 72, 174n68, 206

MacKinnon, Catharine, 55n1, 182, 183n81, 185
Maimonides (Moses ben-Maimon), 202, 204–6, 208
Marx, Karl, 6, 60–61, 63, 65; Marxist/Marxism, 7, 9, 34, 57, 59, 70, 161, 186
Matheron, Alexandre, 35n25, 70, 81n59, 94, 97, 99n16, 100, 101n20, 111–12, 124, 125n32, 132–33
melancholy, 50, 104, 118–19, 152, 194–95, 197–99, 208, 217–19
misanthropy, 4, 18, 24, 173, 184, 187, 193, 199–201, 211, 217, 219
mockery, 46, 171, 173, 197
mode, 26–27, 33, 38–39, 45, 48–49, 67–70, 72–74, 76, 83, 91, 95, 99, 122, 151, 169, 179, 185
model. See exemplar
monarchy, 53, 81, 132
Montag, Warren, vii, viii, 11n19, 27n12, 46, 59–60, 62nn21–22, 69n36, 75, 203n38, 215n56
Montaigne, Michel de, 194–97

Naess, Arne, 4n7, 109–12, 186n3, 190–91
necessity/necessary: of absolute sovereignty (for Hobbes), 131; and affects in finite modes, 41, 91, 205; of being good for one another insofar as we agree in nature, 194; causal/natural, 7, 22, 46, 49, 65n28, 70, 74, 134, 173–74, 197; of the connection between adequate knowledge and joy, 78; contributions of women to society as, 182; of the correspondence between ideas and the bodies of which they are the ideas, 100; of an enduring objective representation of freedom (for Hegel), 127; of exemplars, 188; existence and causal activity of substance/nature as, 68, 74; of fear/domination (in Hegel), 129–32; and freedom, 49, 51, 106; and ideology/imagination (generally), 7–8, 60; and the interdependence of finite modes, 25–26, 70, 91, 106, 205; and judgment/the mind/the will, 46, 70, 106; of negation/negativity (in Hegel), 123; physical, 128; of a provisional morality, 11; of resistance/contestation, 156, 168; of sadness and hatred (vs. joy and love) for Descartes, 31; of the striving to increase one's power to exist, 99, 134; of violence, 166
Negri, Antonio, 11n19, 23n4, 27n12, 37, 62n22, 118n5, 134n61, 146, 179n78, 211n47; and Michael Hardt, 117n1
neo-Hegelian/neo-Hegelianism, 12, 14, 160–61, 164, 180, 182
Nietzsche, Friedrich, 165–66, 168, 170, 183

parallelism, 3, 28, 178
part(s) of nature, 1, 4–5, 8–10, 16, 53, 55, 63, 74, 87, 90, 98–99, 138–39, 146–48, 150, 170, 174, 179–81, 190, 197, 206–9, 218–20
passion(s)/passivity: converted into action(s)/activity, 145, 197; Descartes on the, 29, 31–32; and disagreement, 96, 103, 142, 193–94; and doubt, 45; and ethology, 214; in general, 8, 22–23, 27, 29–31, 33, 71, 80, 85, 90, 192; and glory, 145; and gossip, 48; and ideas, 63, 71, 83; and the imagination, 45, 58; impossibility of fully eliminating/escaping, 33, 41, 46, 76, 88, 90–91, 103–5, 111, 194, 198–99; as intertwined with and enabling action/activity, 33, 40, 75, 111, 181n79, 216; joyful, 30–31, 33, 41, 50, 78; of mind and body in parallel, 69; sad, 4, 6, 14, 30–31, 33, 50, 175, 217; of the social/political body, of the masses, or of a culture, 81, 91, 175; speech as function of, 47, 52–53; and transindividuality, 152
perfectibility/perfectionism, 87, 89, 93
perfect/perfection, 3, 30, 61, 105–6, 136, 141, 147, 153, 193, 201–2, 204–6
person (autonomous subject / bearer of rights), 2, 11–13, 88, 107, 121, 125, 128, 139, 143, 147, 149, 155–57, 159, 161–64, 166, 170, 179, 181, 183, 189, 211–12
philanthropy, 4, 174, 177, 201, 209–10, 219
politics of imperceptibility, 17, 155–59, 163, 166–68, 170, 175–84
posthumanism/posthumanist, 4–5, 11n17,

15, 18, 112–13, 139, 159, 187–88, 209, 212n50, 213, 218–19
power/force: of affects, 32, 34, 48, 50, 52, 78, 140, 204; agreement in, 103, 194, 204; agreement in nature and the amplification of one's, 100–101, 194; and the attributes, 68; coercive, 143; as coextensive with right, 1–2, 11; compositions of / collective power, 10, 13–14, 17, 34, 44, 53–54, 78, 82, 86, 95, 98–100, 103, 112, 141, 148–49, 172, 182–83, 198, 204, 207, 216, 218; of deliberation, 24; differences between Hegel and Spinoza on, 17, 121, 123, 132; equality/inequality in, 53; field(s)/network(s) of, 15, 25, 46, 64, 66, 70, 134, 138, 146, 174–75, 214; and finite modes / singular essences, 33, 54, 72, 92, 95, 99, 132–34, 139, 148, 171, 180, 202, 207, 210–11; and glory/ambition, 142, 144–45; Hobbes on, 131; of ideas (especially as independent of their truth), 46, 56–58, 62–63, 71–73, 77, 79–80, 82–83, 95, 179; as identical with virtue, 56, 72, 86, 95, 147, 197; increase and/or decrease in power of finite modes, 3–5, 10, 13–14, 25–26, 29–31, 33, 39, 41, 46, 79, 96, 98, 101, 103–4, 140–42, 147, 171, 182–83, 188, 192, 197, 200, 203, 205–6, 208, 216 (see also joy; sadness); (inter)relations of, 34, 40–41, 43, 53–54, 63, 78, 82, 112, 120, 133, 141, 145–46, 152, 158, 161, 174, 181, 187, 211, 215; of intuition, 148; -knowledge, 61, 81; mental and/or bodily, 3, 13, 16, 23, 25, 27–30, 33, 41, 57, 60, 64–66, 69–72, 74, 78, 81–84, 86, 92, 96, 99, 104–5, 108, 133, 142, 172, 181, 191, 197, 200; of nature/God, 3, 16, 28, 30, 34, 45, 58, 71, 75, 81, 89, 93, 99, 104, 108, 111, 123, 136, 139, 143, 146–48, 169–70, 174, 177, 180; as necessarily limited in finite modes, 1, 5, 9, 16, 24, 42, 44, 47, 52, 68, 75–76, 148, 204, 208; of negation / the negative, 123, 127, 151; sovereign, 24, 88–89, 131–32; of the state, 44, 129, 131; structures of, 6, 53, 55, 63; to affect and be affected, 27, 49–50, 53, 74–75, 192, 211; to enjoy/realize highest good, 92; to persevere in being / exist, 29, 41, 66, 79, 132–33, 140, 146, 220; transfer of, 88; of the will / self-determination, 2, 5, 21, 23, 28, 44–45, 53, 65–66, 68, 145, 204, 207
preservation/perseverance, 29–31, 38, 66, 71, 73, 79, 90–91, 95, 101, 103, 106, 109, 112, 118–19, 122, 125, 128, 131–34, 136, 140, 146, 171, 192, 208, 215
pride, 33n23, 144, 156

ratio of motion and rest, 90, 95, 101, 215
reason, 2, 5, 15–17, 26, 46, 50–51, 62n22, 71, 81, 83, 85–112, 130, 163, 180–81, 189, 191–94, 197–98, 201, 204, 207, 212, 215, 217
recognition, 6, 11–13, 17, 117–53, 156–68, 170–73, 175, 178, 180, 182–83
religion, 129, 199, 213
representation: epistemological, 45, 56, 57n7, 62, 126, 139, 147–49, 165–66; of oneself (to oneself and/or to others), 126–28, 138–39, 143–44, 147–49, 152, 162, 164–66, 175, 182; political and juridical, 7, 11–15, 17, 37, 42, 44, 121, 128, 131, 138, 148, 152, 164–66, 176, 182
Rice, Lee, 35n25, 100, 103, 111
right(s): of animals and other nonhumans, 10, 25, 110–12, 188, 191, 219; as co-extensive with power, 1–2, 11, 110–11, 191; to the exercise of force, 42; juridical concept of, 6, 110; to life, 125, 171; natural, 51, 110, 217; of persons/humans, 11–13, 125, 157, 159, 171; politics of, 13, 15, 42, 44, 159, 165, 167; to think/speak freely, 51; transfer of, 88; of women, 166

sadness, 30–32, 46, 139, 171, 188, 190, 195, 197
Sartre, Jean-Paul, 165, 176, 198
singular: constitution / ratio of motion and rest, 95, 142, 215; essences/natures, 31, 40, 71, 80, 86, 96, 101, 105, 133, 141–42, 145, 194, 210; ideas, 75, 96; things/singularities, 4, 22, 30, 34,

singular (*continued*)
39–41, 54, 70–71, 75–76, 90, 100, 125, 133–34, 138–39, 146–47, 208, 211–12, 216

slave(s)/slavery/servant(s)/servitude: to biological life (in Hegel), 129; and Butler, 118; consent to one's own, 59–60; dialectic of master and, 60, 118, 127–32, 156–57, 160, 169; excluded from citizenship, 81n59; and exemplars, 208; fighting for one's own, 129; to the flesh (in Augustine), 202; and the imagination, 57, 59, 156; and interdependence, 138; of mind and body in parallel, 29, 69, 179; as opposed to Spinoza's "free man," 173; and the passions, 26; question of the humanity of, 172; and recognition, 118, 156–57, 164; as sociohistorical reality, 60, 78, 129, 161; as something we resist, 198; as topic of *Ethics*, part IV, 30, 106, 192–93, 198; of the tyrant to opinion, 145

Smith, Steven B., 35n25, 51n52, 56n3, 75n45, 87n3

Socrates, 196–97

soul, 7, 29, 31–32, 51, 71, 155–56, 196–97, 211, 219

spirit/spiritual, 3–6, 8, 15, 22–24, 27, 30, 35, 37, 39, 43, 69, 75, 87–88, 90, 100, 108, 111, 124–25, 127–28, 131–32, 137–39, 143, 146, 152, 158, 160, 169, 173, 200–201, 211–14

superstition/prejudice, 26, 42, 49, 58, 65n28, 109, 137, 145, 175, 191–92

Taylor, Charles, 159n16, 160–61, 163–64, 166n45

teleology/purpose/end/goal, 7, 28, 38, 41, 59–60, 64, 106, 136–37, 180, 195

thought, 3, 16, 25–28, 33, 44–49, 57–60, 62–63, 66–76, 85–86, 98–99, 121–22, 190

transcendence/transcendent, 33, 37, 60, 110, 112, 137, 145, 149, 153, 163, 171–73, 177, 180, 198, 216

transindividual/transindividuality, 16, 24, 34–42, 68, 71, 133, 145, 152, 211

utile (advantage/use/interest/good), 83, 89–91, 93, 95, 99, 101–4, 109, 111, 132, 135–36, 139, 191–93, 203

virtue: and *acquiescentia*, 147; in Descartes, 31; and ethology, 216; humility not a, 187n7; Montaigne on, 195–97; nonhuman nature and animals as exemplars of, 186, 195–96, 200–201; and particular affects, 33; and reason, 86, 91–92, 96; self-mortification/self-annihilation as, 124; as synonymous with power, 56, 72, 86, 95, 147, 197; and true/adequate ideas, 56, 72, 74, 95

will/willing/volition: in accordance with universal rule, 12; causes of our, 2, 58, 136; as *conatus* with respect to the mind, 134; freedom of the (*see under* freedom); identity of intellect and, 45; infinity of the, 45 (in Descartes), 170 (in Hegel), 190; and judgment, 45, 60; perfection of, 202 (in Augustine); pessimism of the, 146, 179; the politics of renaturalization and the, 146; as power to control the body/passions, 3, 28, 32, 42; as prior to the good, 124; for self-annihilation/self-harm, 123, 128; the world as product of the, 153

www.ingramcontent.com/pod-product-compliance
Lightning Source LLC
Chambersburg PA
CBHW021941290426
44108CB00012B/920